A History of Thimbles

A History of Thimbles

Edwin F. Holmes

Cornwall Books
New York ● London ● Toronto

© 1985 by Rosemont Publishing and Printing Corporation

Cornwall Books
440 Forsgate Drive
Cranbury, NJ 08512

Cornwall Books
25 Sicilian Avenue
London WC1A 2QH, England

Cornwall Books
2133 Royal Windsor Drive
Unit 1
Mississauga, Ontario
Canada L5J 1K5

Library of Congress Cataloging in Publication Data

Holmes, Edwin F.
  A history of thimbles.

  Bibliography: p.
  Includes index.
  1. Thimbles—History.   I. Title.
NK9505.7.H637   1984   646'.19   82-46084
ISBN 0-8453-4761-6

Printed in the United States of America

Four farthings and a thimble, will make a tailor's pocket jingle.

Old English proverb

Contents

Preface   9
Acknowledgments   11
Early Thimbles   15
Thimbles in Germany   24
Thimbles in England   37
Thimbles in America   54
Thimbles in France   65
Porcelain Thimbles   73
Enamel Thimbles   82
Gold Thimbles   86
Mother-of-pearl Thimbles   93
Ivory Thimbles   94
Tortoise-shell Thimbles   96
Silver Thimbles   98
The Dorcas Thimble   106
Bone Thimbles   115
Horn Thimbles   117
Glass Thimbles   118
Stone Thimbles   120
Leather Thimbles   125
Wooden Thimbles   128
Fabric Thimbles   131
Brass Thimbles   133
Iron and Steel Thimbles   145
Nickel Thimbles   150
Aluminum Thimbles   154
Plastic Thimbles   156
Tailors' Thimbles   163
Children's Thimbles   167
Commemorative Thimbles   173
Keepsake Thimbles   178
Souvenir Thimbles   182
Patent Thimbles   189
Advertising Thimbles   197

Finger Guards   200
Just a Thimbleful   203
Thimble Cases   207
Thimble-Rigging   220
Thimbles in Museums   226
Thimbles for Other Uses   232
Collecting Thimbles   236
Appendixes   243
Bibliography   249
Index   250

Preface

THE QUESTION WHICH I AM MOST FREQUENTLY asked is how I came to be interested in thimbles and the answer is simply that many years ago I happened to be visiting one of the London auction rooms where I saw a small collection of thimbles which was on view prior to a sale. These thimbles intrigued me and later the same day, finding myself in a public library, it occurred to me to look up the word *thimble* in a book of reference. The first book I consulted was the obvious one, namely, the *Encyclopaedia Britannica,* which learned publication, I was surprised to find, bore no mention of the word. So I consulted the next work of reference along the shelves, namely the *Encyclopedia Americana* which, to its credit, did have an entry. According to the *Encyclopedia Americana* the introduction of the thimble into Europe was due to a Dutchman, Nicholas van Benschoten of Amsterdam, in 1684. This was promising but on second thoughts I realized that it must be nonsense because the origin and development of a simple utilitarian object like a thimble could not possibly be ascribed to any given individual. So I next consulted that well-known French encyclopedia, the *Grand Larousse,* which states that the existence of thimbles goes back into antiquity and goes on to mention Roman and Gallo-Roman thimbles in bronze, bone, and ivory. This sounded more plausible, but by then I had my doubts, which led me to inquire further—and wisely so, because I now know that for all its apparent erudition the *Grand Larousse* is also mistaken. So one thing led to another. I soon found that little was known about thimbles,

that what was written about them was mostly fanciful and that I had stumbled, quite by accident, on a new and attractive subject which was largely unexplored.

The next few years of my researches were devoted to combing libraries and museums, examining private collections and putting together a small collection of my own, which I found was essential because it is impossible to become familiar with thimbles without the opportunity to handle, study, and compare at leisure. The notes, clippings and illustrations which I gathered soon accumulated embarrassingly, and it was at that stage that I first thought of writing a book. An indulgent critic reviewing my earlier book, *Thimbles,* wrote that it was the definitive work on the subject, but it was of course nothing of the sort. The reason why I wrote a book is that having reached a first stage in my researches, I wanted to set down what I knew, order my thoughts, and provide myself with a firm basis for further research. I also realized that if my book was published it would open up new sources of information which in the event is precisely what happened. Because of this earlier book I was able to pursue my researches along new paths, and eight years later I find myself in a position to present a better book with a wider range of information.

As was to be expected, I have found that there were errors in my earlier book. A case in point are the so-called Roman thimbles. When I first wrote about them there was ample learned authority, including for instance Saglio's *Diction-*

naire des antiquités grecques et romaines, to support the existence of thimbles in Roman times. There were even several museums specializing in Greek and Roman antiquities which displayed (and continue to display) Roman thimbles in their showcases. Yet I am now convinced that Saglio got his records mixed up, confusing thimbles *(dés à coudre),* with gaming dice *(dés à jouer)* and there is good reason to think that the existence of thimbles in Roman times is, to say the least, doubtful.

Another case in point is the wearing of thimbles on the thumb. There can be no question that the word *thimble* originates from the Old English *thūma* a thumb, from which is derived the word *thȳmel,* and from that thimble, the intrusive letter *b,* arriving under the influence of Middle English *tho(u)mbe* during the fifteenth century. But what is by no means so sure is that thimbles were worn on the thumb. Admittedly there are many authorities to attest that they were, and *Brewer's Dictionary of Phrase and Fable,* for instance, states unreservedly that the thimble is so called because "it was originally worn on the thumb, as sailors still wear their thimbles." The odd feature, however, is that these assertions are peculiar to the English-speaking world and do not arise in countries such as France and Germany where the word for a thimble is derived not from the word for a thumb but from the word for a finger. Equally disturbing is the story that the word *thimble* is a corruption of *thumb bell,* the article being so called because of its shape. This picturesque fancy goes back a long way. Samuel Johnson, for instance, quotes Minshew as supposing that this was the derivation and by inference lends it his own authority.[1] However, such explanation is nonsense, and the Reverend Professor Walter W. Skeat, author of the standard reference work *An Etymological Dictionary of the English Language* and undoubtedly one of the foremost authorities, demolished it in a scathing letter he wrote specifically on this very point.[2] The truth is that there is no possible foundation for the thumb bell story and the proper derivation is as given above. Quite obviously the association of thimble and thumb provides its own pitfalls, and it would be most unwise to accept it at its face value.

Needless to say that wherever possible I have sought to avoid any errors which were contained in my earlier book; where the two books disagree, the later version is to be preferred. However, it would be futile to pretend that all errors have been eliminated or that fresh errors may not have crept in unbeknown. It is in the nature of this kind of research that new facts and ideas are constantly coming to impinge on the old. There is always something new to learn and the only claim I would care to advance is that my present work, taken as a whole, represents some modest contribution toward a better understanding of thimbles and their history.

NOTES

1. Samuel Johnson, *Dictionary of the English Language,* (London, 1773), s.v. "Thimble."
2. *Notes and Queries,* 7th Series, 8 (16 November 1889): 393.

Acknowledgments

THE AUTHOR'S GRATEFUL THANKS ARE DUE TO ALL those who have given permission for photographs to be taken of items in their care or ownership, or have allowed photographs in their possession to be reproduced. Details of such ownership will be found in the notes to each item. Mr. Michael Holford was responsible for much of the color photography and the author is indebted to him for his skill and for his painstaking attention to detail.

A History of Thimbles

Early Thimbles

THE IDEA OF PROTECTING THE FINGER WHEN SEWing with a needle is presumably as old as the invention of the needle itself and goes back into antiquity. It is unlikely however that we shall ever be able to retrace the origins of the needle or the steps which brought the thimble into existence. It is tempting to speculate that the earliest tool resembling a thimble was a piece of stone or bone held in the hand and used to push through a needle. Archaeologists have found evidence which lends support to this theory. Some pebbles and bones found in a neolithic hut at Lazaret in France bear marks suggesting that they were used for the purpose;[1] a pebble found in Algeria is believed to have served likewise;[2] and a small stone implement discovered at El Lisht in the Nile Valley and now in the safekeeping of the Metropolitan Museum, New York, is reputed to be a needle pusher dating from the XXth or XXIInd Dynasty, or approximately 1000 B.C.[3] Such evidence however is far from conclusive, if only because it is by no means certain when needles first came into use. So-called needles made of bone have been found in river caves in the South of France and elsewhere which are of paleolithic origin dating from about 15,000 B.C., but it is doubtful that these needles were used to sew skins in the accepted sense of the word, and they were probably used more in the manner of a bodkin. The likelihood is that holes were pierced through the skins with an awl or similar implement and that the needle was merely used to thread sinew through the holes in order to bind the skins together. If this is correct, and the

evidence provided by primitive societies would seem to support it, then the introduction of the thimble may not have taken place until the development of spun thread and woven textiles.

Spindle whorls which have been recovered from various sites indicate that spun thread was being produced by 5000 B.C., and as regards woven textiles an early picture of a loom on a Mesopotamian seal and a similar picture on an Egyptian painted dish confirm that cloth was being woven by 3000 B.C. In Egypt flax, which is indigenous to the Nile Valley, was used to make linen garments, in China silk was the preferred material, and in northern climates wool was widely used. Certainly by the time of the Middle Kingdom (c. 1980–1800 B.C.) the textile industry in Egypt was well developed, and there is in the Liverpool Museum a small burial tomb model depicting a spinning and weaving scene. One woman stands spinning thread and the other two are weaving on a horizontal loom painted on the base. Pieces of textile material have even been found from this period and among the many treasures in the Cairo Museum there is a light linen garment repaired with a darn so fine that it would do credit to any needlewoman. There is therefore no question that the ancient Egyptians knew how to sew, but strangely enough, among all the many activities of daily life faithfully recorded on the walls of tombs and elsewhere, sewing does not appear nor has a thimble ever been found. The noted Egyptologist Sir William M. Flinders Petrie does record a thimble in his *Tools and Weapons* (London,

15

1917)—a bronze ring-type thimble which he thought might be late Roman—but significantly there is only one and he did not find it himself but purchased it from an unknown source. Similarly, the Cairo Museum has an odd thimble which was not found in a tomb but which, like the Petrie thimble, is of doubtful provenance. Otherwise thimbles are conspicuous by their absence and bearing in mind the wealth of artifacts which have survived, the inescapable conclusion is that if the ancient Egyptians used anything to protect their fingers when sewing it was not a metal thimble as we know it today. It seems therefore that there are only two possibilities.

One is that because of the nature of the needles available the Egyptians found such protection unnecessary. The other is that they used a leather thimble. Leather has been used to make thimbles in many parts of the world, the leather industry was well developed in ancient Egypt, and it is known that Assyrian archers used leather guards to protect their hands and forearms when shooting arrows, so that this would be logical. It would also explain the absence of any remains because unless it is preserved under exceptional circumstances such as in a water-logged deposit, leather will disintegrate into dust. There is little evidence either way and the existence of thimbles must therefore remain a matter of supposition.

The introduction of bronze, which also dates from about 3000 B.C., may have been one of the factors influencing the development of the thimble. Before the age of bronze, needles were necessarily made of wood, bone (including fish bone), or copper, but bronze was an altogether harder and more suitable material with which to make needles. Many of these early bronze needles have been recovered but it is noticeable that the majority are coarse, and in most cases it is obvious from the thickness of the eye that they were not intended for domestic sewing as we know it today. Possibly there were also finer needles which being more delicate and fragile have not survived. However, fine needles made of bronze would not have been able to bear much stress and would never have warranted the use of a metal thimble with all the force that is implied. Thus it is possible that it was the introduction of iron and the subsequent development of the steel needle which led to the adoption of metal thimbles. The art of working iron and steel was developed in China several centuries before Christ, and it is noteworthy that the first thimble about which there is any evidence dates back to the Han dynasty. During the so-called Cultural Revolution, the Chinese people were encouraged to assist archaeologists in unearthing the past, with the result that a wide array of decorative and mostly aristocratic objects—jewels, bowls, silver and gold ornaments of all kinds—were recovered. In the tomb of a minor court dignitary was found a sewing set complete with thimble. Provided this thimble (which featured in a Chinese film and was shown on a British Broadcasting Corporation television program, "Treasures of the Cultural Revolution," by Ken Shepheard) is genuinely of the Han period—and there is no reason to believe otherwise except that China is so cut off from the outside world that it is difficult to verify the evidence—then it is by far the earliest thimble that is known to have survived. It proves that already more than two thousand years ago the Chinese knew the use of metal thimbles and it seems likely that this was associated with the use of steel needles, which so far as can be judged were first introduced about this time.

From China the art of steel making reached

Brass thimble of uncertain origin. Height 3.0 cm.
Egyptian Museum, Cairo

Asia Minor toward the end of the pre-Christian era and Damascus became a center for working steel, mostly swords and armor. It appears that at first iron was too valuable to serve for domestic purposes and that the development of steel needles was relatively slow. From Damascus the Moors brought the art of needlemaking to Cordoba, which became renowned in Europe for its steel needles, and the art later spread to Nuremberg, where steel needles were made in quantity by 1370. Nevertheless it is important to realise that steel needles remained a rare and valuable possession, as is made evident by an early sixteenth-century comedy entitled *Gammer Gurton's Needle*. The plot of this play revolves round the loss of a needle, and it is significant because Gammer Gurton, who was a woman of some substance in her community, nevertheless owned only one needle, the loss of which was a major disaster for her household. Thus it appears that the use of steel needles only spread gradually and that it was not until about the time of the Reformation that the steel needle became at all commonplace.

Going back to the Roman era, it has long been an article of faith among thimble collectors that the Romans used metal thimbles, but more recent research suggests that this is unlikely. Obviously the Romans did engage in needlework, and even assuming that the amount of domestic sewing was limited, needles were used for sail making, for leather work, and for sewing the hides used for packaging. The term pack thread is a reminder that in the days when goods were carried on the backs of animals it was customary to sew them into bales. Thus it is reasonable to suppose that some form of thimble was required, but surprisingly enough the Romans do not appear to have had a word for it. There is no problem about finding the Latin name for a needle or a needlecase, for thread, spools, shears, or a spindle (or dice for gaming, about which more later) but nowhere is the thimble mentioned in Classical Latin. A word *digitale* does feature in Low Latin (also *digitabulum*) with the precise meaning of a thimble, but going back to earlier times the meaning was different and it was originally used to denote a finger stall. Thus a fifteenth-century Anglo-Saxon and Old English vocabulary from a manuscript in the Trinity College Library in Cambridge gives *themyl* as equivalent to *digitale*. Similarly a fourteenth-century Latin/French Glossary has *digitabulum* as the equivalent of *deel a mettre ou doy pour queudre*. We can be sure therefore that during the fourteenth and fifteenth centuries, when we know that thimbles were already in use, the words *digitale* and *digitabulum* had the precise meaning of thimble. However, if we go back to the thirteenth century the meaning changes with Johannes de Janua's *Summa quae vocatur Catholicon* (1286) giving "digitabulum, instrumentum in quo digitus intromittitur, quod et digitale dicitur." And if we go back earlier still the meaning changes even more with the *Glossarium Latino-Grecum*, which dates back to possibly the sixth century, defining both *digitabulum* and *digitale* as *digitum involucrum*, i.e., a wrapping or a case for the finger. It seems therefore that these words were more closely associated with finger covers or finger stalls than with the metal *themyl* or *deel* and that it is only later that they acquired the meaning of thimble, a conclusion which will be strengthened when we come to investigate the subject of leather thimbles (see page 125).

Equally surprising, it appears that no thimbles have so far been discovered among the ruins of Pompeii and Herculaneum. It will be recalled that Vesuvius erupted in A.D. 79, burying the two towns under a thick layer of mud and ashes, and obviously if thimbles were found in the ruins there would be no room left for argument. It has long been held in Britain (though strangely enough not on the Continent) that ring-type thimbles open at both ends were found at Herculaneum. This belief, which was already current by the middle of the nineteenth century, is difficult to substantiate.[4] Early excavation reports (admittedly incomplete) make no mention of thimbles; the Ashmolean Museum at Oxford, which is the leading authority on the subject, has no record of thimbles being excavated, and the Museo Nazionale at Naples, which is the main repository for the objects excavated from the ruins, has only one domed type thimble of doubtful authenticity in its collection. It seems likely therefore that there were no thimbles found, with the obvious inference that they were still unknown in Roman times.

The tentative conclusion that the metal thimble did not exist during Roman times conflicts with accepted ideas on the subject and is difficult to reconcile with the many thimbles on show in museums. It appears however that thimbles have

Brass thimbles of uncertain origin. *Musée des Antiquités Nationales, St. Germain-en-Laye*

never received much attention from archaeologists and what little has been said about them is often nonsense. For instance, Saglio's *Dictionnaire des antiquités grecques et romaines* states that Roman and Gallo-Roman thimbles made of bronze, bone, or ivory are to be seen in the museums at Lyons, Narbonne, Nîmes, Arles, Rouen and in those at Naples and Florence, a statement which was copied widely by learned encyclopedias both in France and elsewhere. The truth is that there are few thimbles of any kind to be found in these museums (in French *dé à coudre*) and none of bone or ivory, but on the other hand they do have plenty of dice *(dé à jouer)* made of these materials, which leads to the obvious conclusion that the two types of *dés* were confused and muddled together. Or again, it may seem presumptuous to suggest that the bronze thimbles in these and other leading museums such as the Musée des Antiquités

Nationales at St. Germain-en-Laye, the Kam Museum at Nijmegen, the Ashmolean Museum at Oxford, and the Rheinisches Landesmuseum at Trier are not Roman, but regrettably they include thimbles which are obviously medieval or later. In fact the museums concerned are seldom able to tell precisely where and under what conditions their thimbles were found. Some are recorded merely as gifts and others have become separated from their antecedents, and it is no coincidence for instance that the Ashmolean Museum which had so-called Roman thimbles on display has withdrawn them to its reserve collection on grounds of doubtful authenticity. But even when an item can be traced back to excavation reports, these are often found wanting. A thimble found on the Châtelet site[5] is obviously sixteenth century on grounds of style, and while modern archaeologists might claim to be more reliable, a thimble which was recently

18

found in an allegedly Roman level at Wroxeter is unmistakably nineteenth century. So little is known about thimbles that the most fanciful attributions have been allowed to pass unchallenged.

The decline of Rome was followed by the rise of Constantinople, which was already a large and thriving city when London and Paris were still little more than a scattering of wooden hovels and mud walls. It is here, or rather in one of its associated cities, that the first concrete evidence of metal thimbles in Europe is to be found. As the capital of the Byzantine Empire Constantinople derived its wealth from trade and manufactures, notably of linen, wool, and silk, which flourished at Corinth and other Greek cities. The history of Corinth need not detain us, but its remains go back to early Grecian times and the bulk is Roman and Byzantine. The site of Old Corinth has been the object of the most extensive and meticulous excavations. A wealth of objects have been recovered including many bronze thimbles, possibly a hundred or more, all dating from the Byzantine era, that is from the ninth, tenth, eleventh, or twelfth centuries and, according to Dr. G. R. Davidson in her book *Corinth* (Vol. 12: *The Minor Objects;* Princeton, 1952), none dating from earlier times. The significance of this statement is of course that it confirms the absence of Roman thimbles and suggests that the thimble began to be used during the Byzantine era.

The period which began with the crowning of Charlemagne in A.D. 800 was to witness some notable innovations such as, for instance, the introduction of riding stirrups, which came to revolutionize the art of horsemanship and even that of warfare generally. It would not therefore be altogether surprising to find that the more widespread use of steel needles and the development of bronze ring-type thimbles came at about this time. Besides the evidence provided by the Corinth excavations, some support for the view that the thimble did not come into current use in Europe until about the ninth century results from the absence of finds among Merovingian remains. The Merovingian dynasty ruled in France from the sixth to the eighth century and many useful discoveries of tools and weapons have been made in Merovingian tombs, but to date no thimbles have been found, which supports the view that they were a later development.

The earliest written evidence about thimbles arises strangely enough from an Arabic poem or word picture entitled "The Thimble," written by a Moorish poet, Al-Liss, in the twelfth century. Al-Liss was born in Seville and lived from 1108 to 1182. In translation his poem reads as follows:

'Tis like a helmet, nicked
Where thrusting lances pricked;
Some sword has dispossessed
The helmet of its crest.

This poem is included in an anthology compiled in 1243 by the Andalusian Ibn Sa'aid under the title of *The Pennants of the Champions and the Standards of the Distinguished*—a splendidly appropriate name for an anthology.[6] Why Al-Liss chose to write about a thimble will remain unknown but there is no question that Hispano-Moresque thimbles looked very much like Moorish soldiers' helmets during the twelfth century and that the comparison is both accurate and justified.

Bronze thimbles found at Corinth. Mostly Byzantine. Height from 1.1 to 2.2 cm. *Princeton University*

19

Hispano-Moresque bronze thimble from Cordoba. Probably twelfth century. Height 5.1 cm. *Victoria and Albert Museum*

Arising from Al-Liss's poem, some useful information may be derived from the etymology of the Arabic word for a thimble. Al-Liss used the word *kustubān* (thumb guard), which is not a true Arabic word but is the arabicized form of a word borrowed from the Persian. In Persian the word is *angushtvān* (finger protector), which is a word commonly encountered in works on archery. An alternative form was *angushtāneh* which was used in India and from which such words as *angushtāna* (Bengali), *angulitra* (Hindi), *anghootyum* (Gujerati), all meaning a thimble, are derived. Archery was of course an overwhelmingly important activity for sport and warfare, and it will be recalled that earlier the Assyrians used leather guards of various kinds for this purpose. The Persians for their part used many different types of thumb rings and thumb guards to suit individual styles when drawing a bowstring, and not surprisingly the thimble's identity becomes lost in this context. Nevertheless the derivation of the Arabic word indicates that the metal thimble may have taken its name from a guard made of leather, or in other words provides some confirmation of the use of leather thimbles in early civilizations. It also suggests that the use of the metal thimble spread westward from Asia Minor and would tend to confirm that its development was associated with

that of the steel needle which spread gradually across to Spain. However, too much should not be read into the derivation and the important point is that by the twelfth century the thimble was evidently well established.

More difficult perhaps is to determine how these early thimbles were used and what they looked like. There are basically two varieties of thimbles, and the first, which is open at both ends and usually referred to as the ring type, is similar in concept to the present tailor's thimble. It is designed to be used sideways and all the specimens found at Corinth are of this variety. The other is sometimes referred to as the sugar loaf or beehive type, though it is more appropriate to refer to this variety as the closed end or domed type, since it includes thimbles of a number of different shapes. Its main feature is that, unlike the ring type, the tip of the finger is enclosed. In earlier thimbles the top may be pointed or else smooth without indentations, indicating that the thimble was designed to be used sideways like a tailor's thimble. The specimen illustrated in relation to Al-Liss's poem is of the latter variety. Subsequently the top becomes rounded or flattened, and from the sixteenth or seventeenth century onward it is covered all over with indentations so that the needle may be driven forward by the tip of the finger in the modern manner.

The fact that the thimbles found in Corinth were all of the ring-type variety suggests that ring-type thimbles came before the closed end or domed type. In all probability the thimble found by Petrie and also the one in the Cairo Museum are Byzantine, not Roman, and so is another ring-type thimble in the Museu Arqueologić in Barcelona which is said to have been found among the remains of the Greek settlement at Ampurias. It is important to remember, however, that the design of ring-type thimbles has remained very much the same over the centuries. Appearance can be deceptive, and just because it is highly corroded a ring-type thimble is not necessarily very old.

Dome-type thimbles are equally difficult to date, but before discussing the more commonplace items there are two designs of special interest. The first is that of the Hispano-Moresque thimbles already referred to, which are so large and heavy that they are obviously unsuitable for normal sewing purposes. They are thought to have been intended for harness making and saddlery. They were made of bronze and cast by the lost-wax process. These thimbles sometimes bear the name of their maker and there are two in the Museo Arqueologico in Madrid, believed to date from the tenth century, which are both inscribed "Made by Al-Sayib." The other is the onion-shaped thimble from the Near East, somewhat reminiscent of the dome of a Greek Orthodox church. The latter, which are presumably late Byzantine, are far too large and bulbous for comfort, and it has been suggested that they were designed to be filled with wet clay, which was then allowed to dry to the right size and shape to fit the wearer's finger. The explanation is ingenious but not totally convincing and gives no hint of the purpose for which these thimbles were used. There is obviously much to learn about both types of thimbles and some need for more research on the subject.

The appearance of an old bronze or brass thimble can be deceptive and depends very much on where it was kept. Under optimum conditions the thimble may retain its original

Bronze thimble from Hungary. Height 2.7 cm. Possibly sixteenth century. A type of thimble more commonly found in Asia Minor and presumably introduced under Turkish influence post 1526. *Collection Musée d'Art et d'Histoire, Genève*

finish, but if the environment is at all detrimental the original surface may be replaced by a layer of corrosion product which will have eaten into the metal and it will be only too painfully obvious that the original surface has been destroyed. Moreover, even in those cases where corrosion does not obscure the surface or where the thimble has been cleaned, color remains a poor guide to the thimble's composition. Under certain conditions the process of corrosion may alter the composition of the surface and so may the cleaning process itself. Even at the best of times it is difficult to differentiate between copper and the various grades of bronze and brass, and the only sure test is chemical analysis.

Another problem is that there are few evolutionary pointers which can be used as guides to date early thimbles. Moreover, the changes in sewing habits consequent on the introduction of more sophisticated needles, the disappearance of the leather thymel, the different uses for which thimbles were intended making for variations in size, coarseness, and thickness of indentations, and finally the international trade in thimbles even during early times make it difficult to establish a pattern. Nevertheless the following notes may be of interest:

Construction

The earliest brass thimbles were either cast or else shaped by hammering into a die. Later thimbles were either cast or else they were made of two pieces with the sides formed from a strip of metal brazed at the joint and the cap fitted separately on top. About the end of the eighteenth century brass thimbles began to be made by pressing (deep drawing) from sheet metal.

Indentations

Early thimbles have hand-punched indentations set in an orderly pattern, for example, vertical lines or more commonly a spiral which begins at the open end and continues up to the crown. Later they may have a stamped mark preceding the first indentations at the commencement of the spiral such as an anchor, a dagger, a flower, a goblet, a key, or some other device denoting the maker. Later still thimbles from about the end of the seventeenth century have the indentations applied mechanically

Medieval brass thimbles mostly 1350–1400. Metal thimbles do not appear to have been used in Britain to any extent before 1350. *Private collection*

Medieval brass thimbles mostly circa 1400. *Private collection*

Medieval brass thimbles mostly early fifteenth century. *Private collection*

round the sides in a wide strip as at the present time. The crown is stamped or indented separately. Modern thimbles have the indentations applied to the sides and the crown together by machine.

Crown

Early thimbles usually have a bare tonsurelike patch on the crown and some have a small hole. If the thimble is indented with a spiral this terminates before reaching the center. Thimbles with a bare crown are unlikely to date from after 1650.

Rim and decoration

The earliest thimbles have no rim or decoration except possibly for a single incised or lightly hand-punched line; by the sixteenth century they may be decorated with some hand-punched or engraved pattern round the sides and by the eighteenth century there may be a solid projecting rim round the edge. From the nineteenth century onward the rim is turned over mechanically.

In one of their catalogs, the British Museum once suggested that the more ancient specimens were less finely pitted on the outer surface than those of later date. There is some truth in this proposition but it can be misleading. The size of the cavities normally corresponds to the thickness of the needle, and since the thickness of the needle is usually a function of the nature of the work it follows that the larger heavier thimbles have large indentations and the smaller lighter thimbles have smaller indentations. The latter, however, are more vulnerable to the ravages of time, with the result that many of the older thimbles have large indentations, but it is by no means a universal rule and early thimbles with small indentations do exist.

In conclusion it cannot be stressed too strongly that the above is mainly a guide to enable the collector to know what features to look for. In practice, the best way to date an early thimble with accuracy is to relate it to other objects with which it may have been found, but even this method has its limitations, and it is possible to go astray.

NOTES

1. H. de Lumley, "Report on Lazaret-Acheulian Man" (unpublished MS).

2. "Note sur un galet paraissant avoir fait aux temps néolithiques l'usage d'un dé à coudre actuel," *Bulletin de la Société Préhistorique Française* 10, no. 4 (April 1913).

3. William C. Hayes, *The Scepter of Egypt* (New York, 1953), 2: 411–12.

4. George H. Townsend, *The Manual of Dates* (London, 1867).

5. Grivaud de la Vincelle, *Arts et métiers des anciens*, vols. 6, 16.

6. A. J. Arberry, *Moorish Poetry* (Cambridge: At the University Press, 1953).

Thimbles in Germany

THE EARLIEST KNOWN REFERENCE TO A THIMBLE IN Germany dates from the twelfth century and is to be found in the works of the blessed Hildegard. Hildegard von Bingen (1098–1190) was celebrated during her lifetime for her piety, her visions, and her learning. She left many writings and among them a collection of nine hundred words translated from an unknown language (perhaps a forerunner of Esperanto) where she quotes the word *ziriskans* as corresponding to *uingerhuth*, which was the early German word for a thimble. The list is made up largely of articles of daily life, so that it may be deduced that already in the twelfth century the thimble was well known and in common use.

Given that thimbles were already used in the twelfth century, the earliest thimble about whose date it is possible to be reasonably sure is one which was found in the course of the excavations of the Raubritterburg Tannenberg which took place in 1848 in the Bergstrasse at Darmstadt. The Burg (castle) was destroyed in 1399 and was never rebuilt, so that the thimble is not likely to have been any later. Unfortunately this thimble, which was in the Hessischen Landesmuseum (Kabinetmuseum) collection, was lost during the Second World War, but it is known from illustrations that it was almost identical to a thimble in the Kam Museum collection at Nijmegen (see illustration) and there is every reason to believe that it was a genuine fourteenth-century thimble.

Turning now to the question of where such thimbles were made, it is important to remember

Medieval brass thimble. Probably circa 1400. *Rijksmuseum G. M. Kam, Nijmegen*

that Lower Saxony was one of the principal sources of brass during the Middle Ages. Hildesheim, Goslar, and Minden were the main brass-founding towns and they obtained their raw materials from the mines of the Harz Mountains, which provided a generous supply of both copper and calamine. Trade in brass was surprisingly widespread and although Nuremberg was a long way away, it drew on these resources and became renowned for its brass work, including its brass thimbles. Nuremberg's prosperity depended on providing for the needs of others and its merchants ranged far and wide on their yearly expeditions to the great fairs of Leipzig, Hamburg, Lübeck and the like. From there Nuremberg manufactures found their way to lesser fairs or to local shops. In a German shrovetide play of the fifteenth century a shopkeeper calls his wares as follows:

Auch habich nadelin, pursten und hem,
Fingerhout, taschen und nestel vil.

(Needles have I, brushes and combs
Thimbles, purses, laces in plenty.)

Or they might be sold by itinerant vendors or peddlers trudging from village to village with their packs on their back and their packstaff in their hand. And beyond the great fairs thimbles were also exported in large quantities. Thimbles are known to have been available in Scandinavia from the thirteenth century onward;[1] these probably came from Nuremberg, and many of the thimbles imported into England came from the same source. There is evidence that by Tudor times England was well established as an importer of thimbles and there is even evidence to suggest that from England some were reexported as far afield as Iceland, where they were exchanged for fish.[2]

The first reference to thimble making in Nuremberg dates from 1373, when an artisan named Praun is mentioned as being a thimble-maker. Nothing more is known about him, but we have information about another thimble-maker who appears to have been a contemporary of his and who ended his days in a home for aged artisans (Mendelschen Institute). In an old register which is now in the possession of the City Library of Nuremberg, may be seen a picture of a thimble-maker at work with a caption reading "The sixteenth brother who died who was called Fingerling and was a thimble-maker". Fingerling died about 1400, so that he was probably exercising his trade at about the same time as Praun. The picture (see color plate) shows him drilling the indentations, and on the table in the background there are a number of thimbles, some of which resemble closely the thimble found in the Burg Tannenberg. In accordance with the fashion of the time, the artist has enlarged the thimbles beyond their proper scale in order to make the illustration more intelligible.

Thus it may be seen that there are three small prongs at the end of the drill. These were intended to support the drill and steady it while the bit bore down in between.

It is probable that neither Praun nor Fingerling actually made thimbles but that they purchased ready cast blanks from a coppersmith and contented themselves with adding the indentations. The members of the guild of coppersmiths (Rotschmiedezunft) made a wide range of cast brass objects, notably clasps and buckles for harness and saddlery. Theirs was a well-established and tightly knit trade and they may well have looked down on the thimble-makers, who lacked guild status and were little more than piece workers working from home. In those days thimble making in Nuremberg was still what was known as a free trade, which is to say that anyone could engage in it and there was no training or examination required. This had certain advantages, but it also meant that those concerned did not enjoy guild privileges nor could they look to the protection which membership in a guild could afford its members. The thimble-makers sought to remedy this situation, and from 1462 (1490 is sometimes mentioned) thimble making came to be incorporated with brass founding in the guild of coppersmiths.

Up to that time most thimbles were still made by casting, but about 1530 improvements in the technique of brass founding resulted in a brighter and more uniform product. Thimble-makers discovered that starting from sheet metal they could make thimbles which were better and more elegant than they could make by the old casting methods. They therefore found themselves at odds with their own guild, and in 1534 (here again the dates sometimes vary) they were allowed to set up a separate guild of their own. The line of demarcation between the new guild and the old was spelled out carefully in 1537 as follows:

Item: Resolved that the coppersmiths alone be permitted to make cast thimbles but that they are not permitted to make thimbles of beaten metal which latter will be made by the thimble-makers and of these only such as have learned the trade.

In the circumstances this was perfectly logical and no one could foresee that within a generation or two there would be a reversion to casting methods and that it would spell the end of Nuremberg thimble making.

Once incorporated into a guild, the thimble-makers became more closely regulated. Traditionally, in order to become a master, an apprentice was required to demonstrate his skill by providing a suitable example of his work, which was known as a masterpiece. According to Christoph Weigel, this also applied to apprentice thimble-makers.[3] He recalls that about 1500 an apprentice named Heinrich Leisen submitted a masterpiece which consisted partly of two dozen domed or pressed thimbles about the size of a thaler and somewhat like the ferrule at the end of a large stick and partly of two dozen silk embroiderers' thimbles of a size suitable to fit on the finger and with small round indentations. The inference is that the former were large thimbles of a size suitable for heavy work whereas the latter were small thimbles designed to fit a lady's finger.

The civic authorities of Nuremberg watched over their artisans and regulated their activities very closely. For instance, an artisan was not allowed to leave the city without special permission, and if permission was granted he could not take his tools with him. Nor was an artisan allowed much independence of action. The regulations might even repress improvements in trade, as happened in 1572[4] when a master thimble-maker named Jörg Endtner who had invented a new kind of lathe was forbidden to use it because other masters complained that it placed them at a disadvantage. There was, however, one valuable rule which was strictly enforced, namely, that no goods of inferior quality or workmanship were allowed to leave the city for fear of injuring its reputation. Perhaps in consequence of so many regulations the thimble-makers' guild never really flourished, and the lack of prosperity of its members is evidenced by a note on a folio sheet dated 1621, as follows:

Die Bader, Küfer, Fingerhüter,
Bringen zusammen nicht viel Güter.[5]

Or in other words, the bathkeepers, coopers, and thimble-makers amassed no wealth.

Returning to the sixteenth century, the well-known illustration by Jost Amman will serve to explain the process for making thimbles starting from sheet metal. This engraving, which was first published in 1564, was reproduced in *Eigentliche Beschreibung aller Stände auff Erden*, by Hans Sachsen, 1568, and was accompanied by a few lines of verse:

Der Fingerhüter
Auss Messing mach ich Fingerhüt
Blechweiss werden in Feuwer glüt
Denn in das Ensen glenck getriebn
Darnach Löchlein darein gehiebn
Gar mancherln art eng und weit
Für Schuster und Schneider bereit
Für Seidensticker und Näterin
Dess Handwercks ich ein Meister bin.

(The Thimble-maker
Out of brass I make thimbles, metal plate
is tempered by fire, then it is stamped
in a die, after which holes are indented:
of many sizes, narrow and broad:
for cobblers and tailors made,
for silk workers and seamstresses.
I am a master of this craft).

The process is not difficult to follow. The basic implement was a heavy iron block with holes of different sizes. The sheet metal (usually brass) was hammered into the holes by means of graduated punches and the metal was heated at intervals in a furnace to soften it and make it more malleable. The latter is known as annealing. Once the final stage was reached the holes were added by hand individually with a punch or drill. The thimbles were then pickled in acid (acid dip) to clean them after the annealing process, following which they were polished and made ready for sale. Alternatively the thimbles might sometimes be tinned, presumably to give the appearance of silver.

Richer and more delicately decorated thimbles were also made of fine metal, normally silver. They were produced by the silversmiths since to make them required a degree of engraving and chasing skill which an ordinary thimble-maker could not be expected to possess. Moreover, not content with making straightforward silver thimbles, the German silversmiths developed a fashion for more sophisticated articles of a kind which a lady might be pleased to receive but which were not intended for practical needlework. Weigel gives the following description:

There are also double thimbles with the inner part being completely smooth and gilded, and

The thimble-maker. After an engraving by Jost Amman (1539–91).

Sixteenth century brass with decorated border. Round the rim the inscription "Glick und Lieb stielt mir kein dieb 1599" (happiness and affection no thief can steal from me). *Kunstgewerbe Museum, West Berlin*

the outer part which fits snugly over the inner part is made of silver and worked in filigree which looks very attractive. They often decorate the lower edge of the thimble by engraving garlands, foliage, animals and the like, in which type of work the craftsmen of Nuremberg remained the leaders because foreigners seldom engage in it.

Weigel was writing in the latter part of the seventeenth century, but the Nuremberg craftsmen were nothing if not conservative, and the description applies equally well to thimbles made a hundred years earlier. A number of thimbles of this kind have survived from the period 1580–1600, and since they usually bear a date there is little room for uncertainty. One

type, for instance, consists of three detachable parts of which regrettably one or other of the parts is often missing. There is an inner cylinder which is designed to fit round the finger; it is smooth without indentations and may be decorated round the base with a coursing scene, a date, or some motto. At the top there may be an enamel crest or a miniature portrait covered with glass or crystal. There is an outer sleeve made of pierced metal or filigree, which fits round the cylinder and covers the lower part of it. And there is an indented cap which fits over the upper part of the cylinder and keeps the sleeve in position. This is only one of several different constructions, each more impractical than the other, and the decoration of thimbles was evidently considered sufficiently important that the Frankfurt copper engraver Jos. Theo. de Bry (1528–98), who engraved ornamental designs for use by jewelers and other craftsmen, also applied himself to the subject. He designed thimbles with engravings based on mythological or biblical themes, and round his thimbles can be found cupids or guardian angels surrounded by mottoes in Latin or French, such as *Vis amoris, Force d'amour*, and the like. Obviously a needlewoman who sought to use thimbles of this kind would not get very far. They were intended as fashionable toys, objects made to look like thimbles but with the cap concealing some added token to enhance the gift. One way or another this was a fashion which was to continue throughout the seventeenth and eighteenth centuries. A common feature is the sleeve of pierced metal which was often decorated with enamel and which persisted throughout with variations in wirework or filigree. The English filigree thimbles from the late eighteenth or early nineteenth century are in the same tradition. A filigree thimble as such is largely useless and the inspiration must surely have originated from those

Silver thimble with removable cap. Nuremberg 1596. *Kestner Museum, Hanover*

28

Design for thimbles. After an engraving by Joh. Theo. de Bry (1528–98).

double thimbles which Weigel thought were so attractive.

There is no obvious reason to account for the decline of thimblemaking in Nuremberg but it is possible that like the decline of the guilds it can be traced back to too much adherence to old traditions and to the disregard of changing conditions. The importance of thimble making at the turn of the eighteenth century was still considerable, but within a hundred years it had vir-

Silver gilt thimble with removable cap (missing) and inside under a transparent cover a shield with flowers and near it the date 1606 and the letters VGMN. The sides surrounded by ornamentation and at the rim the inscription IVNKFRAW (Miss) IVSTINA VON HERTEN. Height 2.0 cm. *Kunstgewerbe Museum, West Berlin*

tually disappeared. Gatterer reviews this development as follows:

> They [the thimble-makers] were a very important craft in olden times, . . . but even here they sought to impose restrictions to their own greatest disadvantage. So sure is it that their craft has greatly declined in recent years that in 1784 there were only two masters left, namely Pouner and Hautsch, with the former working on his own and the latter with only one apprentice. Whereas around 1720 there were still ten masters working. The reason for the decline is the following: In Nuremberg thimbles and finger rings were still finished by the old traditional method whereby the indentations were applied by hand with a punch, as a result of which the work was very slow and by no means so well finished as by the modern method. Then in the neighborhood of Aachen where the majority of thimbles are now made they started to make indentations mechanically under pressure. The Nuremberg thimble-makers would not accept the new method or that the Aachen thimble-makers were capable of supplying finer and cheaper wares. They continue to operate under strict prohibitions to this day which they are not prepared to change, even though it would obviously be to their advantage. That the Nuremberg thimble-makers were formerly held in very high esteem is true, but unfortunately it is equally true that the Nuremberg merchants ordered many thimbles from Aachen and then dispatched them far and wide passing them off as Nuremberg merchandise.[6]

While Gatterer's account of the decline of thimble making in Nuremberg may be factually correct, it probably overlooks some more fundamental problems. Already by 1698 Christoph Weigel had noted the competition from thimble-makers in Holland as well as from other parts of Germany. By the time Gatterer was writing in 1784 not only had the Dutch thimble-making industry reached its zenith but from Holland it had spawned to England, where the English thimble-making industry had taken root and in its turn had displaced the Dutch. During the eighteenth century it was the Birmingham thimble-makers who were in the ascendant, thimble making was becoming industrialized, and the move away from Nuremberg was part of a wider development. Moreover Gatterer failed to realize that very much at the time he was writing the thimble-making industry in Germany was in

The thimble-maker's workshop. After an engraving in Christoph Weigel, **Abbildung der Gemein-Nützlichen Haupt-Stande**, Regensburg, 1698.

the throes of complete reconstruction. On the one hand, that part of the industry concerned with iron and brass was establishing new roots, notably in South Westphalia, in the region of Iserlohn, Hemer, Sundwig, and Altena, in the area of the River Lenne and its tributaries where machinery could be put into motion by water power. There it would develop and flourish in conjunction with other kindred activities and there it remains to this day. A full account will be found below in the chapter on brass thimbles. On the other hand, that part of the industry concerned with fine metals remained with the silver-smiths and marked time while waiting for more favorable circumstances. There was still extreme poverty throughout much of Central Europe, so that unlike Britain the demand for silver thimbles remained limited. What demand there was tended to be concentrated more on gifts and toys such as those elegant thimble and needlecase pedestal combinations which are so typical of the German silver industry during the eighteenth century. In the more common form, the thimble covers a small bobbin for thread, the stem serves as a needlecase, and the foot is adapted as a letter seal. These, however, were luxury items and

Silver—putti playing musical instruments. Circa 1700. Height 2.1 cm. There is an almost identical thimble in the Colonial Williamsburg Foundation collection. *Private collection*

for silver thimbles increased, new techniques were developed which brought the mass production of thimbles within the realm of possibility, and it was then only a matter of time before some enterprising silversmith found it worthwhile to specialize in making silver thimbles and to set up as a full-scale thimble manufacturer.

In the event, it was Johann Ferdinand Gabler, who was born in 1778, the son of a tailor, and became a silversmith at Schorndorf in Württemberg, who set up the first thimble manufactory. Possibly because of his family associations, he gradually came to concentrate on making thimbles and in 1824 the King of Württemberg granted him a charter (patent) for a special machine designed for thimble making. The original business started in 1825 and his sons built on these beginnings to establish the company of Gebrüder Gabler GmbH. About 1850 the business occupied a millhouse, but these premises became inadequate and new premises were built to accommodate a production which by the second half of the century was being exported worldwide. At its peak in 1914, just before the start of the First World War, Gebrüder Gabler employed 150 workers. In fact Gebrüder Gabler remained the largest manufacturers of thimbles in Germany, including thimbles of gold, silver, brass, nickel, aluminum, and even at one time plastic, for well over a hundred years. Their thimbles sometimes bear the mark of a letter *G* in a rosette, or they may have a star-shaped pattern woven into the indentations at the top, but more often than not they are completely unmarked. Gebrüder Gabler continued to make thimbles until 1963 when owing to falling demand they abandoned the production of thimbles, and turned their attention to more profitable activities.

it was not until after the end of the Napoleonic wars that economic conditions began to improve and that as a result silversmiths began to redeploy and flourish in such centers as Pforzheim, Schwäbisch-Gmünd, and Hanau. The demand

Silver thimbles from Germany and neighboring territories. The marks 12 and 13 refer to the silver content reckoned in loths and indicate that the thimbles were made before 1860. *Private collection*

Muster-Tabelle I.
der Pforzheimer-Fingerhut-Fabrik von Lotthammer & Stützel.

Für mit Silberböden sind nachstehende Nummern gültig.
„ „ Steinböden ist zur Nummer ¼ beizusetzen.
„ „ Stahlböden „ „ „ ½ „
„ „ glanz gekratzte „ „ „ ¾ „

Innere Grössen-Maase.

7 6 5 4 3 2 1 0

Gangbarste Grössen.

101	102	103	104	105	106	107	108	109	110
Matt ganz weifs	Matt mit Schild ganz weifs	Matt innen vergoldet	Matt mit Schild innen vergoldet	Matt, Hohlkehlen u. innen vergoldet	Matt m. Schild. Hohlkehlen Schild u. innen vergoldet	Matt. Bordur u. innen vergoldet	Matt m. Schild. Schild. Bordur u. inen vergoldet	Ganz vergoldet	Matt ganz weifs ganz gelöchert
111	112	113	114	115	116	117	118	119	120
Matt ganz gelöchert innen vergoldet	Matt, ganz weifs	Matt inen vergoldet	Matt, Hohlkehlen und innen vergoldet	Crvolen, glanz nur oben gelöchert ganz weifs	Crvolen glanz nur oben gelöchert inen vergoldet	Matt mit Schild emaillirte Borduren innen vergoldet	Matt mit Schild emaillirte Borduren Hohlkehlen u. inen vergoldet	Matt m. aufgelötheten Gallerien, emaillirt u. innen vergoldet	Matt mit aufgeloth. Gallerien, emaillirt u. inen u. inen vergoldet
121	122	123	124	125	126	127	128	129	130
Matt m. aufgelötheten Gallerien innen vergoldet	Matt m. aufgelötheten Gallerien u. innen vergold.	Matt m. aufgelötheten Gallerien innen vergoldet	Matt m. aufgelötheten Gallerien innen vergoldet	Matt m. aufgelötheten Gallerien u. Hohlkehlen innen vergold.	Matt m. damascirter Bordur ganz weifs	Matt m. damascirter Bordur, inen vergoldet	Matt m. Schild damascirter Bordur Hohlkehlen Schild u. inen vergoldet	ANDENKEN — Matt innen vergoldet	ANDENKEN — Matt mit Schild Hohlkehlen, Buchsta Schild u. inen vergold.
131	132	133	134	135	136	137	138	139	140
GOTT SCHÜTZE DICH — Matt innen vergoldet	GOTT SCHÜTZE DICH — Matt m. Schild. Hohlkehlen Schild u. innen vergoldet	SOUVENIR — Matt innen vergoldet	SOUVENIR — Matt m. Schild Bordur. Hohlkehlen u. inen verg.	AMISTAD — Matt m. Schild. Hohlkehlen Schild u. innen vergoldet	RECUERDO — Matt m. Schild. Hohlkehlen Schild u. innen vergoldet	MEMORIA — Matt m. Schild. Hohlkehlen Schild u. innen vergoldet	DIOS TE PROTEGA — Matt m. Schild. Hohlkehlen Schild u. innen vergoldet	NO ME OLVIDAS — Matt m. Schild. Hohlkehlen Schild u. innen vergoldet	CON AMOR — Matt m. Schild. Hohlke Schild u. innen vergolde

Catalog of Lotthammer und Stützel circa 1875. *Private collection*

Needless to say that other silversmiths sought to emulate the success of the Gabler business and set up in competition. Among these was the firm of Wilhelm Lotthammer of Pforzheim, which was founded in 1850 and continued in production until the end of the Second World War, and that of Soergel and Stollmeyer of Schwäbisch-Gmünd which was founded in 1863 and continued until 1969. The mark of Soergel and Stollmeyer was a letter *S* in a triangle which may be found at the top of the thimble, but many of their thimbles merely included a star-shaped pattern similar to that of Gebrüder Gabler. Both Lotthammer and Soergel became specialized thimble-makers and competed with Gebrüder Gabler at home and in overseas markets. Other thimble manufacturers who followed included Helmut Greif of Winterbach, who was the successor to Gebrüder Gabler until the factory was destroyed by fire in 1966, and Friedrich Eber, of Pforzheim, which latter continued to make thimbles until 1980 when they finally closed down.

It is impossible to understand the workings of the German thimble-making industry during the second half of the nineteenth century and the first half of the twentieth century if it is not first understood that throughout this period the German thimble manufacturers were competing fiercely among themselves both at home and abroad. They watched over each other jealously to ensure that none of their competitors stole a march on them and they had little hesitation in copying each other's designs, trademarks, or advertisements if they thought it was to their advantage. In this connection, thimble collectors have come to associate the star-shaped pattern often to be found at the top of German thimbles with Gebrüder Gabler, but in fact this mark was copied by other manufacturers, notably by Soergel and Stollmeyer. As a general rule, sales were conducted through wholesale distributors who bought in bulk for resale to customers in their given territory. The range of choice was enormous: Gebrüder Gabler are reputed to have made some four thousand different models over the years, but even that is not the whole story. Starting from any given model, thimbles could be ordered with different kinds of tops: plain tops, stone tops of different colors, or steel; they could be made with indentations of different shapes and sizes; they could be gilded inside, outside, or both; the overall weight of a thimble could be varied by reducing the gauge of the metal; they could be ordered in a different range of sizes; and lastly, since in Germany there were no regulations governing the standard of fineness of silver above a minimum of 800 parts per thousand, the silver content could be lowered to reduce the price. In other words, given the basic model, there was an infinite number of ways in which production could be tailored to fit the customers' precise requirements.

The tremendous variety and flexibility which the German thimble manufacturers were able to offer their customers may be held an advantage, and indeed it did a great deal to promote the sales of German thimbles in many parts of the world. The negative aspect is that it encouraged lower standards. Rightly or wrongly German manufacturers before the war acquired a reputation for sacrificing quality for the sake of price, and it is not altogether unfair to apply this to thimbles. Some German thimbles were made to the highest standards using high grade silver (.925), but under the pressure of competition most manufacturers were tempted to reduce the silver content or to resort to nickel silver (alpacca). Moreover, in order to lower costs still further the weight of silver alloy itself was often reduced, with the result that the thimbles were less sturdy. It can be argued that the latter was justified because a lower silver content makes for a stronger alloy and that consequently the weight of metal could be reduced without impairing serviceability. This is fair comment, but in the process the thimble loses much of its appeal, and it is equally fair to say that there is precious little difference visually between .800 silver or silver-plated alpacca. High grade silver is attractive in a way which neither .800 silver nor alpacca can possibly hope to emulate, and to compensate for this failing the German thimble-makers tended to resort to gilding. Both .800 silver and alpacca thimbles were gilded extensively both inside and also sometimes outside as a means of decoration. This certainly improved the appearance of the thimbles but the disadvantage is that gilding soon wears off, and it is un-

German silver thimbles circa 1930. Note early-twentieth-century influence (*Jugenstil*) on design. *Private collection*

33

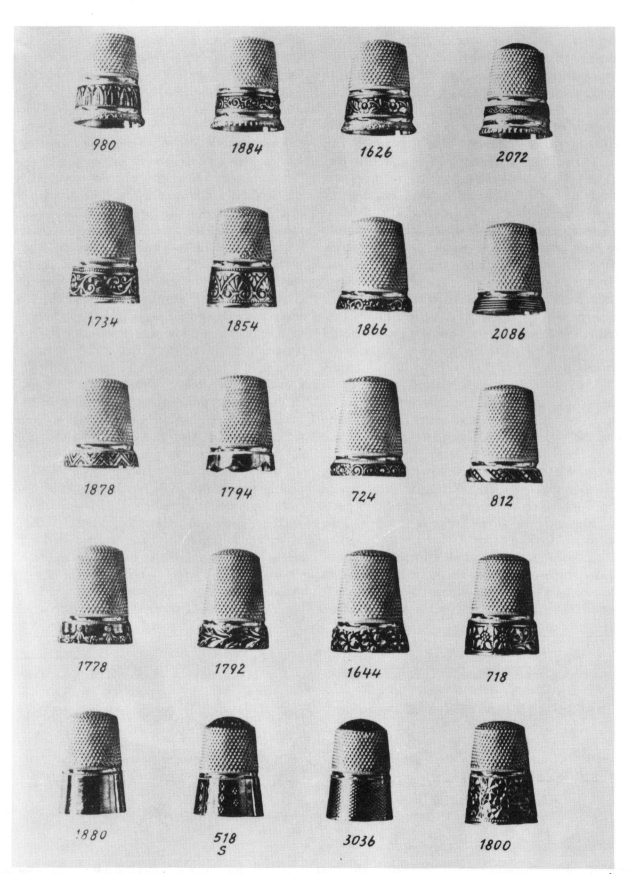

Modern German thimbles. Two plates from catalog of Friedrich Eber of Pforzheim, 1978. *Private collection*

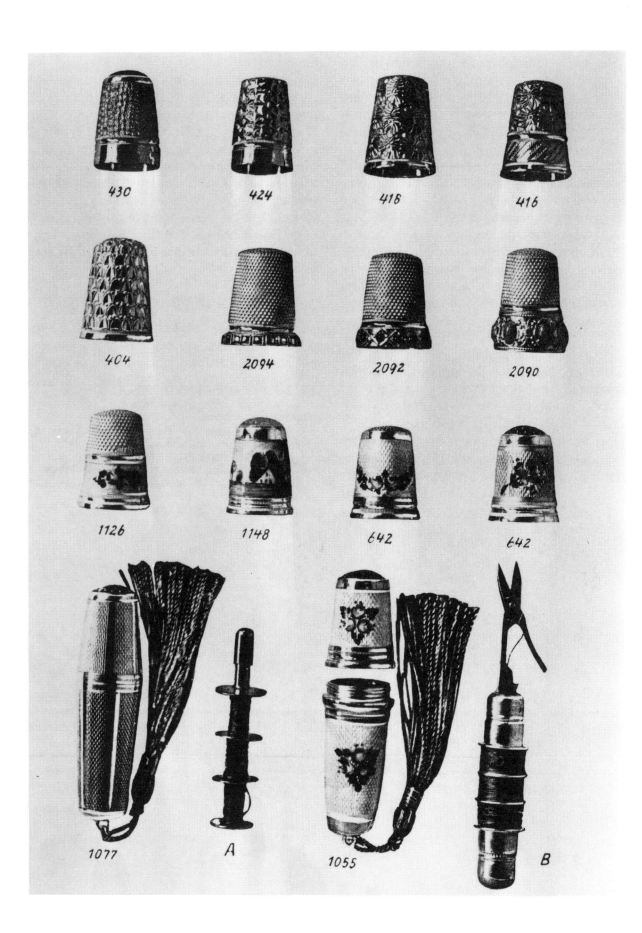

430 424 418 416

404 2094 2092 2090

1126 1148 642 642

1077 A 1055 B

doubtedly the reason why there are so many thimbles of so-called Continental origin which have little appeal. In mint condition German thimbles can be a magnificent sight and they are rightly sought after, but once they have been used only the better quality ones are likely to have kept their attractiveness.

German thimbles never found their way in any great number to Britain or to the countries which were part of the British Empire because Britain had its own thimble industry, which was strongly based and which enjoyed tariff protection. Similarly, German thimbles found it difficult to compete in the United States, although Gebrüder Gabler's Masta brand sterling silver and enamel thimbles did manage to find a limited market. But outside these two countries the German thimble industry had the field almost entirely to itself and it made the best of it. Thimbles were exported throughout the world, but not content with supplying the usual type of thimbles, the German manufacturers sought to increase sales by supplying keepsake thimbles, souvenir thimbles, and a range of religious thimbles specially designed for the purpose. Thimbles with a religious motif are a peculiarly German development (see page 188) which has no counterpart either in Britain or in the United States.

German silver thimbles continued to be sold until recently in many countries, notably those made by Friedrich Eber of Pforzheim. The maker's mark showing twin figures linked together belongs to J. A. Henckels of Solingen, who sold Eber thimbles under their own name but do not manufacture. Unfortunately Eber have now discontinued production and although the tools and equipment were acquired by a son of Helmut Greif who is also a thimble-maker, it is unlikely that production will return to its former scale.

NOTES

1. *Kulturhistorik Lensikor for Nordisk Middelalder,* vol. 4. (Copenhagen: Rosenkilde og Bagger, 1959).

2. Icelandic archives MS (DI XVI s.89).

3. Christoph Weigel, *Abbildung der Gemein-Nützlichen Haupt-Stände* (Regensburg, 1698).

4. Johannes Janssen, *History of the German People after the Close of the Middle Ages* (London, 1905–25), vol. 25.

5. J. and W. Grimm, *Deutsches Wörterbuch.*

6. Christoph Gatterer and Wilhelm Jacob, *Technologisches Magazin,* vol. 1, pt. 2 (Memmigen: Andreas Seyler, 1790).

Thimbles in England

THE EARLIEST MENTION OF A THIMBLE IN THE ENglish language dates from about 1412 and concerns a (th)emel of lea(th)er.[1] The reference to leather will be noted and is not altogether surprising because unlike Continental countries such as Germany and the Low Countries, medieval England did not possess an indigenous brassware industry. Consequently most articles made of brass, including thimbles, had to be imported from abroad, and the fact that thimbles are mentioned in an early customs publication dated 1550 is evidence that they were a major item of trade. This publication, known as a Book of Rates, the original of which is in the custody of the London Customs House Library, carries the following entry:

Thymbles the M   v.s.

Thus the official valuation of thimbles for import duty purposes (poundage) was five shillings per thousand, which besides giving some indication of the value of thimbles at the time also suggests that the trade was considerable, since the imports were numbered in thousands. The next Book of Rates to have survived is dated 1582, by which time the valuation had been increased:

Thimbles the M   xiijs iiijd

That is, thirteen shillings and fourpence per thousand. Thereafter the records become more plentiful: in 1610, for instance, the valuation appears as twenty shillings per thousand and in 1642 as three pounds per thousand. Then in 1690 a subsidy or additional duty was imposed on the wrought-iron content of all imported merchandise with the result that the thimbles heading needed to be divided into two separate headings, one for brass thimbles and the other for iron thimbles. The significance of the division is that it presupposes that both brass and iron thimbles were imported in fair quantities.

The above refers essentially to the assessed value of thimbles for customs purposes and not to their retail value. The inventory of James Backhouse at Kirby in Lonsdale dated 20 September 1578 includes:[2]

—j dosson and a d. o Thimbles	viijd
—Halfe a hundreth of Thimbles	xvjd
—Halfe a hundreth of Thimbles	xvjd
—ij. dos. of Thimbles	xijd

These values are not much higher than the assessed value current at the time, which seems low if allowance is made for duty, inland transport, financing, and profit. Nor do we know the quantities imported because early customs returns were not consolidated and it would be an impossible task to go through the available records in detail. It is known, however, that the list of goods entered in and cleared out, to and from the City of London, from 29 October 1682 to 1 February 1683 as extracted from the Bills of Entry included 19,500 thimbles.[3] A similar list covering the period from 1 February 1683 to 1

37

March 1683 included 10,500 thimbles; elsewhere John Houghton states that 145,000 thimbles were imported from Holland during the year 1694. In all probability the latter refers to the number imported through London. The general trade of England was about a third again of London trade, so that the annual importation for the country as a whole may have been as much as 200,000 thimbles per annum. Meanwhile, however, England had been developing its own indigenous brassware resources, and in 1693 John Lofting seized the opportunity to bring the technique of making cast brass thimbles across from Holland. His success encouraged others to set up in competition, the focus of the industry shifted to Birmingham, and during the nineteenth century Birmingham became one of the leading brass thimble-making centers. A full account of the English brass thimble-making industry will be found in the chapter on brass thimbles.

Coming back to the sixteenth century, the increased supplies of gold and silver which became available following the discovery of the New World and the growing prosperity of Elizabethan England led to a demand for silver (and occasionally gold) thimbles which had not existed previously. There is little information available regarding the growth of silver thimble making during this time or much knowledge of the goldsmiths (or silversmiths) involved, though presumably they were centered chiefly on London, with a few possibly in York, Norwich, and Bristol, which were the larger and more prosperous towns at the time. What is known however is that the use of silver for domestic purposes grew enormously and a hundred years later had become so widespread that it was commonplace among the middle classes. In particular, whereas during the first half of the sixteenth century a silver thimble was still a rare item, by the time of the Commonwealth even lesser folk might be expected to own one. Samuel Pepys in his diary for 3 April 1663 refers to a sermon in the course of which the minister, Dr. Creeton, "ripped up Hugh Peters (calling him that execrable skellum) his preaching and stirring up the maids of the city to bring in their bodkins and their thimbles." Peters, an Independent minister, had been the leading preacher of the New Model Army and had often preached begging

Seventeenth-century English silver thimble inscribed "Soe not sleeping." Height 2.8 cm. *Private collection*

sermons cajoling gifts. These donations are well documented. May wrote:

> The poorer sort, like the widow in the Gospel, presented their mites also; in so much that it was common jeer of men disaffected to the Cause, to call it the Thimble and Bodkin army.[4]

This also led to a belief that Sir John Barkstead, who was one of the major-generals who ruled England under the Commonwealth, was a thimble-maker.[5] In fact he had been a goldsmith in the Strand, but Lilburne and the Royalist pamphleteers so taunted him with selling thimbles and bodkins that it became accepted that he made them. Being one of the regicides, he fled abroad at the Restoration but was extradited from Holland and executed in 1662.

Following the Restoration there was a new surge in demand for domestic articles made of silver, so much so that it affected the coinage, and special laws were passed which, for instance, prohibited the use of silver tankards in taverns. Obviously under these conditions large quan-

38

tities of silver thimbles were undoubtedly made and some have survived. There is, however, very little information about them or about the men that made them, because the silversmiths concerned were still operating largely as individuals or in loose partnerships that came and went and have left little trace save the odd maker's mark.

Thimbles being in constant use, the demand was widespread and they were therefore very much an article of trade. In the towns brass thimbles could be purchased from mercers, haberdashers, milliners, and even from some general stores, which appear to have stocked them in considerable quantities; in the countryside they could be obtained from peddlers (so called for their "peds," or packs) and itinerant vendors who traded objects of this kind, and of course thimbles would also be available at country fairs. Brass thimbles were usually supplied in three sizes corresponding to girls', maids', and women's fittings. Silver thimbles on the other hand were somewhat different. Originally they were custom-made, but as demand increased it became worthwhile for a jeweler or silversmith to accumulate a small stock in different sizes and, as demand increased still further, for some silversmiths to specialize in making thimbles and

Portrait of John Lofting. After an engraving by J. Kip in the *London Prospects Portofolio*, circa 1690.

to resell them to the trade. Thus from London thimbles found their way to the provinces and could be bought from local jewelers and also from itinerant vendors, who by the second half of the eighteenth century featured silver thimbles among other ladies' requisites. In London during the eighteenth century they could be bought from shops such as Jho. Jackson Jewellers at Ye Crown and Pearl, George Street (1734), or John Fossey, Goldsmith and Jeweller at the Blackmoore's Head and Sun, Ye Corner of Ball Alley, Lombard Street (1748), whose trade cards both included thimbles. Large numbers of silver thimbles were also exported to the American colonies and elsewhere. Thimbles for export were normally handled by London indenting houses which purchased them for their own account and consigned them to their correspondents overseas.

The fashion for expensive trifles, *galanterien* and the like, which swept the Continent during the eighteenth century, found a following in the British Isles. Among a wide range of goods, expensive thimbles and thimble novelties could be bought from the so-called toy shops, the equivalent of the modern gift shop, which specialized in small articles, useful or ornamental, but often of a luxurious and costly nature. Among a list of objects stocked by Bellamy, a Holborn toy-seller "at the Green Parrot near Chancery Lane" in 1762 were "steel topt and other thimbles," and Deard's, a famous toy shop in Pall Mall, is also known to have stocked needlework accessories. "Deard's deluding toys" are mentioned by both Garrick and Horace Walpole. Still more expensive thimbles, such as custom-made gold or jeweled thimbles, would have been available from a goldsmith.

English silver thimbles during the seventeenth century were mostly long and cylindrical and they often bore some kind of pious exhortation or improving text. Religious fervor during the time of Puritan rule manifested itself by a wearisome obtrusiveness of scriptural phrases and virtuous maxims for every common act of life. Needlework was no exception, and it is not surprising therefore that thimbles might be inscribed with mottoes such as "Feare God," "Labour is profitable," and the like. However, following the Restoration, the practice gradually fell out of favor and with trifling exceptions during the Victorian era was never revived.

Silver filigree work, English, eighteenth century. There is an inner sleeve which is detachable. Height 2.0 cm. *Private collection*

Toward the end of the seventeenth century silver thimbles became shorter and rounder. This change may have been associated with fashions in needlework because most of the longer thimbles had bare crowns and were evidently designed to be used sideways, whereas the shorter thimbles were indented at the top. There was also a change in the nature of the indentations themselves. During the seventeenth century the indentations were either waffle shaped or else in the form of small circles, but with the turn of the century the indentations gradually evolved from the small circles into a more modern form. The design of thimbles of this period usually incorporates a shield or cartouche for the purpose of engraving the owner's cipher or monogram. A maker's mark may often be found above the shield. Sometimes the shield may consist of two hearts joined together and supported by attendant cherubs or cupids, a favored motif until well into the eighteenth century. Alternatively a plain shield might be supported by a pair of eagles or the like. The thimbles are usually made of two parts soldered together and are relatively heavy. It was not until the latter part of the eighteenth

century that silver thimbles began to be made in one piece by deep-drawing and—because deep-drawn thimbles tended to be lighter—that steel tops were introduced to ensure that they did not wear out in use.

Following the introduction of deep-drawing, short thimbles appear to have gone out of fashion in England and English styles lengthened. By 1770 the American silversmith Richardson, who was importing English silver thimbles to Philadelphia, was complaining repeatedly that the thimbles he was receiving were too long for American taste. Among those known to have made thimbles during the latter part of the eighteenth century, the best known is undoubtedly Hester Bateman, the famous eighteenth-century lady silversmith who was active from 1761 to 1790 and whose mark may be found on thimbles. An unusual feature is that instead of being stamped with a punch, Hester Bateman's mark was engraved as part of the design on the special rollers used to decorate the thimbles, which suggests that Hester Bateman made thimbles in substantial quantities.

During the latter half of the eighteenth century Birmingham also became an important center for the manufacture of silverware, and largely through the efforts of Matthew Boulton, a Birmingham businessman, and despite the opposition of the London Goldsmiths' Company, an act of Parliament was passed authorizing the opening of the Birmingham Assay Office in 1773. Thimbles came to be made increasingly in Birmingham and such prestigious firms as Samuel Pemberton and Matthew Linwood made them, as well as a host of lesser firms. Many of these thimbles were plain silver thimbles, with or without a steel top, but Birmingham was also known for its toy-makers, and these evolved some more fanciful designs. The favorite medium was filigree, which is a form of decoration, one could almost call it a construction, made from fine silver wire. Early filigree thimbles dating from the mid-eighteenth century are somewhat stubby, with a rounded hemispherical dome and well spaced and distinct indentations. The later filigree thimbles, dating from the end of the eighteenth or the beginning of the nineteenth century, are longer, with the scrolled pattern usually stretching out to include a shield shape or oval panel, which could be engraved with the owner's crest or cipher. The Birmingham toy-makers also combined filigree thimbles (and sometimes plain thimbles as well) with some kindred object to form a small compact. A typical example is that of filigree needlecase and thimble case combined, with a filigree thimble inside. Another is a filigree thimble which acts as a cover for a scent bottle and screws into a yard measure. A third is a thimble which forms the cover and screws into a base holding a small cut-glass scent bottle, the underside being engraved to provide a letter seal. There are other combinations. The association of thimbles and letter seal may appear puzzling until it is remembered that skill in the art of letter writing was held in the same esteem as proficiency in needlework—both were regarded as essential ladylike accomplishments—and it is not therefore unusual to find writing and sewing accessories combined. During the eighteenth century ladies were accustomed to use the top of their thimbles to seal a letter, and if we are to believe Robert Louis Stevenson, so were seafaring men, since it will be recalled that the map of Treasure Island was found to be sealed in several places with the captain's thimble. It is tempting to ascribe all such toys and novelties to the eighteenth century, but this is not necessarily correct. There are specimens bearing the mark of Joseph Taylor of Birmingham, who flourished well into the nineteenth century; there is a thimble, yard measure, and scent bottle combination in the Colonial Williamsburg Foundation collection which bears the date 1811; and, exceptionally perhaps, a filigree thimble in a private collection bears the date 1867.

During the first half of the nineteenth century thimbles became even longer than they had been immediately following the introduction of deep-drawing. The reasons are not entirely clear. It is possible that the longer thimbles were made in response to a demand from customers who found them more attractive or more comfortable when worn with long fingernails. Or alternatively customers may have been encouraged to accept longer thimbles by thimble-makers keen to prove their skill and to realize the full potential of deep-drawing as applied to their trade. Either way as the thimbles grew longer, so the metal walls necessarily became thinner, to the point that there was not sufficient substance left round the rim to bear anything except the most superficial of surface decorations. Thus for the more elaborately decorated thimbles it became necessary to introduce a new and more complicated method of manufacture whereby the design was die-stamped into a flat piece of silver, which was then rolled up and seamed into a ring and the ring was then in turn soldered onto the top piece of a thimble made in the conventional way. These somewhat elongated thimbles, which appear to have enjoyed their heyday about the time of the Great Exhibition of 1851, can be most elegant. The designs, which were sometimes chased after stamping, are of many kinds, but possibly the most significant from the collector's point of view are those with views of royal castles and the like. They can be very similar to the designs to be found on other small silverware of the period, notably snuffboxes. There is, for instance, a design showing Windsor Castle com-

English steel-topped silver thimbles from about 1775. *Left to right:* **SM, possibly Samuel Massey 1787–88; ASH; WT, possibly William Turton 1773–91; cursive HB, Hester Bateman 1761–80; SM (see earlier).** *Private collection*

plete with a bent pine tree, which is typical of the work of the well-known silversmith Nathaniel Mills, but the similarity can be misleading. Some firms in Birmingham specialized in the supply of ready-made die-stamps and the same design, or family of designs, did not necessarily originate from the same silversmith.

A wide range of designs was evolved during the nineteenth century and special mention should be made of a popular thimble introduced in about 1860 which was known to thimble-makers as the "scollop" model but which has since become known to collectors as a "cable" thimble. It was a relatively light thimble (average weight about 30 dwts per dozen) with an engraved border and a galerie rim. It earned its name because in 1866 a thimble of this kind was used to make an improvised battery which served to send an electric current through one of the first transatlantic cables. The story is that, after several failures, the Great Eastern had finally laid a cable between Ireland and Newfoundland and the conductors of the two lines had been joined at the Newfoundland end, thus forming an unbroken length of 3,700 miles, when the problem arose of testing the circuit. No battery being readily available, a thimble was borrowed from Miss Emily Fitzgerald, the daughter of the Knight of Kerry on whose land stood the terminal known as Telegraph House, and with its help a battery was improvised with a scrap of zinc and a few drops of acid. By this primitive agency signals were conveyed twice across the breadth of the Atlantic Ocean and were still strong enough to be recorded on a reflecting galvanometer such as had recently been devised by Professor W. Thomson (later Lord Kelvin). The thimble used for the experiment was presented to the British Science Museum in 1949, where it is on display. It is an attractive type of thimble and has become very popular with collectors. It is not rare, however, and thimbles like it continued to be made until the First World War.

The changes which have taken place in the design of English thimbles during the last hundred and fifty years or so will be evident from the illustrations, but it will help to a better understanding if care is taken to examine each example systematically. Besides the general shape and construction of a thimble, it is neces-

Cable thimble. The silver thimble used to generate current through the Atlantic Telegraph Cable. *The Science Museum, London*

sary to distinguish three main parts, namely the top, the border and the rim. Each part should be considered separately.

Top. What constitutes the top or crown of a thimble is obvious until it is remembered that in German, *mit Steinboden* means "with a stone bottom" or "flooring," but either way it is that part of the thimble which bears the indentations or holes as they are commonly known to thimble-makers. For silver thimbles there might be three sizes of holes, fine, coarse, and extra coarse, to correspond with different sizes of needles. A thimble with a plain top would have holes running down to the border. Instead of holes the thimbles could have a steel top or a stone top. There is also the style of thimble which became popular toward the end of the nineteenth century, which no longer had holes in the accepted sense of the word but instead relied on some heavily indented pattern reaching all over the thimble. These were known as chased thimbles.

42

It is easy to be deceived by the regularity and exactness of the design on chased thimbles, which suggests that they were impressed mechanically, but in fact the reason why they are so bright and attractive is that the design was not rolled on but was struck with a cutting tool. Moreover, to achieve the necessary degree of sharpness, the tools were built up of individual components so that in the case of a flowered pattern it can almost be said that each petal was struck separately. Similar considerations apply to other designs and the chased thimbles produced by James Fenton, for instance, are particularly fine and attractive.

Border. The border may be defined as that part of the thimble which lies between the rim and the holed portion of the thimble and which usually carries the decoration. There are innumerable ways of decorating the border of a thimble, with each thimble manufacturer having his own designs. In many cases manufacturers made no attempt to describe the border of their different models, merely giving the thimble a code name or a number and allowing for variations in the nature of the top and allowing for different rims. The border is the part which carries a shield if the thimble is intended to have the initials of the owner engraved on it. It is also the part which carries any lettering, as in resort thimbles. The most common pattern during the latter half of the nineteenth century was an engraved border featuring a bright cut wavy design of the kind which would readily be worked with a rose machine, or even by hand with a graving tool. Subsequently many English thimbles came to have a chased border with a more pronounced pattern. Alternatively the border might carry applied decorations of the galerie type (cable thimbles), small individual incrustations such as semiprecious stones, or be decorated with enamel. The very simplest kind of border consists of a plain band between two hollow rings.

Rim. Top or bottom, there can be no argument about what constitutes the open end of a thimble or the rim running round it. The usual way of making the rim of a thimble is to turn it over, after which it can be finished flat, round, cut (faceted), beaded, or chased. If the rim is not turned over it can be left flat, plain, or with a design or else it may have a decorative edging applied round it. A rim which is not turned over and deep enough may sometimes take the place of a border. The rims of English thimbles tend to be plainer than those of either German or French thimbles.

Having examined these aspects of a thimble, a thimble-maker would also look for some more specialized features. By and large, English thimbles are not gilded on the outside, the makers preferring to rely on the appeal of plain silver, though quite often they are gilded on the inside to give a warmer effect. Some of the designs may also have been oxidized for contrast or else

English silver thimbles. *Left to right:* **1851 Great Exhibition showing registered design mark; plain top and decorated border; plain top, engraved border, and galerie rim; cable type with Manx shield; daisy pattern with engraved border and galerie rim.** *Private collection*

HALL MARKED SILVER THIMBLES.

215	303	404	474	532 D	671
213	302	403	447	531 G	656
213 S	300	400	443	530 A	654
213	289	334	440	519	653
212	287	328	427	504	650
206	279			500	642
205	270 S	400		485	640
204	270	327	423	483	590
204	249	323	420	481	585
203	235	320	418	480	570
202	233	307	412	476	550
201	229	304	407	475	536 B

Charles Horner catalog of hallmarked silver thimbles circa 1900. *Private collection*

Hall Marked Silver Thimbles.

No.	TOP.	BORDER.	RIM.	Average Weight Per Doz. in Dwts.					Fashion Per Doz.	All Out Per Doz.
201	Plain	Two Hollow	Flat, Turn Over	20	30	40	50	60	1/4	
202	,,		,, ,, ,,			40	50	60	1/4	
203	,,	Plain, Narrow	Round, ,, ,,	20	30	40	50	60	1/4	
204	,,		,, ,, ,,			40	50		1/4	
204	,, Tailors		,, ,, ,,			40	50		1/4	
205	,,	,, ,,	Faceted, ,, ,,	20	30	40	50	60	1/6	
206	,,		,, ,, ,,			40	50		1/6	
212	,,	Deep, Engraved	Round, ,, ,,			40	50		2/6	
213	,,	,, ,,	Faceted, ,, ,,	20	30	40	50		1/8	
213 S	,, Stone End	,, ,,	,, ,, ,,	20						6/6
213	,, Child's	,, ,,	,, ,, ,,	16					1/8	
215	,,		Threaded, ,, ,,			40	50		1/6	
229	,,	Daisy	Flat, ,, ,,		30	40			2/-	
233	,,	Diamond	,, ,, ,,		30	40			2/-	
235	,,	,,	Faceted, ,, ,,		30	40			2/2	
249	,,	Engraved	Galerie		30					9/-
270	,,	,,	,,		30					9/-
270 S	,, Stone End	,,	,,		30					11/-
279	,,	Princess May	Flat, Turn Over		30	40			2/-	
287	,,		Beaded, ,, ,,			40	50		2/-	
289	,,	Deep, Engraved				40	50		4/-	
300	Daisy		Flat		30	40			3/6	
302	,,	Plain, Narrow	Round, Turn Over	20	30	40			3/6	
303	,,		Faceted, ,, ,,	20	30	40			3/8	
304	,,	Diamond	Flat		30	40	45		4/-	
307	,,	,,	Faceted, Turn Over			40	45		4/2	
320	Diamond	Two Hollow	Flat, ,, ,,		30	40	45		4/-	
323	,,	Plain, Narrow	Faceted,			40	45		4/2	
327	,,	Daisy	,, ,, ,,			40	45		4/2	
328	,,	Persian	Flat, ,, ,,		30	40	45		4/-	
334	,, and Bead	Plain, Narrow	Faceted, ,, ,,			40	45		4/2	
400	Princess May	Two Hollow	Flat		30	40	45		4/-	
403	,, ,,	Plain, Narrow	Faceted, Turn Over			40	45		4/2	
404	,, ,,	Diamond	Flat		30	40	45		4/-	
407	,, ,,	,,	Faceted, Turn Over			40	45		4/2	
412	,, ,,		Flat, Louise				45		5/6	
418	,, ,, and Bead	Plain, Narrow	Faceted, Turn Over			40	45		4/2	
420	Shell		Flat		30	40	45		4/-	
423	,,		Faceted, Turn Over			40	45		4/2	
427	,,	Diamond	,, ,, ,,			40	45		4/2	
440	Louise		Flat		30	40	45		4/-	
443	,,	Plain, Narrow	Faceted, Turn Over			40	45		4/2	
447	,,	Diamond	,, ,, ,,			40	45		4/2	
474	Princess May	1 Row, Ottoman	Louise				45		6/-	
475	Plain	,, ,,	,,			40			4/-	
476	Diamond	,, ,,	,,				45		6/-	
480	Plain	Stamped	Flat				45	60	3/-	
481	Daisy	,,	,,				45	50	5/6	
483	Diamond	,,	,,				45	60	6/-	
485	Princess May	,,	,,				45	60	6/-	
500	Diamond	1 Row, Ottoman	,,				45		5/-	
504	Plain	,, ,,	Faceted, Turn Over		30	40			2/2	
519	,,	,, ,,	Flat, ,, ,,		30	40			2/-	
530 A	,,	Galerie	Round, ,, ,,			40				12/6
531 G	Daisy	,,	,, ,, ,,			40				15/-
532 D	Diamond	,,	,, ,, ,,			40				15/-
536 B	Princess May	,,	,, ,, ,,			40				15/-
550	Plain	Hammered	Flat,							4/6
570	Daisy	Fancy			30				4/-	
586	Plain	Plain, Narrow	Deep, Polygon				45		6/-	
590	Queen	Two Hollow	Flat		30	40	45		4/-	
600	Plain, Whisky Measure	Lettered	Round, Turn Over							60/-
640		Plain, Narrow	Cut Vandyked			40				10/6
642	Daisy	,, ,,	,, ,,			40				12/6
650	Plain	,, ,,	,, Annular			40				10/6
653	Diamond	,, ,,	,, ,,			40				12/6
654	Princess May	,, ,,	,, ,,			40				12/6
656	Louise	,, ,,	,, ,,			40				12/6
671	Plain	Enamelled Hammered	Flat			40				W/T

Charles Horner price list circa 1900. *Private collection*

highly polished. Hallmarks and maker's marks may call for comment, but another important feature is the size and weight of the thimble. Some models can run from 20 dwts. per dozen to 60 dwts. per dozen for an identical assortment of sizes so that one thimble can be three times heavier than the other. Obviously the lighter thimble is a puny thing, whereas the heavier one is a quality item which is likely to prove more durable and resistant. Since obviously neither the weight nor indeed the silver content can be judged from an illustration, this serves to underline the need to see and handle a thimble before it is possible to pass a valid judgment.

The strict regulations which govern the activities of goldsmiths and silversmiths in Britain have had the result that unlike in Germany, there is a clear division between the manufacturers of gold and silver thimbles on the one hand and those of base metals on the other. In Germany most thimble manufacturers making silver thimbles also made thimbles of nickel silver and what with lower grade silver (800), silver-plated nickel silver (alpacca) and the possibility of applying gilding to both indiscriminately, the two have come to overlap. In England however where a thimble-maker could not sell a thimble as silver unless it was sterling (925), there was no option but to make virtue out of necessity. The silver thimble was featured as a quality item and did not seek to compete with nickel silver, the latter being left in the hands of the brass thimble manufacturers, who produced nickel silver thimbles and marketed them with their other production at the cheaper end of the market. This lack of competitiveness was damaging to the English silver thimble industry in the sense that it found it difficult to stand up to the Germans when selling abroad, but on the other hand it does mean that there were fewer temptations to compromise, and English silver thimbles are generally speaking of the highest quality.

It would be pointless to seek to list all the silversmiths who are known to have made thimbles because in many cases theirs was only a passing interest and because such a list would necessarily remain incomplete. It is estimated that a full list to cover the nineteenth century would comprise well over a hundred names. On the other hand there are certain names which remained associated with thimble making over several generations, the oldest being undoubtedly Charles May of London, who were first recorded as thimble-makers in Bethnal Green as early as 1805 and who continued to make thimbles, mainly of gold and silver, at various addresses in the East End of London until about 1929. The other important name in London is Henry Foskett (later Samuel Foskett) who are first recorded in 1865 and continued making thimbles until about 1912. Most of the silver thimble-makers however were situated in Birmingham and they include two outstanding names. The first, James Fenton, who was listed in 1839 as a thimble-maker occupying premises in Constitution Hill, subsequently moved first to Great Hampton Street, and then to Hockley Hill. The firm was still in existence in 1921 though they no longer made thimbles. The other is the firm of Henry Griffith, which is noteworthy because it was set up specifically to be a thimble manufacturer and became a leader in the field.

Henry Griffith started the business which bore his name in 1856 and occupied premises in Leamington Spa. Under his direction the firm prospered and he became one of the biggest thimble manufacturers in the country. His sons, Fred Griffith and John Henry Griffith, took over when he retired and in 1916 the business was formed into a public company. However, two years later, Fred Griffith (the older son but by a different wife) bought back the share of his half brother and it reverted to a private company. Fred was born in 1866, joined the family firm in 1880 and died in 1951 at the age of eighty-five, after seventy-one years with the company. Henry Griffith and Sons' business was largely with British firms, having a close working relationship with Sanders the jewelers, and they did little export trade. They were badly hit by the depression, but by that time the company had been successful in developing other lines and had become a large manufacturing silversmith. Henry Griffith and Sons continued making thimbles until 1955, when sales no longer justified the amount of factory space required and production was discontinued. In 1974 Henry Griffith and Sons were taken over by another group but they remain in existence to this day. Thimbles were the beginning of Henry Griffith and Sons and they continued to make them for one hundred years.

Silver thimbles from James Fenton catalog circa 1900. *Private collection*

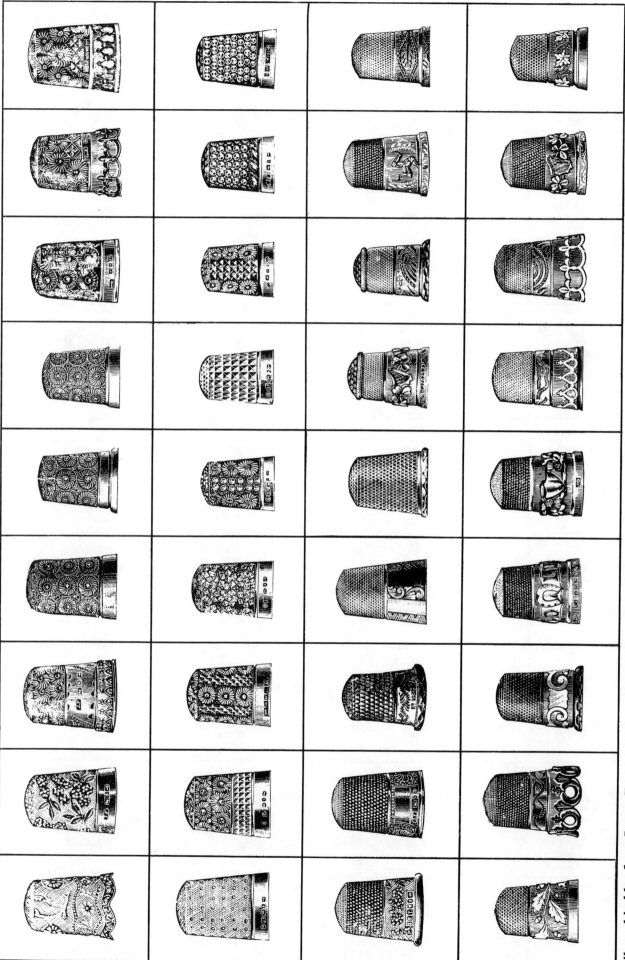

Silver thimbles from James Fenton catalog circa 1900. *Private collection*

Besides James Fenton and Henry Griffith, the firm of James Swann should also be mentioned. The latter were first listed in 1890 when James Swann (gold and silver thimble manufacturer, late with James Fenton) was occupying premises at 59 Bramston Street. After the founder's death his son and then his goddaughter carried on the business always under the original name. They are said to be the only gold and silver thimble manufacturers left in Britain, but this would appear to ignore the claims of F. Field.

Other Birmingham silver thimble manufacturers who were active during the middle part of the nineteenth century included Joseph Addis, who is known to have been active in thimble making from about 1828 to 1865, James Collins from about 1828 to 1870, and James Webb from about 1843 to 1890. However, since most silver thimbles before 1885 remained unmarked there is little point in delving too deeply, but mention must also be made of Charles Horner of Halifax, who started in 1885 and produced the Dorcas thimble (see relevant chapter). By the turn of the century Charles Horner, James Fenton, Henry Griffith, Samuel Foskett, and James Swann (and also Charles May who by that time concentrated more on gold thimbles) dominated the market and between them they account for most of the English silver (and gold) thimbles in the hands of collectors.

The absence of marks on early English thimbles is somewhat confusing and requires some explanation. Under the Plate Offences Act of 1738 (12 Geo.II c.26), described as an act for the Better Preventing of Fraud and Abuses in Gold and Silver, thimbles were specifically exempted from hallmarking in common with other objects weighing less than ten pennyweights. The act remained in force until the act of 1790 (30 Geo.III c.31) which reduced the exemption limit to five pennyweights (about 8 grams), but as most thimbles weighed less than this amount, thimbles remained unmarked for the next hundred years. Then from about 1885 or thereabouts English thimble manufacturers started to send thimbles for hallmarking at the assay offices. The reasons for this are not entirely clear. It is a practice which appears to have grown gradually and it was not until 1895 that it was adopted on a regular basis. It is possible that the activities of Charles Horner may have had something to do with it. Charles Horner made both silver thimbles and silver thimbles with steel lining, so that he may have been tempted to have his silver thimbles hallmarked as a means of distinguishing between the two. Alternatively, the success of Charles Horner's steel-lined (Dorcas) thimbles may have led his competitors to have their thimbles hallmarked in the knowledge that steel-lined thimbles could not be hallmarked because of the steel-lining. There is some support for this latter suggestion to be found in an advertisement by James Fenton about 1900 which featured "hallmarked sterling silver thimbles" rather as if hallmarking conferred some advantage or privilege. Either way it is rare to find a hallmarked English silver thimble dating from before 1885; the few that do exist usually

Chased silver thimbles circa 1900. *Left to right:* **Olney, Amsden & Son 1898; James Fenton 1899; Henry Griffith 1895; James Fenton 1900; Henry Griffith 1907.** *Private collection*

formed part of a sewing case, and for practical purposes unmarked English silver thimbles date from 1900 or earlier.

Before leaving the subject of silver thimbles, it should be recorded that some silver thimbles without hallmarks were made in imitation of English designs in Commonwealth countries. Despite the principle of Empire free trade which captured imaginations during the interwar years, there was never much chance that the dominions would lower their tariffs on British goods; on the contrary, they were just as much concerned to protect and encourage new industries as to benefit their farmers. It is in this context that, taking advantage of protective tariffs, several silversmiths in Australia sought to emulate the established thimble manufacturers in Britain by making branded thimbles of their own. The brand names Elgin, Nifty, and Palfrey have been noted in this connection, but the quality was not as good as that of the imported article, which, despite the imposition of a duty, re-mained competitive. The decline in demand, coupled to the severity of the depression, eventually led to their production being abandoned.

Turning now to base metal thimbles, there are two main firms which need to be mentioned. The first is Edwin Lowe Ltd., which celebrated its centenary in December 1952. It is recorded that Edwin Lowe, a young man of twenty-six, took leases together with his father-in-law, Thomas Pratt, on plots of land at New Street and Whitehead Street, Aston, and started the company as thimble-makers in 1852.[6] He engaged in the manufacture of ferrules about 1880 and continued until about 1910. The company also engaged in the manufacture of shawl pins, but at the turn of the century the fashion for shawl pins was going out and the use of the sewing machine lessened the demand for thimbles. Many thimbles were exported to the United States but the imposition of tariffs brought the trade to an end. Nevertheless the production of pins and thimbles was maintained and one of the

Left, **Australian Nifty thimble;** *Right*, **English Daisy pattern. The thimble on the right is evidently better quality.** *Private collection*

50

company's regular customers for thimbles was the Royal Army Clothing Department, for whom some sizes had to be produced for as low as 15 pence per gross. The production of thimbles has since been discontinued, but the company remains in Aston in the hands of the Lowe family as manufacturers of ferrules and metal pressings.

The other company is Charles Iles, whose origins can be traced back to the firm of Peyton and Iles, which produced metal haberdashery goods as well as brass thimbles about 1840. The partnership was subsequently dissolved and Charles Iles, Sr., took over the tools and machinery for thimble making and set up on his own account. Little is known about Charles Iles's business career, except that at the Great Exhibition of 1851, he displayed some thimbles and was awarded a prize medal. Then, in 1857, he took out a patent for the manufacture of thimbles with a nonmetallic lining, which was the first of the many patents which came to be associated with the Iles name. He was awarded another medal at the Kensington Exhibition of 1862, when besides thimbles (both plain and patent enamel-lined), he exhibited specimens of hooks and eyes, solid-headed pins, hairpins, and fancy boxes, the last-named foreshadowing the interest which the Iles Company would take in the packaging of thimbles.

Charles Iles, Jr., took over from his father, when the latter died in 1870, and that same year the business was moved to Highgate Street, Birmingham, where it was to remain for the best part of a hundred years. In 1877, at the International Exhibition in Brussels, Charles Iles, Jr., also gained a prize medal for his thimbles. The company continued to prosper under his direction, and by the turn of the century it had reached a production capacity of 3–4 million thimbles per annum. There were many models, some of which were protected by patents, including patents covering thimbles with metal outershells, metal thimbles with noncorrosive linings, plastic molded thimbles in casein, or celluloid named "Ivorine," and "Alurine" thimbles made of aluminum (see "Patent Thimbles"). Many employees were engaged in box making, and good presentation and packaging were a feature of "British Iles" thimbles.

Following the First World War, the machine shop consisted of about fifty bench lathes and five grating lathes which were kept fully occupied making a wide range of thimbles, including thimbles in brass, in steel lined with brass, white metal, or "enamel," in nickel silver, in aluminum, and in celluloid. Then, in 1921, a major reorganization took place with the acquisition of two horizontal forming presses of the type which had served to make cartridge cases during the war, and with the installation of roll feed and cupping presses to make thimble "cups" from sheet metal rolls. The effect of these changes was to double the capacity.

When Charles Iles died in 1927, the business was continued by his son-in-law, Alfred E. Cox. With a recession in prospect, Alfred Cox felt it wise to diversify the company's activities, and he acquired the electroplate and souvenir business of Gomms. Many types of souvenirs were manufactured and sold at holiday resorts. Aluminum advertising thimbles were in great demand during the thirties and millions were made. So were nickel silver thimbles in presentation cases, including "Threader" thimbles with a hook attachment. Another development was the replacement of ivorine thimbles by nonflammable cellulose acetate molded thimbles, the moldings purchased in bulk from outside and processed at the works (see "Plastic Thimbles").

During the Second World War, the production of thimbles was restricted, and the company devoted itself to war work. Immediately after the war, production was concentrated on nickel-plated brass thimbles and on the processing of injection moulded plastic thimbles, but in the following years the company gradually resumed its traditional activities, and production was increased to over one hundred thousand thimbles per week. In 1947, the company was registered as a limited liability company under the name of Charles Iles and Gomms Ltd.

When Alfred E. Cox died in 1955, his two sons took over as managing director and works manager respectively. Under their direction, the quality of the Iles industrial thimbles was improved by nickel-plating steel thimbles and offering chrome-plated steel thimbles as a separate line; packaging was modernized by the introduction of carded thimbles, first twelve to a card, and then carded singly; and the aluminum range was strengthened by the introduction of anodized and colored aluminum alloy thimbles. In 1962, the City of Birmingham compulsorily acquired the Highgate Street site for redevelopment and the company moved to a new factory on Tyseley Industrial Estate, where it now resides. In 1971, the business passed into the hands of new owners, but the production of thimbles continues unchanged.

Before concluding this account of English thimbles it may be useful to mention thimbles made of miscellaneous alloys or constructions which do not conveniently fall under other headings and which were mostly produced in Britain. The first is Prince's metal which was a new metal alloy developed shortly after the English Civil War and said to have been invented by Prince Rupert of Bavaria, grandson of James I of England. It was more coppery than brass in appearance and is stated variously to have been an alloy of copper and arsenic or copper and bismuth. The name of Prince's metal also came to be attached to brass with a copper content in the range of 75–85 percent. An example of a thimble made of Prince's metal was described in the *Journal of the British Archaeological Association* for March 1879:

> The slightly domed top is smooth, with a ring round its margin; the upper part of the sides is indented, the lower decorated with a scroll pattern and there is a trifling rim at the base. This thimble is really a tasteful little thing in its way.

The subject of this description may be seen in the Cuming Museum in South London.

Less certain is the use of Sheffield plate, as invented by Thomas Bolsover in the 1740s and consisting of silver and copper fused and hammered or rolled together. Reports that Bolsover started by making small articles including thimbles remain unconfirmed. On the contrary it would seem that technically it would be difficult to apply the indentations without damaging the thin silver surface, and moreover that such surface would not resist the wear of the needle. There is reason to believe therefore that even if Bolsover may have experimented with thimbles, these were never produced commercially.

Similar uncertainty surrounded the use of pewter, which is an alloy of four parts of tin and one part of lead. Besides being more expensive than brass, pewter is relatively soft and there has

Pewter thimble, English, eighteenth century. Height 1.8 cm. *Private collection*

always been considerable doubt whether it was ever used to make thimbles. The discovery of several pewter thimbles found in archaeological layers dating from 1700–1750 has settled the question once and for all, but it does not necessarily mean that pewter thimbles were in general use. On the contrary, the size of the thimbles concerned would suggest that they were designed as tokens or for children's games. Certainly they serve to confirm that pewter is too soft to make thimbles, and given that both brass and silver thimbles were readily available, it is unlikely that they were ever intended for practical sewing.

A more practical development from the point of view of thimble making was that of Britannia metal, an alloy of 80 percent or more tin, 5 percent or more antimony, and 1 percent copper. Britannia metal may be regarded as the modern equivalent of pewter but it is less malleable and for that reason was also called hard metal. It is not known whether any thimbles were ever made of Britannia metal, but subsequently W. Tutin (c. 1780) developed Tutania, which was a kind of Britannia metal, and an entry in Pigot & Co.'s commercial directory for 1822–23 indicates that Francis Lowe, who was a thimblemaker in Birmingham, made thimbles of Tutania. Presumably some of these thimbles have survived but so far none has been identified. Collectors should be warned that the ease with which pewter and related materials can be cast has encouraged the production of many so-called pewter thimbles which are of no conceivable interest or value.

Finally, some reference needs to be made to porcelain thimbles which, although first developed by Meissen as an *"objet de galanterie,"* gradually came to be adopted by English porcelain manufacturers as their own. For the last two hundred years English manufacturers, notably Royal Worcester, have made porcelain thimbles, and it is only recently, because of the vogue for thimble collecting, that some foreign manufacturers have followed suit. A full account will be found in the chapter on porcelain thimbles.

NOTES

1. Thomas Occleve, *De Regimine Principium*, ed. Thomas Wright (London: Roxburghe Club, 1860).
2. *Wills and Inventories in the Archdeaconry of Richmond,* Surtees Society, vol. 26 (1853).
3. John Houghton F.R.S., *A collection of letters for the improvement of husbandry and trade*, rev. ed. (Richard Bradly), vol. 2 (London, 1727/8), Letter 14, dated 13 March 1683.
4. May, *Hist. Parl.* II vi, 97.
5. *Burton Diary*, 1 : 331.
6. *Our Centenary Year. A Historical Note on the company of Edwin Lowe Ltd.*, compiled by Frank Lowe (1952).

Thimbles in America

IF THIMBLES HAD BEEN KNOWN ON THE AMERICAN Continent before the arrival of the Spaniards, there might be evidence among the more advanced civilizations such as the Mayas and the Aztecs, but none has been discovered. Moreover, a possible explanation for the lack of thimbles may be found in the writings of Garcilaso de la Vega.[1] Garcilaso, who was born in 1539 and was known as El Inca because his mother Princess Isabel Chimbu Occlo was of royal blood, wrote of his native Peru as follows:

> Married women were generally dedicated to the care of their homes; they knew how to spin and weave wool or cotton according to whether they lived in cold or hot regions. They did little sewing, however, for there was hardly any needed, Indian garments both masculine and feminine, being generally woven in one piece in the proper length and width.

If there was little sewing, there could hardly be any need for thimbles, and in all probability it was Christopher Columbus and his ship's company who in 1492 first brought thimbles to the Americas. Besides the obvious need to darn and mend clothing on a long voyage, the thimble was an essential tool for the sailmaker and it was equally essential for sewing leather harness and other military accouterment. We can be sure therefore that there were thimbles aboard the *Santa Maria*, but such thimbles would be men's thimbles made of heavy brass or iron and with large indentations to match the heads of large needles. Later, when the Portuguese and the Spanish colonists had established themselves, it became necessary to arrange for regular supplies of thimbles to be sent from home. Thus, following the conquest of Mexico by Hernando Cortés in 1521, the supply of thimbles is mentioned in colonial records for 1566: "500 dedales de muger . . . 800 maravedís," or again "Dedales para sastres a rreal y medio la dozena."[2]

It will be noted that these were not men's thimbles for sailors or leather workers but ladies' thimbles and thimbles for tailors, as befitted the settlement of the country. It is probable that by this time Spain had developed its own thimble-making industry derived from the Moors, whereas elsewhere on the Continent most thimbles were still produced in Nuremberg and possibly also other centers in the Low Countries.

Meanwhile England had embarked on its war with Spain, and the fierce loyalty of Elizabeth I's subjects is evidenced by reports of thimbles inscribed "God save the Queene" and like mottoes. It was the victory over the Spanish Armada which settled the naval supremacy of England and paved the way for the establishment of English-speaking settlements. Jamestown was founded in 1607 and the Pilgrim Fathers settled in New England in 1620. The new settlers were obliged to bring with them everything they needed to live, and the first thimbles as well as other sewing tools were imported from Europe. One of the first commercial ventures in what was to become the United States, was in 1603 and

Seventeenth-century silver thimble. The tulip design suggests a Dutch association. *Colonial Williamsburg Foundation*

included sewing tools. A group of merchants in England financed a ship full of goods for trading with the natives. It carried needles, thread, thimbles, and scissors to exchange for sassafras, the bark of the root of a laurel-type tree, which is a powerful stimulant and which was much in demand as a remedy in the Elizabethan pharmacopoeia. The ship sailed to the coast of the present state of Maine and went south as far as the future Plymouth Harbor. At this time Germany and the Low Countries were the chief suppliers of thimbles, England imported large quantities and it continued to do so throughout the seventeenth century.

One of the few mentions of thimbles in North America in the early seventeenth century arises in 1649 concerning the estate of Mr. William Whiting (". . . thimbles, boxes and knives")[3] and five years later in 1654 thimbles were again mentioned: "For other his undertakinges [he] is a thimble-maker . . .",[4] but this latter in a figurative way. Most of the thimbles reaching North America by then were probably Dutch, but the Dutch influence was waning; it suffered a serious setback following on Charles II's acquisition of the region that became New York, New Jersey, and Pennsylvania (1667), and by the beginning of the eighteenth century much of the

trade, including the trade in thimbles, had shifted to London. There are few authenticated American thimbles dating back to the seventeenth century, but the Rhode Island Historical Society is fortunate in possessing three thimbles of that period. One belonged to Esther Willitt, daughter of Thomas Willitt (or Willett), the first mayor of New York. It was found on the site of the old Willitt dwelling place on Rhode Island (Aquidneck Island). It is a topless silver thimble of the colonial period and around the base it bears the name of its former owner. There is every reason to believe that this thimble dates from between 1662 and 1672. The other two thimbles, also made of silver, were found in the grave of Princess Ninigret (otherwise known as Weunquesh, chief sachem of the Narragansett Indians) and were buried with her. She succeeded her father in 1676 and reigned until her death in about the year 1690. There must be other seventeenth-century American thimbles in museums or private collections, but the Rhode Island Historical Society thimbles are exceptional in that the date and the provenance are fully authenticated.

So far as one can judge, it was the practice in the early part of the eighteenth century for

Silver sewing ring engraved on one side with a heart, on the other with a flower. Inscribed Esther Willitt. 1660–65. *The Rhode Island Historical Society Photo by Richard Cheek, Cambridge, Massachusetts.*

American silversmiths to make silver thimbles individually by hand according to their customers' requirements. Some gold thimbles were also made, as witness the gold thimble dating from about 1730–40 by Jacob Hurd of Boston which belongs to the Yale University Art Gallery. At that time the basic tool for thimble making was still a thimble stamp. These are mentioned in several inventories of the period, notably that of John Coney of Boston dated 1722, that of Francis Richardson of Philadelphia taken on his death in 1729, and that of John Burt of Boston dated 1746. John Burt's thimble stamps were valued at £4 10s. 0d., which was a considerable sum at the time. These thimble stamps were probably imported, as may be deduced from an advertisement in the *Boston Gazette* dated 28 October 1765, which published an announcement by Daniel Parker, who had imported from London a variety of goldsmiths', jewelers', and watchmakers' tools and wares including "silver thimble steel ends" and "thimble stamps." Similarly the *Boston News-Letter* of 29 August 1771 featured an announcement by Daniel Boyer, jeweler, who had imported a variety of merchandise including "thimble stamps," but by then new ways of making thimbles were already on the horizon and the days of thimble stamps were numbered.

A study of the advertisements which appeared in newspapers during the latter half of the seventeenth century suggests that quantities of thimbles were imported but that until about 1760 those that were imported were mostly made of brass. The first recorded advertisement of this kind occurs in the *Weekly Post Boy* of New York on 19 May 1746, where Thomas Brown, cutler at the sign of the Cross Daggers near the Fly Market, advised that he had moved to new premises and offered a variety of ironmongery and cutlery including "thimbles, pins and needles." These may or may not have been imported but only a week later the *Boston Gazette* of 27 May 1746 carried an advertisement from Edmund Crowley (general merchant) offering "thimbles" among a variety of imported merchandise. This same Edmund Crowley advertised in the *Boston News-Letter* of 18 October 1750, announcing the arrival of merchandise "in the Sloop Mary late Capt. Hussey's from London, and to be sold . . ."; among items of needle-

work figure "Men's and Women's Common Thimbles." In the *Boston News-Letter* dated 15 May 1760, Mary Jackson & Son (hardware) "having open'd their shop, since the late fire, a few doors from the Court House" advertised "brass and iron thimbles" together with a great variety of London, Birmingham, and Sheffield cutlery ware. It is unlikely that the production of brassware could be developed successfully in the face of the competition from the long-established Dutch brassware industry and also from the more recently established English brassware industry, which was competing with it. Imported brass manufactures flooded in, and among them thimbles which came first from Holland, then from John Lofting's newly established factory in England, and then from the Birmingham thimble-makers who followed in his footsteps. The selling price of these thimbles may be gauged from an inventory dated 1711: "Three dozen and one thimbles at 2d ye thimble."[5]

The picture which emerges with regard to silver thimbles is somewhat different. The demand for silver thimbles in colonial times was relatively small and the local artisan silversmiths making thimbles to order were better placed than their English counterparts. The latter therefore made little progress until the middle of the eighteenth century, when with the introduction of mechanization, which resulted in a better article at a cheaper price, imported English silver thimbles began to sweep the market. It would be pointless to quote the many advertisements which appeared in contemporary newspapers from 1760 to about 1800 advertising imported silver and steel-topped thimbles. There was an unending stream of them and it will be more instructive to turn to the records of the Richardson family, a well established firm of silversmiths whose records have survived and who were engaged in the wholesale importation of silver thimbles.[6]

Three generations of Richardsons lived and worked as silversmiths in Philadelphia during the eighteenth century. The first was Francis Richardson (1681–1729) who made and sold thimbles in his shop and whose inventory, as already mentioned, including thimble stamps. Next came Joseph Richardson (1711–84), who is noteworthy for the detailed accounts which he left of the business. The thimbles made by Joseph Richardson were mostly of gold rather than silver, they weighed about four penny-weight, and they cost about six shillings to make. No thimble bearing his mark has survived but presumably they looked something like the Jacob Hurd thimble in the Bostom Museum of Fine Arts. Joseph sold his goods from a glass case, and in 1744 he had nine silver thimbles and no gold in the case, which suggests that silver thimbles were held in stock and that gold thimbles were only made to order.

Since steel needles will wear out and eventually puncture a gold or silver thimble, one of Joseph Richardson's most frequent repair jobs was the "topping" of thimbles, and it was presumably to avoid this inconvenience that many of the silver thimbles which he imported from England had steel tops. His several English correspondents, Wagstaffe, Ritherdon, and Mildred, all sent him thimbles both plain and with steel tops, and dozens came to him from the Masterman firm. They were of different sizes and Joseph Richardson requested repeatedly that they should not be very deep. His sons, Joseph, Jr. (1752–1831) and Nathaniel (1754–1827), found themselves compelled to write to Masterman at the end of 1773 to say that "the thimbles you sent us tho good in their quallity are so very deep that common people cannot wear them wish the next may be in moderation."

This dispute about the depth of the thimbles supplied by Masterman appears to have started about 1769 and lasted until 1783 or thereabouts. It is of considerable interest as helping to date the changeover from the short stubby thimble which was in vogue in England and in the early part of the eighteenth century and the long thin thimble which was commonplace toward the end. Clearly the fashion in America was lagging behind that in England, Masterman was no doubt doing his best but the Birmingham silversmiths had taken it into their heads to make longer thimbles, and hence Richardson's cries of distress.

It will help to give the flavor of Richardson's business to reproduce some extracts from the correspondence. It should of course be understood that the letters addressed to the various correspondents would not be ordering thimbles alone but would include other items as well.

7.12.1758   Thomas Wagstaffe

	4 doz silver thimbels
	4 doz steel topt do
1.2.1759	Daniel Mildred
	6 doz silver thimbels sorted sizes
	6 doz of steel top do
9.8.1759	George Ritherdon
	3 doz silver thimbels & 3 doz steel topt do
9.2.1760	Thomas How & John Masterman
	6 doz of steel topt thimbels lined with silver
6.6.1760	Daniel Mildred
	6 doz silver thimbels & 6 doz steel topt do lined
19.10.1764	How, Masterman and Archer
	Please to add 4 doz of steel topt silver thimbels
4.6.1766	Masterman & Archer
	Please to send per first convenient opportunity:—
	6 doz steel topt thimbles
11.4.1769	John Masterman
	6 doz of steel topt thimbles lined Not very Deep
11.10.1770	John Masterman
	6 doz steel topt thimbles & 4 doz silver do not very Deep
29.2.1772	John Masterman
	6 doz steel top thimbles

An inventory of the goods belonging to Joseph Richardson, Jr., and Nathaniel Richardson on 31 May 1790 included 39 steel top and 9 plain silver thimbles. Joseph Richardson, Jr., is known to have made gold thimbles about 1796. The partnership came to an end with the death of the brothers about 1830.

While evidently the use of silver thimbles with or without steel top was growing enormously it should not be assumed that more fancy materials such as were becoming popular in Europe were necessarily ignored. The *New-York Journal* of 6 August 1767 carried an advertisement on behalf of Charles Shipman, ivory and hardwood turner, lately from England in which "Ivory thimbles" appeared among a long list of turners' articles. Similarly the *New-York Gazette* of 6 January 1777 published an advertisement on behalf of Richard Sause, hardware, jewelry, and cutlery store offering "silver, pinchbeck, brass and taylors' thimbles," but these were the exception. As the eighteenth century came to its close, wealthy Americans who could afford it preferred gold.

The *Pennsylvania Pocket* of 31 May 1791 published an advertisement on behalf of Claudius Chat, goldsmith and small worker in gold from Paris, who made and sold thimbles, and the *Federal Gazette* of 27 November 1797 published an advertisement on behalf of James Jack, jeweler and watchmaker in Philadelphia, who offered merchandise imported from London including "ladies' strong gold and silver thimbles." Evidently the United States was still importing thimbles, but the country was gradually building up toward a period of industrial expansion. It could only be a matter of time before some innovating and practical-minded thimble-maker introduced new machine techniques in order to take advantage of the economies of large-scale production and thereby establish a locally based thimble manufacturing industry.

It is possible that the first silversmith who sought to specialize in thimble making was Benjamin Halstead, who was born in Elizabeth Town in 1734. Benjamin Halstead was apprenticed in New York, and a curious incident occurred in August 1764 when his master, Andrew Browne, caused an advertisement to appear in the *New-York Gazette* warning the public to beware of Benjamin Halstead as a dangerous character who had "hit him for no reason." Nevertheless, despite this contretemps Benjamin Halstead was admitted as a Freeman Silversmith of the City of New York, he married in 1765, and he was employed in New York until 1766 when he returned to Elizabeth Town to start his own business. Back in Elizabeth Town he was associated with his brother Matthias as a partner, and although there is no evidence that he was specially interested in thimbles at this early stage of his career, nevertheless when advertising the opening of their shop in the *New-York Gazette* on 25 September 1766, Matthias took the opportunity to mention that he had "a few best steel top thimbles" for sale. It is not known how long Benjamin Halstead remained in Elizabeth Town but he worked in Philadelphia from 1783 to 1785, by which time he had presumably developed his interest in thimbles, and then removed to New York where from 1786 to 1814 his name featured in the City Directory under the heading of "thimble-maker." The following notice was printed by the *Diary, or Evening Register* for 10 August 1794:

Benjamin Halstead—Thimble Manufactory. Benjamin Halstead informs his Friends and the Public in general, that he still continues carrying on the Gold and Silversmith business No. 67 Broad Street; he has brought the manufactory of Gold, Silver and Pinchbeck Thimbles with steel top to great perfection and thinks he could make sufficient quantity to supply the United States. Citizens, consider your interest, and encourage American Manufactures.

Those imported are of the Slightest kind, I will engage that one of mine, will do more service than 3 of them, and I know by experience that imported ones of the quality of mine cost 18 shillings per doz. and could not be sold by 25 percent, as low as mine. Every dealer in this article will soon find the advantage of keeping Halstead's Thimbles and have the satisfaction of knowing that he does his customers justice. Silver and steel Bodkins, tooth and ear picks by the doz. or single.

About 1815 Halstead's second son had his own factory on Varick Street, New York, a few years before his father's death in 1817.

As is well known, the eighteenth century was an age when correct spelling was held of little account and it is not surprising to find, there-

Silver thimble with steel top inscribed "Halsted N.Y." Probably by Benjamin Halsted, Jr. Early nineteenth century. Height 2.4 cm. *Private collection*

58

fore, that Benjamin Halstead came to spell his name Halsted. The latter is the spelling he adopted in his later years and it is also the spelling practiced by his son. The mark "Halsted N.Y." in a rectangle will occasionally be found on a silver thimble or sewing ring and it remains to be decided whether the mark belongs to the father or to the son or to both. Either way those thimbles are of keen interest and presumably date from somewhere between 1795 and 1815. A noteworthy feature is that they were made in different sizes with the size of each stamped on the rim. Stamping in this way may seem an obvious development, but it is not adopted by the English thimble-makers until 1885 or thereabouts. A puzzling feature is that so few Halsted thimbles appear to have survived, but this may have something to do with their quality. Despite the somewhat bombastic nature of Halsted's advertisement the fact remains that Halsted marked thimbles are relatively slight and fragile, they compare badly with English thimbles of the same period and for that reason may not have enjoyed much success. But whether the Halsted thimbles were successful or not, this should not be allowed to detract from Halsted's merit in being one of the forerunners of large-scale production and from his possible claim as the first thimble manufacturer (as opposed to thimble-maker) in the United States.

From about 1800 many American silversmiths began to designate themselves as thimble-makers, but it would be misleading to think that this was necessarily their principal activity. On the contrary, most silversmiths making thimbles also made other products and thimbles were only one of their specialties. There would be no point in mentioning all the firms whose names have been associated with thimbles or in seeking to unravel the history of such firms as they evolved with the passing of time. Anyone interested can do no better than to consult Mrs. Sickels's articles on "New York Thimble-Makers from Huntington, Long Island,"[7] a scholarly account of that part of the subject that will serve to illustrate its complications. The fact is that until about 1880 American thimble-makers did not normally mark their thimbles, so that there is no easy way of relating a thimble to its maker, and it will be sufficient to mention those thimble-makers who are known by their marks.

The mark which is most frequently encountered among American thimbles is that of Simons Brothers Company of Philadelphia, which consists of a letter S set in a shield. There are several varieties of the mark, which has been in use continuously since 1880, and it sometimes appears together with the trade names "Priscilla" or "Quaker." The firm of Simons Bros. was originally started by George W. Simons in 1839 and it differed from its contemporaries because from the start its principal activity was thimbles. It was also fortunate because three years later the passage of a protective tariff in 1842, whereby duty of 30 percent was levied on all imported gold- and silverware, provided a welcome shield against foreign competition. George had four sons who were all in the business and the company remained in their hands and in the hands of their descendants until 1969, when the family sold out to Mr. Nelson Keyser, a former employee who had started with Simons Bros. as an apprentice. The Keyser family now run the company. Needless to say that over the years Simons Bros. have made many items other than their famous thimbles, but thimbles were always their specialty and they pioneered many designs including the well-known "Liberty Bell" thimble. In 1876 the company was honored by being awarded a Centennial Medal and a Diploma for thimbles. Simons Bros. are the only manufacturers who continue to make silver and gold thimbles in the United States, and as such they are the last remaining representatives of a long and honored tradition.

The next mark most commonly found in American thimbles is that of Ketcham & McDougall of Brooklyn, N.Y. It is estimated that between them Simons and Ketcham & McDougall account for nearly two-thirds of the marked American thimbles in the hands of collectors. Ketcham & McDougall had their beginning in 1832 when John Roshmore opened a small silversmith shop in New York. Two years later he moved to larger premises at 6 Little Green Street (now Liberty Street) and it is here that a young orphan, Edward Ketcham (1820–92), began working for him as an apprentice. A few years later, another apprentice, Hugh McDougall (1834–1901) was learning the thimble-making trade in Huntington; he left Huntington to come to New York and joined the firm

Silver thimbles from the United States, mostly 1890–1920. *Top Row (left to right):* Stern, lady with flowing hair; Simons, raised grapes; Goldsmith Stern, small cupid faces round rim; Waite Thresher, anchors; Webster, raised lions. *Middle Row (left to right):* Simons, Christmas bells; Stitch in Time; Ketcham and McDougall, holly leaf and berry with ruby; Simons, birds (patented 30 September 1881); St. Louis World Fair 1904. *Bottom Row (left to right):* Ketcham and McDougall, Florida; Ketcham and McDougall, Washington, D.C.; Columbian World's Fair 1892; Simons, Washington, D.C.; San Francisco World's Fair 1939. *Private collection*

American gold thimbles from the nineteenth century. *Left to right:* 1879, 1888, 1866, 1895, 1871, 1877. *Private collection*

which was by now known as Roshmore and Ketcham.

When John Roshmore retired in the 1850s, Edward Ketcham's brother Ebenezer Ketcham joined him and the firm's name became Ketcham and Brother. Meanwhile Hugh McDougall was still learning the business, but in 1875 the brothers invited him to become a partner and the firm was named Ketcham & McDougall. Its retail shop became known as "The Thimble House." Hugh McDougall was an inventor as well as a silversmith and in 1881 he patented a new method of manufacturing sewing thimbles, "consisting in first so rolling a blank as to form a thick portion for the rim, or a thick portion and embossed ornamentation, next trimming said blank to the desired form, afterward bending said blank into tubular form and soldering its meeting edges together, and finally closing the end of the tube, substantially as and for the purpose specified." In 1882 he extended his patent to cover "new and useful improvements in the art of making thimbles." Some of the finest thimbles made by Ketcham & McDougall had raised designs on the band and were made by this process.

As New York grew, the partners decided that Manhattan was becoming too crowded for their factory and in the 1890s they put up a plant in Brooklyn. The company began a massive expansion and developed a popular and successful device for holding a pince-nez known as the Automatic Eyeglass Holder as well as other inventions. Nevertheless thimbles remained their specialty. They continued to make them successfully until changes in public taste in the early years of the depression led to enforced rentrenchment, and the making of thimbles was discontinued in 1932 after exactly one hundred years of leadership in that field.[8] The trademark K&McD was used continuously from 1892 until 1932 when Ketcham & McDougall discontinued production of thimbles.

Other marks which may be encountered include those of Stern Brothers & Co., New York (1890–1912) and their successors Goldsmith Stern & Co., New York; Webster Company, North Attleboro; H. Muhr's Sons, Philadelphia; Thomas F. Brogan, New York; Untemeyer Robbins Co., New York; and Waite Thresher & Company, Providence, Rhode Island. Waite Thresher bought the designs and tools of the Barker Manufacturing Co. (also of Providence, Rhode Island) when the latter went out of business toward the end of the nineteenth century. The company was established by Daniel B. Waite in 1860 under the name of D. B. Waite & Co., which in 1869 changed to Waite, Smith & Co. In 1884 Henry Thresher who had been a salesman for the company was taken into partnership and in 1892 the business was incorporated. The firm produced low quality gold ornaments and gold-filled jewelry as well as gold and sterling silver thimbles. The designs and tools were in turn bought by Simons Brothers when Waite Thresher went out of production in 1927. Not all the names which appear as suppliers of thimbles were necessarily manufacturers: for instance, Baird North, which issued illustrated catalogues of thimbles during the first quarter of the twentieth century, were only distributors, selling thimbles made for them by an established manufacturer.

As might be expected the American thimble manufacturers developed a style of their own, and this is so distinctive that an experienced collector should be able to recognize an American thimble at a glance. They are normally shorter and squarer than thimbles from other countries and the size markings are small, precise, and easy to differentiate from those found elsewhere. American styles are also less ornate and more conservative than their counterparts in Europe. The early introduction of mass production methods may have influenced the design but the finish is unusually good and ornamental scrollwork, beading, and channelings are almost invariably of a high standard. It is possible that the squatness of American thimbles may have been of some advantage by imposing less stress on the metal during manufacture and allowing greater thickness. Some of the more noteworthy are the nineteenth-century scenic silver thimbles with stylized panoramic views—coast scenes with harbors, lighthouses, and sailing boats; town scenes with buildings, rivers, and bridges; and country scenes with farmhouses, trees, and mountains. There is a pleasing simplicity about many of the designs and the scenic thimble is unmistakably American.

The dating of American thimbles presents the usual difficulties, though the practice of marking

Silver thimbles from Stern Bros & Co. catalog circa 1900. *Private collection*

thimbles with the name of the manufacturer or merchant may be a useful clue. So is the word *sterling* denoting the standard of gold or silver purity. American gold and silver thimbles did not normally carry a mark until the 1860s, when the word *sterling* was introduced to show 92.5 percent fine metal content. There are no hallmarks in the United States and the "sterling" mark thus merely provides an indication of the country of origin and suggests that the article in question cannot be much more than a hundred years old. Another type of marking which is sometimes found on American thimbles is a pat-

ent date (see "Patent Thimbles"). Quite obviously the thimble cannot be older than the date of the patent. Thimbles marked "coin" are also American and the mark purports to establish that the silver content is that of silver coinage.

No account of American thimbles can be complete without some reference to advertising thimbles (see separate chapter). Since the First World War advertising thimbles in aluminum and plastic have been used to a greater extent in the United States than in any other country, and not content with advertising goods and services, the political campaign thimble is a peculiarly

STERLING SILVER WITH GOLD BANDS STERLING SILVER

Silver thimbles from Stern Bros & Co. catalog circa 1900. *Private collection*

Silver thimbles made by Simons Bros. *Left to right:* Rococo, egg and dart, polychrome enamel, cupids, butterflies. *Private collection*

Silver thimble case with thimble. This type of case is not normally found outside the United States. *Private collection*

American development. Added to this, the vogue for thimble collecting has created a demand for so-called personal thimbles and also for a wide range of thimbles, including commemorative thimbles, of a kind which are best described under the generic name of "collectibles." The sheer volume of these so-called collectibles makes it necessary to mention them, but they are mostly trifling and of no lasting value.

NOTES

1. Garcilaso de la Vega, *Comentarios Reales* (Madrid, 1607).
2. Peter Boyd Bowman, "Indice y extractos del archivo de Protocolo de Puebla" (Unpublished MS, vol. 2).
3. Conn. Rec. 1:497
4. Nicholas Papers (Camden), 2:116.
5. Springfield Rec. 2:42.
6. Martha Gandy Fales, *Joseph Richardson and Family, Philadelphia Silversmiths* (Middletown, Conn., 1974).
7. Elizabeth Galbraith Sickels, "New York thimblemakers from Huntington, Long Island," *Antiques Journal*, Sept., Oct., Nov., 1964.
8. "The Story behind 'Since 1832' . . . The 125 years of Ketcham & McDougall, Inc." (1957).

Silver thimbles with gold bands by Ketcham and McDougall. At left outsize thimble, height 2.6 cm., at right normal size for comparison. Large thimbles were made specially to order. *Private collection*

Thimbles in France

THE THIMBLE MAKING INDUSTRY IN FRANCE NEVER reached the same proportions as did that in Britain, Germany, or the United States, nor did it achieve the same international significance. Nevertheless French thimble-makers developed some distinct and attractive styles of their own and the early history, which can be traced back to the thirteenth century, is the best documented. It is therefore well worth examining on its own account.

We do not know when thimbles were first introduced into France, but since the steel needle came to Europe via Spain it is possible that the thimble followed the same route. The word for a thimble in old French was *deel,* which became contracted to *del* and should have led to *deau* (a form which exists in dialect) but its phonetical development was impeded by, and it became assimilated with, the word for gaming dice, which led to the modern forms of *dé à coudre* and *dé à jouer.* If we compare the romance forms of these two words, on the one hand *dedal, ditale, deel,* on the other *dat* and *dacho,* it will be seen immediately how they diverge. This distinction is important and the similarity of the two words has led to repeated confusion. The word *deel* itself is derived from the Latin *digitale,* the neuter of *digitalis,* "belonging to the finger," and probably emerged during the eleventh or twelfth century. Other forms include *deaul, deis, deez, deyl,* and other variants. A thimble-maker was known as a *deilier.*

Detailed evidence that thimble making was already well established in Paris during the thir-teenth century is to be found in Etienne Boileau's famous *Livre des métiers.* King Louis IX of France appointed Etienne Boileau, who was Provost of Paris, to set in order the rules of the various trades, and in 1260 the latter published his ordinances under that name. The activity of thimble making was apparently not sufficiently important to warrant separate rules of its own and for reasons which are not entirely clear thimble making was assigned partly to the claspmakers *(Fremailliers)* and partly to the buttonmakers *(Boutonniers).* The relevant clauses in the *Livre des métiers* read as follows:

—Titre XLII Cist titres parole des Fremailliers de laiton et de ceus qui font frémaus à livres.
[item ix refers to thimbles]
  Nus du mestier dessus dit ne puet faire deux pour home et pour fame, establis à coudre, qui ne soient bons et loyaus, bien marcheans, de bon estoffe, c'est assavoir quil soient de bon laton et de fort et bien ouvrés loyaument.
  (This section refers to claspmakers and to those who make book clasps.
  . . . The members of the above-mentioned trade are only allowed to make men's and women's thimbles for sewing if these are good and true, serviceable and of sound material that is to say of good and strong brass and of true workmanship.)
—Titre LXXII Cist titres parole des Boutonniers et des Deyciers d'archal, de quoivre et de laiton.
[item i refers to thimbles]
  Quiconques veut estre Boutonnier d'archal et de laiton et de coivre neuf et viez, et feseres

de dex a dames pour coudre, a Paris, estre le puet franchement, pour tant que il soit preu-d'om et loial et que il face le mestier bien et loialment, et que il face creable que il ait fait envers le mestre qui appris l'a ce que il doit.

(This section refers to the button-makers and to makers of dice [already dice and thimbles were confused] of latten, copper and brass.

Whoever wishes to be a button-maker of latten, copper and brass including scrap brass, or a maker of ladies' sewing thimbles, can do so freely provided that he is a good and loyal citizen, that he works well and dutifully and that he can show that he has fulfilled his obligations toward the master who taught him.)

It will be seen that there is no obvious line of demarcation between the clasp-makers and the button-makers. Some notes in the margin of one manuscript suggest that the clasp-makers may have been more active, but this is uncertain. The *Livre des métiers* does not mention the mercers *(merciers)* in connection with thimbles though it is possible that the mercers were involved in their distribution. A thirteenth-century poem entitled the "Dict du mercier" starts:

Moult a çi bele compaignie
Merciers sui, si port mercerie

Then follows a list of the articles the mercer has for sale:

J'ai les deex à costurieres.

As early as the twelfth century the mercers were one of the most powerful guilds in France and in due course they must have acquired the right to sell thimbles, because Jacques Savary des Bruslons in his *Dictionnaire universel du commerce* (vol. 3, column 850) quotes thimbles in a long list of products for which the mercers held the rights at the end of the seventeenth century.

Information regarding individual thimble-makers living in Paris at the time of Philippe-le-Bel is available from old taxation records *(Livres de la taille)*. Thus there was a thimble-maker called Gile le Deelier who lived in rue au Lion and paid taxes amounting to ten sols (1296), Jehan le Deelier who lived in rue Pavée and was assessed at two sols but failed to pay (1297), and another called Guiart le Deillier who lived in rue Mauconseil and who paid nine sols (1313) by

Bronze with pointed top. This type of thimble is mostly found in France. Probably medieval. Height 2.6 cm. *Kunstgewerbe Museum, West Berlin*

which date his colleague Gile from the rue au Lion had been increased to twelve sols which were duly paid. Moreover, comparing these assessments with those of artisans in other and more wealthy trades, it becomes obvious that the thimble-makers were rated very low. It is probable therefore that they were relatively humble artisans who pursued their calling with the help of an odd apprentice or two but were otherwise largely insignificant. Besides brass, the thimble-makers were allowed to work with wood, bone, and ivory and in the early fourteenth century there were sixteen of them altogether in Paris.[1]

That the thimble was in common use at the time of Philippe-le-Bel is further borne out by a somewhat bawdy story about a procuress entitled "D'Auberée la vieille maquerelle."[2] The tale revolves around the evidence of a thimble belonging to the madam in question which was left with a needle attached to a man's waistcoat. Obviously a thimble would never have been chosen to fill such a key role in the story if the listeners were not completely familiar with it. A tale of this kind was not designed for the nobility in their castles but for the common mass of townspeople, and it serves to confirm that by the thirteenth century the metal thimble had become commonplace.

From the fourteenth century onward the thimble was obviously in such common use that it was taken for granted. In 1462 François Villon was awaiting execution when he wrote his famous "Ballade des pendus" and was moved to picture his own corpse swinging in the wind: "Plus becquetez d'oyseaulx que dez à couldre" (more hole-pecked by the birds than a thimble). And in 1518, Villon's dark thoughts are echoed in "Le Calendrier des bergers":

Car comme moy tu deviendras en poudre
Tout picote comme est ung des à couldre"

(For like me you will turn to powder,
All pecked over like a thimble)

Clearly neither François Villon, who although he associated with rogues and vagabonds was nevertheless an educated man, nor the anonymous writer of the Shepherd's Calendar would have employed these similes if the thimble had not been an accepted part of everyday life.

Indeed by the sixteenth century the word for a thimble had become so commonplace both in France and in England, that English students learning French would be expected to know it as part of their vocabulary. In an English textbook published about 1530 by a certain G. Duwes, whose real name was Gilles de Gruez, under the title of *An introductories for to learne French*, the student is bid to memorize the following in a list of words relating to a lady's belongings:

Le Does   The Thymble

And Palgrave's Grammar, published about the same date, quotes the inverse:

Thimble to sowe with, deyl

During the sixteenth century the goldsmiths who made thimbles of gold and silver began to produce more luxurious thimbles, replacing the indentations by foliated scrolls and other ornamentations in relief, or alternatively decorating their thimbles with precious stones. In the *Inventaire des joyaulx et pierreries du cabinet du roy de Navarre*, established by Jehanne de Foix in 1583, is mentioned "un petit coffre de cuir noir, là où est dedans deux dés d'or à coudre garnis de rubis." By the seventeenth century the use of silver thimbles was widespread among the middle classes. The *Inventaire de Claudine Bouzonnet Stella* (Paris, 1693) is a case in point. It featured "un viex auchet (hochet) d'argent; plus trois déz d'argent à coudre; plus un petit cuilier d'argent pour un enfant nouveau-né"—very much the same items as might figure in a latter-day inventory.

Thimbles made of precious metal became increasingly popular during the eighteenth century, particularly gold thimbles ornamented

Two gold thimbles with red velvet-lined shagreen cases. Late eighteenth or early nineteenth century. *Private collection*

with flowers or other decoration worked with golds of different shades. Such thimbles would normally be presented in small cases made of shagreen (*galuchat*). The gold, silver, and gilded brass (ormolu) thimbles made in Blois about 1700 were highly prized, and large consignments were not only sent to Paris but also exported to foreign countries. However, possibly as a result of the French Revolution, thimble making at Blois subsequently ceased, leaving scarcely a trace. During the Revolution, the authorities encouraged patriotic citizens to contribute to the cause and some donated their thimbles, much as had happened in England during the Civil War:

> Nor are Patriotic Gifts wanting, from those that have aught left; nor stingily given; the fair Villaumes, mother and daughter, Milliners, in the Rue St. Martin, give "a silver thimble, and a coin of fifteen sous" with other similar effects; and offers, at least the mother does, to mount guard.[3]

But once the Revolution was over, the love of luxury soon reasserted itself, and there is at Castle Douglas in Scotland a beautiful enamel compact which was the property of Stephanie of Beauharnais, the niece of Napoleon I, who married a Duke of Hamilton. The gold thimble is set with small opals in the shape of a heart with initial *S* inside. However following the fall of the Empire, there was a great dearth of precious metals. In the absence of gold, mother-of-pearl became fashionable and some fine mother-of-pearl thimbles were made about this time (see relevant chapter). So also did cut steel, and cut steel thimbles are a particularly French development. According to a contemporary fashion journal, the *Miroir des Grâces,* it was a certain Master Dumény, from Saint-Julien-du-Sault, who had the best reputation for this type of article. Trade fairs and exhibitions were popular in France during the first half of the nineteenth century and thimbles featured regularly among the exhibits. At the exhibition which was held in Paris at the Palais du Louvre in 1819, Messrs. Rouy et Berthier, 17 rue Chapon, showed steel thimbles and at the same exhibition M. Michaud Lalanté, goldsmith, 4 rue Neuve-Saint Eustache, submitted thimbles whose interior was lined with

French eighteenth-century porcelain (soft paste) probably Crépy-en-Valois. *Private collection*

French silver thimbles from the eighteenth and early nineteenth century. *Private collection*

platinum and the exterior in silver. At the exhibition of French manufactures in 1823, Messrs. Delaporte frères & Cie., 18 rue des Deux-Portes Saint Sauveur in Paris, presented tailors' thimbles, known as *verges de fer,* as well as thimbles lined with silver and lined with gold. At the Paris Exhibition of 1834, Messrs. Mathieu-Danloy gained a bronze medal for their thimbles and later, following the decease of her husband, Mme Veuve Mathieu-Danloy continued the business at Vouziers in the Ardennes.

During the mid-nineteenth century several firms started to produce thimbles in the old-established pins and needles manufacturing center of Laigle in the Orne region. One of the leaders was A. Lebas, who distributed his steel and brass thimbles through L. Chatelain at 4, rue de Mauconseil. In 1865, a few doors away, E. Leroux, at 14, rue de Mauconseil, was also engaged in the thimble industry and the attentive reader will recall that it was in this same street that Guiart le Deillier lived in 1313. The street still exists but unfortunately the thimble-makers have now moved away.

The vogue for steel thimbles did not prevent goldsmiths and silversmiths from setting up as thimble manufacturers, much as they did in other countries, but they found themselves uncomfortably squeezed between the emerging British manufacturers on the one side and the German manufacturers on the other, both of which were rapidly moving toward mass production. One of the more successful was A. Féau,

which was the successor to an earlier company called Lorillon and was established at 59, rue Turbigo, Paris, and subsequently removed to 4, rue Portefoin. This firm specialized in gold and silver thimbles and in accordance with the practice of the time it participated in the Paris Exhibition of 1878 and in the exhibitions of Sydney in 1879, Melbourne 1880, and Amsterdam 1883. It is known from a catalog dated 1896 that at that time the firm's range was made up of 140 different models of thimbles, comprising 40 models in gold, including some models decorated with different colored gold or platinum or both, 95 models in silver, including some models in plain silver and others with borders of silver gilt, and 5 models in gold-lined silver. It also appears from the catalog that because the price of gold and silver might be expected to fluctuate and because the fine metal content represented such a substantial proportion of the total cost, A. Féau, in common with other thimble-makers at the time, established its prices partly according to the weight of metal and partly to the cost of workmanship. Thus its price list included two columns, one showing the weight of each model and the other the cost of manufacture. Given the price of fine metal, it was then a simple matter to calculate the price of the finished thimble.

For silver thimbles the weight of metal and the cost of production were quoted per dozen and were based on an assortment of the more common sizes, which ran from size 6 to size 11. If necessary, A. Féau was prepared to produce

DÉS ARGENT

1 Ordinaire	2 Ordinaire Ecusson	2 bis Ordinaire fond plat	3 Piqué bas	4 Ciselé
5 Créole	6 Ciselé feston	7 Souvenir relief	8 Souvenir ou autre inscription émail	9 Fleuron Feston
10 Fleurs relief	11 Feuillage relief	12 Grecque relief	13 Etoiles relief	14 Ceinture

Silver thimbles from A. Féau catalog circa 1900. *Private collection*

thimbles of a heavier or lighter weight than those provided for in its price list. The firm always held some thimbles from size 5 to size 13 available in stock to meet any sudden demand. Above size 13, thimbles were only made to order and there was an extra charge. All silver thimbles sold from stock had polished indentations, but if necessary thimbles could be made to order with a mat finish. A few models were available with extra large indentations but there were normally only three sizes: fine, medium, and large. The larger indentations could only be used on thimbles of sufficiently strong construction. Unless otherwise ordered, thimbles were normally supplied with medium size indentations. Five models were available in children's sizes, 4 to 0. Another model was available in five different weights running from 25 grams per dozen to 90 grams per dozen. A small extra charge was made

to gild the interior of thimbles. All models could be made with stone tops, with the choice of two sizes of indentations, and they could also be made with steel tops. Stone tops and steel tops were priced extra. Finally, A. Féau's sales terms were net 30 days and the cost of packing and transport was for the account of the buyer.

Somewhat similar circumstances applied to gold thimbles, except that whereas silver thimbles were normally quoted a dozen at a time in an assortment of sizes, gold thimbles were ordered and made individually. It follows that in the price list, the weight column referred to a single thimble only, which was chosen as size 8, and there was an adjustment provided for larger or smaller sizes in the range from size 5 to size 10. A supplement was payable beyond size 10. Because gold is so much more costly, the extra charge for stone tops was less than for silver

Nickel-plated brass thimble with a bust of Napoleon flanked by two bees. French circa 1900. Height 2.1 cm. *Private collection*

thimbles. Gold thimbles were normally supplied with polished indentations but could be supplied with a mat finish if required. Finally, for those models set with gemstones, the cost of the stones and the setting for them was not included and needed to be allowed for separately.

In addition to gold and silver thimbles A. Féau also sold nickel thimbles in two models. These were sold by the dozen and the price was the same irrespective of the size.

Besides providing a useful insight into the commercial aspects of the thimble industry at the turn of the century, the catalog in question is also useful in the sense that the illustrations it contains serve to emphasize the extent to which the shape and style of French thimbles had evolved over the years. In the early part of the nineteenth century, French thimbles tended to have a somewhat rounded top similar to that usually associated with mother-of-pearl thimbles, but later, no doubt to facilitate production and cut costs, the top became somewhat more flattened. The rounded top incidentally accounts for the fact that, in contrast to the situation in Britain, there were relatively few steel-topped thimbles made, because a rounded steel

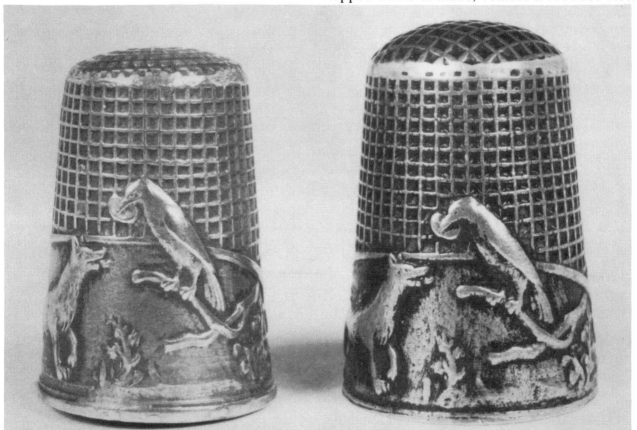

Silver thimbles illustrating La Fontaine's fable of the fox and the raven. *Left,* **French original;** *right,* **German reproduction. Circa 1920.** *Private collection*

71

Prix du Dé d'or. Silver gilt thimble awarded to Hubert de Givenchy January 1982. Height 7.5 cm.
Helena Rubinstein

this has persisted ever since. More recently French manufacturers evolved another distinctive style of their own based on a seamed construction, a wide decorated band, and waffle-shaped indentations down the sides. The range of thimbles decorated with illustrations from the La Fontaine fables is typical of this style, though more traditionally such thimbles are usually decorated with flowers, garlands, and other conventional designs.

Appropriately enough, in a country famous for its *haute couture*, the Prix du Dé d'or was introduced in 1976 as France's highest award for achievement in the field of high fashion design. It is sponsored by *Le Quotidien de Paris,* a daily newspaper, and by Helena Rubinstein, the well-known suppliers of cosmetics, and is awarded in January and July each year. A large silver gilt (vermeil) thimble is presented to the winner of the award.

top would have been more difficult to match for size and curvature than a steel top with a relatively flat surface. French thimbles, however, retained their relatively slender construction, and

NOTES

1. Lebeuf, édit. Cocheris, vol. 2 (Paris, 1883).
2. *D'Auberée la vieille maquerelle, Contes, dicts, fabliaux des XIII, XIV et XV siècles, recueilli par A. Jubinal,* (Paris, 1839), 51:220.
3. Thomas Carlyle, *History of the French Revolution,* vol. 2 Bk. 1, chap. 1.

Porcelain Thimbles

THE MANUFACTURE OF PORCELAIN THIMBLES WAS first introduced at the famous Meissen factory, which pioneered the production of porcelain in Europe and which rapidly became famous for the quality and beauty of its wares. Meissen started production in the early part of the eighteenth century, and the first thimbles date back to about 1735 when together with other small objects they were offered for sale under the heading of "*Galanterien.*" As this name implies, Meissen thimbles were never intended for use in the household. They were merely elegant and tasteful trifles of a kind which a gentleman might care to donate to a lady as a token of affection or esteem. A great many books have been written extolling the virtues of Meissen porcelain, but suffice it here to say that there are only an estimated 250 Meissen thimbles known to survive, each one is a small masterpiece painted in accurate and exquisite detail, and taken together they cover the whole range of Meissen's decorative styles, including all the known ground colors and all the varying types of decoration ruling from 1725 to 1780. In 1975 the world-renowned auctioneers Christie's sold in Geneva a collection of 103 Meissen thimbles, and one of the features of this remarkable sale was that in some cases Christie's were even able to identify the names of the artists who had painted the decoration. The record price paid was 21,000 Swiss francs for a thimble 2.4 centimeters high, which was finely decorated in *Schwarzlot* and gold with galleons in a continuous landscape by Ignaz Preissler at Breslau. Anyone interested in Meissen thimbles

Meissen porcelain decorated in *schwarzlot* and gold by Ignaz Preissler at Breslau with galleons in a continuous landscape. Height 2.4 cm. *Private collection*

should consult the sales catalog for the auction, which is fully illustrated.[1] This record price however was easily surpassed when a further small collection of 10 Meissen thimbles was sold by Christie's in London in 1979.[2] A small thimble decorated with harbor scenes reserved in panels against a lemon yellow ground and dating from about 1740 was sold for £8,000.

A distinctive feature of Meissen thimbles is that they are normally gilt on the inside. A few exist which were left plain white, some of the latter with the Meissen crossed swords in underglaze blue and the rest unmarked. Exceptionally, one specimen is known to have a plain black interior. There is a quantity of Meissen thimbles in the hands of museums in North America (see "Thimbles in Museums") but so far as is known only three in Europe, including one at the Kunstgewerbe Museum, Hamburg, one at the Hermitage, Leningrad, and one at the Swiss National Museum, Zurich.

Besides Meissen several German factories produced thimbles during the eighteenth century. For instance, it is thought that the Fürstenberg factory made thimbles, because in a list of Fürstenberg's products dated 1769, thimbles are mentioned under the heading of *"Galanterien."*[3] The Ludwigsburg factory definitely made thimbles, because there are two in the Schloss Ludwigsburg Collection which were made as part of the table service designed by Gottlieb Friedrich Riedel and presented by Count Carl Eugen to the Marchioness Giovanelli-Martinengo in 1763. The narrow rocaille relief border on the rim matches the rest of the service and the factory mark (CC) appears on the inside of the thimbles.

The Nymphenburg factory probably made thimbles, because a pattern book dated 1767 includes the design of a thimble.[4] Other major German factories which probably made thimbles are Höchst and Vienna (Du Paquier). Some of the minor factories such as Gera or Gotha may also have made thimbles. It should be noted however that besides Meissen, the number of German thimbles to be found is small, they are normally unmarked, and with the exception of the two Ludwigsburg thimbles already mentioned none has been positively identified.

The fashion for porcelain thimbles was not confined to Germany, and several of the Continental factories are known to have made them. From a price list dated 1769 it is known that the Swiss factory at Schooren near Zurich made thimbles and that plain ones were sold at 18 kreuzers and decorated ones at 50 kreuzers.[5] There is no evidence that the other Swiss factory, at Nyon (1781–1813) on the Lake of Geneva, made thimbles, but since Nyon produced other needlework items such as knitting-needle protectors it is by no means unlikely.

In France several factories made thimbles, but there are few records and it is difficult to identify them. The Mennecy-Villeroy (Essone) factory (1734–73) made thimbles which are so typical of

Eighteenth century English porcelain. *Left,* **Chelsea, a bird perched in a branch and another in flight beneath the inscription "Fidelle en Amitié," the indented rim enriched in green and gilt, circa 1760, height 1.8 cm.** *Center,* **Chelsea (damaged) with garlands of purple flowers, inscribed "Gage de mon amour," possibly by James Giles circa 1755, height 1.9 cm.** *Right,* **unknown, possibly Chelsea-Derby, a bird perched in a branch and another in flight with gilt border, height 2.0 cm.** *Private collection*

French porcelain. *Left*, Vincennes, bird in a branch within purple lined border 1750–55, height 2.0 cm; *center*, Sèvres with gilt foliage and carnation garlands entwining red lines 1760–72, height 2.0 cm; *Right*, Mennecy, very small, with a band of trailing roses, height 1.5 cm. *Private collection*

this factory's work as regards the paste, decoration and coloring that no other attribution is possible. Other thimbles have been variously ascribed to the Crépy-en-Valois (Oise) factory (1762–70) and more generally to Vieux Paris. Some thimbles are known to have been made in imitation of Meissen and a porcelain thimble in the shape of a finger and with an impressed CH mark may have been the work of Henri Florentin Chamoie at Barrière de Reuilly (1779–85). The Sèvres factory's records suggest that Sèvres never made thimbles, but there exists a thimble which is undoubtedly from this factory; moreover there is another from the Vincennes factory before it. But these are exceptional and may well be unique.

In Denmark the production of the Royal Copenhagen Porcelain Manufactory is better documented, with an order book for 1778 which includes about one dozen thimbles of various kinds, among them plain thimbles, thimbles decorated in purple enamel, and thimbles gilt with name.[6] A works list dated 1779 also refers to purple enamel. There is a Copenhagen Porcelain thimble in the collection of the Museum of Decorative Art at Copenhagen and two blank undecorated thimbles in the Royal Porcelain Factory's own collection, besides others in private hands.

In Italy the Royal Factory at Naples (1771–1806) made thimbles, and the "Duca di Martina"

Royal Copenhagen porcelain circa 1780. Purple flowers with a green top. Height 2.1 cm. *Private collection*

Museum in the Villa Floridiana at Naples owns an enameled thimble case with gold mounts containing a small porcelain thimble which is attributed to it. There is also a magnificently painted thimble with a continuous landscape depicting the Bay of Sorrento in the possession of the Colonial Williamsburg Foundation, which is typical of this factory's production. No doubt thimbles were also made in other Continental factories not mentioned above, but thimbles were regarded as such trifles that the factories seldom bothered to mention or to list them separately and the evidence is therefore elusive.

Turning now to England, soft paste thimbles are known to have been made at the Chelsea factory. Among other evidence, extracts from the Chelsea weekly bills for the period 1770 to 1773 include one item "96 thimbles, painted overtime by Boardman and Co., £0.12.0," or in other words 1½d per thimble for the cost of decoration.[7] There is an attractive specimen, though unfortunately repaired, in the Victoria and Albert Museum in London whose shape was probably copied from a lesser known type of Meissen thimble. It is painted with a bird perched on a branch and another in flight with the inscription *Gage de mon Amitié* and an indented rim enriched in green and gilt. Part of the famous Schreiber Collection, it is ascribed to Chelsea about 1765, on grounds of material and style of painting. There is another like it in the collection of the Musée des Arts Décoratifs where it is masquerading as *"porcelaine tendre de Mennecy."* And yet another passed through the sales room inscribed *Pour ma Belle* and thought to be about 1760.[8] There are also several other Chelsea thimbles in private collections, including a lovely example, probably by James Giles, who was an out painter for the Chelsea factory about that time, but which is unfortunately badly damaged.

There is good reason to think that the Worcester Porcelain Company made thimbles, because during archaeological excavations carried out in 1977, a spiral fluted shape thimble waster was found fused to its support and dating from about 1785. Thus it appears that thimbles were made at Worcester during the Flight Period but more certainly they were also made at the rival Worcester factory of Chamberlain. Here the evidence is much stronger because many of the

original order books dating from the early 1790s have survived and their pages include many orders for thimbles. Typical orders are as follows:

Miss Stears, Malvern Wells—1 thimble, plain gold edge 1/6d, to be paid for next week.

Lady Coventry, Croome Court, Worcestershire—2 thimbles to size of silver one, BC and Coronet.

William Merryfield, Grantham—Thimbles initialled CM, MW, DSW (large), LW, AW, SW (small).

William Botfield, Dawley, Shropshire—One thimble SB sent as present.

Thomas Emery of Bristol—6 dozen thimbles pattern 55.

Miss Bowen of Bath—6 dozen thimbles, Royal Lily pattern.

Honourable Mrs. Kepple of Malvern—1 thimble with ducal coronet and letter M (two shillings cost).

John Richardson of Cirencester—24 thimbles assorted patterns.

These and other entries from the order book indicate that Worcester was accepting individual orders for ciphered thimbles or thimbles with initials as well as supplying bulk quantities to dealers in neighboring towns. It will also be noted that some attempt was made to cater for differing finger sizes but this was obviously not a matter of major importance, confirming that porcelain thimbles were never seriously intended for sewing but were more in the nature of a fashionable gift. The stock taking on 1 January 1796 disclosed 25 dozen thimbles at one shilling per dozen in the biscuit room, i.e., undecorated thimbles, and 6½ dozen thimbles at one shilling and sixpence in the shop.

The above is ample proof that at the end of the eighteenth century the Chamberlain Worcester factory was conducting a brisk trade in thimbles. On the other hand the situation with regard to the rival Derby factory is more open to doubt. Quite apart from anything else, Derby frequently modeled its wares on other factories, notably Chelsea, so that there is room for confusion. We do know that in the "list of moulds and models which belonged to the estate of the late Mr. Duesbury in 1795, as estimated by Messrs. Soar, Longdon, Fransworth and Hardenburg"

Sampson Hancock Derby porcelain with H&S mark, late nineteenth century. *Private collection*

one of the entries reads "8 thimbles."[9] Duesbury was proprietor of the Derby factory, so that there is strong likelihood that these thimbles came from Derby, but one cannot be sure.

With the advent of the nineteenth century the vogue for porcelain thimbles gained ground in Britain, in contrast to Germany, where it had all but disappeared, and France, where it was dying out rapidly. An occasional French porcelain thimble and an even more occasional German one may be found dating from the early part of the nineteenth century, but these are exceptional and the vast majority of nineteenth-century porcelain thimbles came from Britain. Indeed it is possible to go further and to state that the Worcester factory established for itself a tradition for thimble making which has persisted to this day. The problem is that these thimbles, unlike the Meissen, were relatively insignificant items which were aimed at a mass market. They were seldom marked and they were also easy to imitate by other factories. It is thought that the style of thimbles during the nineteenth century underwent the same development as other Worcester porcelain—Japans or Imaris during the period 1800–1810, fancy birds 1810–15, flowers and landscapes 1815–50, figure subjects in the French style 1850–70, stained ivory and Japanesque 1870–90, and blush ivory with birds and flowers 1890–1914. Most porcelain thimbles continued to be bought for gifts and might be sold in a presentation case: the Worcester factory's records indicate that from 1810 to 1820 Worcester thimbles were sold in thimble cases supplied by a Mr. Graves. It may also be noted that in 1819 the factory sold two so-called Swansea thimbles, suggesting that it may have purchased and decorated blanks supplied from the Swansea factory. Obviously thimbles were made in quantity, and yet the strange feature is that few Worcester thimbles of the early nineteenth century have been identified with any certainty. It is necessary therefore to project inquiries to the end of the century, where it is possible to tread on firmer ground.

By the end of the Victorian era, porcelain thimbles were made chiefly in Worcester and also some in Derby. To start with the latter, when the Bloor Derby factory closed down in 1848, a few employees removed to King Street where they started the business which was to become Sampson Hancock. From 1863–1935 the King Street factory employed the Sampson Hancock (S&H) mark and this mark may be found in

Worcester porcelain. *Left to right:* Grainger mark for 1893; Royal Worcester mark for 1876–91; Royal Worcester mark for 1876–91; unmarked but evidently earlier than the two preceding thimbles; unmarked Japanesque style probably Grainger. *Private collection*

a well-defined type of thimble. As mentioned elsewhere there is a small collection of half a dozen Sampson Hancock thimbles belonging to the Colonial Williamsburg Foundation, some of which are relatively modern, dating from the earlier part of the twentieth century, but others appear older and may well go back to the early days of the King Street factory. In 1875 another company started production in Derby in competition with Sampson Hancock and with premises located in Osmaston Road. The company proved successful and in 1890 the Queen granted it the title of Royal, when it became the Royal Crown Derby Porcelain company. This company also made thimbles; they are of somewhat different shape but they are marked so that there is no question that both the King Street factory and the Osmaston Road factory produced them. In 1935 the Royal Crown Derby Porcelain Company took over Sampson Hancock, the King Street factory was closed, and Osmaston Road assumed the mantle of continuity. The Derby Crown and Royal Crown Derby record of shapes includes an entry (No. 349) in respect of a thimble but unfortunately no drawing is available.

Turning now to Worcester, a somewhat similar situation existed because in addition to the Royal Porcelain Works two other factories operated at the end of the nineteenth century, namely, Grainger & Co., and James Hadley & Sons, which subsequently merged with the main group. It is not known whether Hadley's made thimbles, but Grainger & Co. certainly did, as evidenced by a thimble bearing their mark and the date code for 1893. The Grainger thimbles are characterized by delicately ornate gilding and include some rare examples dating from about 1875 which are decorated in the Japanese style associated with James Hadley when the latter was still working for Grainger before he set up on his own. When Grainger was taken over by the Royal Porcelain Works in 1889 bird thimbles continued to be made but the gilding was curtailed and the potting became heavier. From about 1890 to 1914 Royal Worcester made thimbles in their so-called stained ivory and also in blush ivory (sometimes known as biscuit Worcester) which were decorated with birds and flowers, as well as thimbles with a plain white background. Later examples usually bear the Royal Worcester mark applied in purple colored transfer and include a date mark which is incorporated into the factory mark by means of an elaborate system of dots and symbols.[10] Those marked "Royal Worcester England" date from about 1900 to 1928 and those marked "Royal Worcester—Made in England" from about 1928 to 1963, when the date system was abandoned on thimbles. One charming series produced during the interwar years was decorated by William Powell, who worked at the Royal Worcester factory from 1900 to 1950. William Powell specialized in British birds and flowers. He was a hunchback and a dwarf, but in spite of these disabilities he is remembered as a remarkably friendly and cheerful man who loved birds and painted them with great understanding and affection. Other artists whose signature may appear on Worcester thimbles include Kitty Blake, who painted flowers about 1924, and Ron Godfrey, an apprentice who painted thimbles in the 1930s but left Worcester after the war.

The Royal Worcester factory's technique for making a porcelain thimble follows very much the same lines as for other production. A roll of the prepared clay body is forced through a nozzle and cut out into short lengths for jollying into a thimble shape. This process is really nothing more than mechanical molding. The clay is pressed into a plaster mold revolving on a turntable or wheel and a template is gradually brought down into the mould as it revolves, removing any surplus clay. The mold with the jollied thimble inside is left to dry out, the moisture is taken up by the plaster, and the thimble, which at this stage is larger than normal size is slipped out of the mold. After the edges have been trimmed with a fettling tool, the thimble undergoes its first (biscuit) firing, during which it shrinks down to normal size and emerges as fused bone china. It is then coated with glaze and undergoes its second (glaze) firing, after which it is ready for decoration. Most of the Worcester thimbles made between 1860 and 1939 were in the glazed parian body, a creamier, smoother body than bone china, which is very white and translucent, and are readily recognizable on that account.

The hand decoration of porcelain is a highly skilled operation. Besides the more obvious need for artistic merit, the painter must allow for the fact that the colors change when the pigments are fired into the glaze and that different colors may require different temperatures. For a simple object such as a thimble a first firing for the background colors and then a second firing at a slightly lower temperature to fuse the brighter colors is normally sufficient. After the decorative firings comes the gilding, which is again done by hand. Gold mixed with oil in a suspension of mercuric oxide is painted on the thimble, which

English porcelain of unknown origin. Presumably late nineteenth or early twentieth century. *Private collection*

English porcelain of unknown origin. Presumably late nineteenth or early twentieth century. *Private collection*

is then sent to the kilns for the last time to fire the gold, and when the thimble has cooled the gold is burnished over to a finish.

Royal Worcester continue to make porcelain thimbles which are hand decorated with birds, flowers, and fruit, and each bears the signature of the artist. Since 1963 such thimbles bear the factory mark in black transfer with the letter *R* in a circle underneath. Being relatively inexpensive they are in great demand and the Royal Worcester factory produces them in imposing quantities. Besides hand decorated thimbles, Royal Worcester also make thimbles with printed subjects produced by decals (transfer prints), which are of course less expensive than painted ones and remain unsigned.

Other factories besides the Derby and Worcester factories probably made thimbles during the nineteenth century, because there is a wide range of thimbles of that date which have no obvious attribution. It is thought that Coalport for instance may have made thimbles but no real evidence that they did has so far emerged and the supposition could well be mistaken.

Some porcelain thimbles were made in the United States toward the end of the nineteenth century. The Brooklyn Museum, New York, has a belleek porcelain thimble made by Ott and Brewer, Trenton, New Jersey (1883–92) decorated with a flowered band enclosed by gold bands on a white ground. Moreover another

Trenton firm, the Ceramic Art Co., is also thought to have made belleek thimbles. This company, which was formed by Walter Lenox in 1889 in partnership with Jonathan Coxon, Sr., specialized in belleek ware and according to trade advertisements its products included vases, inkstands, parasol handles, menu slabs, candelabras, and also thimbles. In 1894 Lenox acquired Coxon's interest and he operated alone until 1906 when the present Lenox Co. was incorporated.

In modern times the success of the Royal Worcester thimbles has prompted other porcelain manufacturers to follow their example. Modern porcelain thimbles, mostly with printed designs, are made by Crown Royal Adderley, Caverswall (also A. W. Harrison), Coalport, Countess, Royal Doulton, Masons, Spode, Royal Stafford, Sandford, Royal Windsor, etcetera. Several factories abroad have also followed suit, including Bing and Grøndahl in Denmark in traditional Danish designs, the Hungarian porcelain factory at Herend, which makes some pleasantly hand decorated thimbles reminiscent of Continental styles, Kaiser in Germany, Ginori in Italy, and a factory in Argentina. Needless to say that the hand-painted designs are normally far superior to the printed article and collectors should beware of unscrupulous suppliers who offer series of so-called hand-crafted porcelain thimbles and whose advertisements serve to conceal the only

Derby porcelain. *Left*, Royal Crown Derby circa 1895; center Sampson Hancock, date unknown; *right*, Royal Crown Derby 1934. *Private collection*

fact that really matters, namely, that the design is only printed. Nevertheless it should be remembered that when Meissen began to make thimbles, from 1735 onward, these were considered mere trifles, and the discerning collector will not therefore discard all modern thimbles necessarily out of hand.

The vogue for thimble collecting has encouraged some artisans to make thimbles or to decorate ready-made blanks for sale to collectors. These are usually hand decorated but far too often they are the work of relatively unskilled amateurs. There are some exceptions such as the thimbles decorated by the British artist Graham Payne, which are finely worked and reach a high standard, but otherwise this class of work is frequently coarse and tasteless.

The subject of porcelain thimbles is not complete without some mention of thimble shapes. The latter are referred to again in the chapter on "Just a Thimbleful," but meanwhile it will be sufficient to explain that the term applies to those items which, although molded in the shape of thimbles, have little more than token indentations. In this category are plain thimble shapes without indentations, made at Limoges, and a thimble shape decorated with flowers with small pimples instead of indentations, made by the English firm Hammersley. Thimble shapes of this kind can have little appeal to collectors but they cannot be dismissed altogether—if only because Meissen is known to have made one during the eighteenth century which, needless to say, would now be welcome in any collection.

What can be made in porcelain can usually also be made in earthenware, and this includes thimbles. The Stoke-on-Trent Museum has an earthenware thimble whose origins are unknown, but otherwise earthenware thimbles are rare. Possibly earthenware as a medium proved too soft or too brittle, though if earthenware is baked at very high temperatures and treated with an appropriate glaze it can be very hard. Somewhat surprisingly, there is evidence that Josiah Wedgwood made some thimbles of jasperware at the end of the eighteenth century. An entry in the "Ovens Book"—the name given to day-to-day manuscript records preserved at the Wedgwood Museum, of ware fired at the Wedgwood factory at Etruria—first mentions the firing of 18 dozen jasper thimbles in August 1791, and the final entry is 3 dozen jasper thimbles in October 1800. Presumably these thimbles were sold, but it is not known why production was discontinued and none is known to have survived. Some contemporary earthenware thimbles are made for sale to collectors, including more recently some Wedgwood thimbles, but these are more in the nature of thimble shapes.

NOTES

1. "Christie's Catalogue: Fine Porcelain Galanterie Sale held at Geneva on 10th November 1975, Lots 1 to 103" and illustrations.

2. "Christie's Catalogue: Important Continental Porcelain Sale held at London on 3rd December 1979, Lots 136 to 145" and illustrations.

3. S. Ducret, *Fürstenberger-Porzellan* (Zurich, 1965), Vol. 2.

4. Friedrich H. Hofmann, *Geschichte der Bayerischen Porzellan Manufaktur Nymphenburg* (Leipzig, 1922), 3:593.

5. S. Ducret, *Züricher Porzellan*, (Zurich, 1944), 99

6. B. L. Grandjean, *Kongelig Dansk Porcelain* (Copenhagen, 1962).

7. L. Jewitt, FSA, *Ceramic Art in Great Britain*, vol. 1 (London, 1878).

8. "Christie's Catalogue: English and Welsh Porcelain Sale held at London on 31st October 1980, Lot 109" and illustrations.

9. Wm. Bemrose, *Bow Chelsea and Derby Porcelain* (London, 1898).

10. G. A. Godden, FRSA, *Encyclopaedia of British Pottery and Porcelain marks* (London, 1964).

Enamel Thimbles

THE ART OF COATING A METALLIC SURFACE WITH A vitreous substance and fusing it as a means of decoration was already well established during the Middle Ages and was probably used to decorate thimbles as early as the sixteenth century. However, the evidence is elusive and the earliest enameled thimbles that are known to have survived date from the eighteenth century. Needless to say that enamel is easily damaged, which is no doubt the reason why early enamel thimbles are scarce.

During the eighteenth century English enamelers sought to imitate the small porcelain boxes and other small porcelain articles which were proving so popular in Germany. After a somewhat tentative start at Battersea, the art of enameling copper was mastered and came to flourish in South Staffordshire (Bilston) about 1770. A wide range of small painted boxes, etuis and the like were produced, including chatelaines, needlecases capped with thimbles, Easter eggs with matching thimble inside, and a variety of painted thimbles on their own. It goes without saying that, like the porcelain thimbles they were designed to imitate, these enameled thimbles were not meant to be used. They were far too delicate and were intended more as tokens for display.

Bilston enamel thimbles are usually small and rounded, with the top only indented and the sides reserved for decoration. The indentations at the top may be enameled over or there may be a brass cap which bears the indentations. The thimbles themselves are usually decorated with posies of flowers on a white ground or with a miniature landscape in a cartouche against a colored ground. More rarely they may be decorated with a miniature portrait. There are four fine Bilston enamels in the Schreiber Collection at the Victoria and Albert Museum in London. Good examples of English eighteenth-century painted enamels are not easy to find and when they do reach the market command high prices.

The English fashion for South Staffordshire enamels found its echo on the Continent, and a type of eighteenth-century enamel thimble will occasionally be found which was probably made either in France or Germany. There is a fine example in the Colonial Williamsburg Foundation collection and others in private hands.

Enameling has long been practiced in Russia, where it became a traditional form of art. Some beautiful thimbles have been made, and those illustrated are typical of the kind of enamel thimble most commonly found. The splendor of Russian enamel recalls the name of Fabergé, but genuine Fabergé thimbles are extremely rare. Only two or three authentic examples are known, including one made by Henrik Wigström, who headed Perchin's shop when Perchin died in 1903 and who from that date assumed responsibility for making the imperial eggs. Some enamel thimbles have been produced in Russia since the Revolution, but the work is coarse and has little artistic merit.

Enameling was also a traditional art form in

Eighteenth-century enamel. *Left and right*, **South Staffordshire (Bilston);** *center*, **French style but unknown origin.** *Private collection*

Persia (Iran). In 1975 two fine Persian gold enamel thimbles passed through the salesroom,[1] the first dating from the mid-nineteenth century, decorated with three portrait medallions of a European, an Indian, and a Persian lady, alternating with flowering vine reserved on a blue

Persian enamel on gold. *Above*, **third quarter nineteenth century, height 2.2 cm;** *below*, **mid-nineteenth century, height 2.5 cm.** *Christie, Manson and Woods Ltd.*

ground, and the other from the third quarter of the nineteenth century with three portraits of Persian ladies alternating with flowering branches with perching birds. More commonly silver enamel thimbles will also be found.

Returning to Europe, Norway is another country which specialized in enameling and where during the nineteenth century some very beautiful silver enamel thimbles were made. Norwegian thimbles may be recognized from their style and also because they are usually fitted with a moonstone top. The older thimbles are decorated in traditional designs with shades of blue or green enamel and white beading. When still in mint condition, such thimbles will be seen to have been lightly gilded both inside and out. Later thimbles may be plain with light blue, light pink, or light mauve transparent enamel over a guilloche. Another series is decorated with reindeer, snow scenes, fjords, or pine trees in black over a background of light blues and pinks which are set over a guilloche and achieve an attractive Northern lights effect. Norwegian manufacturers now appear to have abandoned the moonstone top in favor of a flat waffle-indented top and the thimbles are decorated with a printed pattern of roses and foliage against a white background.

As already mentioned, the German thimble-makers have long used enamel to decorate thimbles and a noteworthy eighteenth-century specimen made of silver with enamel decoration will be found in the Fondazione Artistica Poldi-Pezzoli (Poldi Museum) collection in Milan.

Russian enamel on silver about 1900. Note that hallmarks are invariably struck on the rim. *Private collection*

From the nineteenth century onward, various factories produced gold and silver thimbles with a hand-painted design round the base, and this type of thimble is still popular. Unfortunately the quality of the work has declined. Printed designs have replaced hand painting and in recent years the standards have deteriorated further. The silver is more heavily machined, simulated stone tops made of glass are used instead of cornelian, the printed nature of the design has become more apparent, and the enamel has a plastic look about it. Nevertheless, these thimbles sell successfully in many countries and help to maintain Germany's position as a traditional exporter. The usual decoration nowadays consists of posies of roses with a light blue ground, and modern German enamel thimbles are also produced with printed reproductions of famous monuments in different parts of the world, where they are sold as tourist souvenirs. Collectors may also have met the silver thimbles which are decorated with hand-painted or printed blue enamel Delft-like scenes. These are not Dutch as may be thought, but are imported from Germany.

Finally, some mention should be made of Chinese cloisonné thimbles. During the nineteenth century silver thimbles were made in China for the export market which were decorated with a kind of applied filigree enhanced with occasional touches of enamel, usually green or blue. There is a thimble of this kind to be found in the collection of the Colonial Williamsburg Foundation. But more recently, and presumably in response to the demand from collectors, some handsome and colorful brass thimbles made by the cloisonné process have been emerging from mainland China. In this process, brass wire is soldered on a thimble-shaped body to form a design, enamel of different colours is painted between the wires, and following two or more firings the thimble is polished and polished again until the surface is bright and uniform and the enamel level with the retaining wires. Chinese cloisonné thimbles are modern but they are attractive and well made. They are produced by the same traditional methods which have made China famous for its cloisonné work and they are well worth pursuing.

The above covers the main types of enamel

Norwegian enamel on silver. Early twentieth century. *Private collection*

German enamel on silver. Early twentieth century. *Private collection*

thimbles, but besides these there are countless thimbles decorated with enamel which do not fall into any recognizable category. In England for instance both gold and silver thimbles were decorated with enamel during the eighteenth century, usually in monochrome, dark blue being a favourite color. Then during the nineteenth century enamel appears to have been used more on gold thimbles, often in polychrome, and more recently still it was used again on silver thimbles. There is no established pattern and most countries have produced enamel thimbles of one kind or another. It is a beautiful form of decoration and its only drawback is that it damages easily. Great care should therefore be taken when purchasing enamel thimbles, since the value of a repaired item is obviously less than that of the same article in pristine condition.

Moreover, in the same way that the vogue for thimble collecting has encouraged the production of a wide range of porcelain thimbles, so it has also led to the production of some modern enamel thimbles. The English firm of Crummels & Co. from Poole, Dorset, for instance, makes enamel boxes and also thimbles. The latter have a distant resemblance to eighteenth-century Bilston thimbles but the decoration, which is painted over a transfer outline, has less character and they are not difficult to tell apart.

NOTE

1. "Christie's Catalogue: Islamic Art Sale held at London on 14th July 1975, Lots 63 and 64."

Gold Thimbles

GOLD HAS ALWAYS BEEN COVETED BY MANKIND BEcause of the wealth it represents, because of its rich, warm color, and because it does not tarnish. Pure gold being too soft to work on its own, it is usually alloyed with other metals when it takes on a variety of shades: water-green, dead-leaf white, gray, red, blue, and so forth. In former times the weight of alloy was defined in twenty-fourths, so that 24 carat gold is fine gold and 18 carat gold is 750 parts gold per thousand weight. As the gold content declines so the color tends to become less attractive and thimbles made of 9 carat gold for instance are best avoided. The purity (also known as the fineness) of gold can be tested with a touchstone, but this normally requires the services of a jeweler or goldsmith.

It is tempting to imagine that the ladies who lived in medieval castles and occupied their leisure by embroidery or tapestry making owned gold thimbles, but there is little evidence to support it. A painting by Mantegna (c. 1431–1506) at the Petit Palais in Paris shows the Infant Christ with the Virgin holding a gold needle, which suggests that already by the fifteenth century gold was associated with needlework tools, but this is obviously inconclusive. It is possible that the odd gold thimble did grace the finger of a queen or princess but it is unlikely that gold thimbles were made in any number until the sixteenth century, when because new sources of gold were discovered in Africa and because of the gold which the Spaniards were bringing back from the New World, gold became more plentiful. It is during the sixteenth century that silver began to be used to make thimbles, and some gold thimbles were also made about that time.

The first recorded mention of a gold thimble occurs, as already noted, in 1583 and concerns a gold thimble garnished with rubies which belonged to the King of Navarre. At about the same time another two royal thimbles are mentioned in an inventory of the possessions of Queen Elizabeth I, which included "a nedell case of cristall garnyshed with silvergilt with twoo thimbles in it." The inventory does not reveal whether the thimbles were made of gold, but among the personal possessions of the queen preserved at Burghley House, Stamford, was a plain gold thimble. Regrettably this was stolen a few years ago and there are no records available. There is also another thimble associated with Queen Elizabeth I, made of gold set with rubies and sapphires, which is preserved in the Dorothy Howell collection. The latter, according to family tradition, was given by the queen to a lady-in-waiting. If correct, this would suggest that gold thimbles were not unusual. Lastly, in the Doisteau collection, before it was dispersed, there was a very fine gold thimble set with rubies and thought to be Oriental from the sixteenth century. Little is known of the Doisteau collection except that certain items, including the thimble in question, are illustrated in H. R. D'Allemagne and that some of them are now in museums and in private collections.

The use of gold thimbles grew during the seventeenth and eighteenth centuries, particularly in France where gold thimbles were in great de-

French gold thimbles. *Left to right:* **mid-eighteenth century, late eighteenth century, early nineteenth century, mid-nineteenth century, late nineteenth century.** *Private collection*

mand. It is noted that the gold, silver, and gilded brass thimbles from Blois were highly thought of and were supplied in large quantities both to Paris and abroad. In England, according to Therle Hughes, a raised gold thimble cost 50 shillings in 1714, which was a high price considering that a brass thimble only cost one penny.[1] The eighteenth century, however, was an age of extravagance and only a year later in 1715 Lady Mary Wortley Montagu recorded a gold chatelaine for sale at fifty guineas in a fashionable toy shop (see page 216). The earliest gold thimble on record in the United States was made by Samuel Vernon, Newport, R.I., circa 1720 and is owned privately.

Until about 1830, when specialized thimble manufacturers took over the production of both silver and gold thimbles, it was customary for anyone wishing to purchase a gold thimble to have it made specially by a goldsmith. The latter, who was probably also a silversmith, would normally have stocked silver thimbles which he might or might not have bought wholesale from a specialist thimble-maker, but gold thimbles he would make himself in his own workshop. This was the practice of the American silversmith Joseph Richardson (1711–84), who as mentioned earlier left detailed accounts of his business. Most of the thimbles he made were made of gold, they weighed about 4 dwts each, and the price was calculated by adding the value of the gold plus approximately 6 shillings for the cost of workmanship. It also appears to have been the practice of Paul Revere (1735–1818), the well-known silversmith and patriot who was cele-

brated by Longfellow for his exploit in riding on horseback to warn the inhabitants of Middlesex County of the approach of British troops. The Museum of Fine Arts, Boston, owns a plain gold thimble which is said to have been one of a pair and which was made with his own hands in 1805 for his daughter.

Coming back to Britain, by the end of the eighteenth century artisan thimble-makers had all but disappeared. In 1815 two well-known Birmingham manufacturing silversmiths, namely, Taylor and Perry and Edward Thomason, were advertising themselves as makers of gold thim-

Gold thimble with vinaigrette. The thimble is decorated with blue enamel and the underside of the base serves as a letter seal. Probably English about 1800. *Private collection*

Gold thimble of Continental origin. Early nineteenth century. *Colonial Williamsburg Foundation*

bles and already by that date Charles May in London were set on their long career. Obviously gold thimbles continued to be purchased individually and were mostly made to order, but soon only those who manufactured silver thimbles as a matter of routine could produce a gold thimble economically. Many of the leading makers of silver thimbles also made gold thimbles. In England for instance well-known names making gold thimbles included James Fenton, Samuel Foskett and later Henry Foskett, Henry Griffith, Joseph Price, James Swann, Alfred Taylor, and Joseph Willmore. There may have been others but those mentioned undoubtedly account for the bulk of the gold thimbles which were manufactured in Britain during the nineteenth century.

During the nineteenth century English gold thimbles were produced with a great variety of decoration but their shape remained basically unchanged throughout the period. The more expensive gold thimbles were set with precious or semiprecious stones, and among the most beautiful were those decorated with posies of turquoise and worked in different colored golds. More simply a gold thimble might carry turquoise, pearls, coral, or stones inset as a beading round the rim and, simpler still, the thimble might be worked in plain gold with the

Three gold thimbles of Continental origin. Early nineteenth century. *Private collection*

88

goldsmith relying entirely on design to achieve his effect. Some thimbles of this kind are distinctly fussy but others reveal a surprising sobriety of design not usually associated with Victorian taste. Indentations formed by the intersections of two systems of parallel lines are a feature which is often found on English gold thimbles and date from the second half of the nineteenth century.

In France the Revolution brought a pause in the production of gold thimbles, but the love of luxury soon reasserted itself. In the early part of the nineteenth century thimbles continued to be produced in the rounded beehive shape which was characteristic of Continental thimbles at the end of the eighteenth century, with the thimbles made of reddish gold with yellow gold ornamentations round the base. Gradually, however, it came to be realized that this shape was not practical, either in use or in the process of manufacture, and a more elongated shape with flattened top came to be adopted, which one way or another has persisted in France to this day. Meanwhile the French silver thimble industry found it difficult to prosper, being encompassed on one side by the English thimble industry based on Birmingham and on the other side by the German thimble industry based on Baden-Württemberg. These were powerful and uncomfortable neighbors, but gold thimbles were less affected. Since these were mostly sold individually to order, it was more difficult for foreign manufacturers to compete, and consequently business in gold thimbles was more prosperous.

As for the United States, the growth of specialized thimble manufacturers such as Simons Bros. soon led to their appropriating the market for gold thimbles. The artisan thimble-makers dropped out and, as in Britain, the production of gold thimbles came to be concentrated in the hands of the silver thimble manufacturers, notably Ketcham & McDougall and of course Simons Bros., which continue to make them to this day. American gold thimbles have been produced in

Gold (15 carat) thimble and finger guard decorated with turquoise. Made by Charles May, London, 1867.
Private collection

Gold and multicolored enamel inscribed "Profitez du temps," nineteenth century. Height 2.4 cm. *Private collection*

great variety, some in the same style as silver thimbles and others in a style of their own. If there is one criticism, however, it is that they tend to be too bright and glittery. There is not enough of the goldsmith and too much of the factory in their makeup. This was perhaps inevitable seeing that in the latter part of the nineteenth century gold thimbles had become so commonplace that they were advertised in the Sears Roebuck catalog and that Simons Bros. were making to order gold thimbles set with diamonds at $150 a piece.

Not surprisingly, gold thimbles being so attractive, the practice of gilding silver was extended to thimbles from an early date. For instance there are two silver thimbles in the Kunstgewerbe Museum in Berlin which date from about 1600 and show traces of the original gilding. The trouble with gilding thimbles, however, is that the gilding soon wears out in use. This did not deter some French manufacturers in the nineteenth century who made gilded thimbles, nor did it deter the French and German manufacturers from experimenting with the use of gilding as a means of decoration. Dur-

ing the nineteenth century many French and German thimbles bore some gilding on the outside, and it also became the practice for silver thimbles to be lightly gilded inside, the latter being more in the nature of a finish. The practice of gilding thimbles inside continues in use and it is not unusual to find modern German thimbles finished in this way.

Somewhat different is the material known as pinchbeck, which is an alloy of five parts copper and one part zinc. It was invented by Christopher Pinchbeck (1670–1732) and was used as a low priced substitute for gold. During the eighteenth century pinchbeck was used to make thimbles, sometimes with a steel top to give added strength, and its use was continued until well into the nineteenth century. In the United States, Benjamin Halsted advertised thimbles of pinchbeck with steel tops in 1766, as well as thimbles of gold and silver.

Care must be taken when purchasing a gold thimble because of the danger that it may be a plain silver or brass thimble which has been gold plated and which is being passed off as solid gold. There is also the danger that it may be a gold-filled or a rolled gold thimble. Gold-filled denotes a layer of base metal to which a sheet of gold has been fused or rolled. Similarly, rolled gold is gold bonded to a base metal but usually in

Gold with Russian hallmark, possibly made in Scandinavia, nineteenth century. Height 2.1 cm. *Private collection*

even lesser quantities. A gold-filled thimble may be recognized from its style or its lack of weight, but the sure method is to cut a small notch and to apply a drop of aqua regia (a mixture of nitric acid and hydrochloric acid). If there is base metal underneath, the acid will bubble away as it eats into it, but of course the thimble will be damaged, however slightly. Aqua regia, incidentally, is highly corrosive and must be handled only with great care. The above should not be confused with silver gilt thimbles, which being intended as such are perfectly genuine and easy to distinguish. A genuine silver gilt thimble may be an attractive and worthwhile acquisition, but a gold-plated thimble which is intended to pass as gold is a worthless fraud. Collectors must therefore satisfy themselves about what they are buying and when in doubt seek expert advice. Some gold thimbles are hallmarked, which besides offering a measure of guarantee also provides useful information regarding the date and provenance of the thimble. The question of hallmarks is discussed in more detail in the chapter on silver thimbles. As always when one is dealing with thimbles, the more interesting items are often those that are unmarked, but nevertheless some guidance may be obtained from the following:

Great Britain. With few exceptions gold thimbles were seldom marked until the end of the nineteenth century. The marks incorporate the gold content in carats and there is also a date code similar to that for silver. The standard for gold was 22 carat until 1798, when both 18 carat and 22 carat were permitted. In 1854 three lower standards were introduced, namely 9, 12, and 15 carat, and in 1931, 12 carat and 15 carat were replaced by 14 carat. It follows that a thimble marked 12 or 15 carat was necessarily made between 1854 and 1931.

France. Gold thimbles dating from after the time of the Revolution are mostly marked, and the mark most frequently found is that of an eagle's head, which was introduced in 1838. Coincidentally in 1838 the French authorities introduced the practice of striking hallmarks against a specially prepared anvil (*bigorne*) which bears a design in relief, with the result that some part of this design is reproduced on the reverse side of the hallmark. Only France makes use of this type of reverse marking and it is therefore a useful way of identifying French thimbles.

One mark which may occasionally puzzle collectors is a small oval hallmark with the figure of an owl which is sometimes found on some of the older French thimbles. This hallmark (*le hibou*) which was introduced in 1893, is applied, *inter alia*, to objects which do not bear any other means of identification and which are sold through public auction.

Germany. Gold thimbles made in Germany are normally unmarked except for a figure denoting the gold content in parts per thousand.

United States. The more recent thimbles are normally marked with a gold content in carats and they usually bear the maker's mark inside.

Sweden. Gold thimbles normally carry a full set of marks, including the state mark consisting of

South American gold thimbles. *Colonial Williamsburg Foundation*

the three Swedish crowns, the gold content in carats, a date code, and a maker's mark. Since 1901 the Swedish crowns may figure in a clover-shape mark which denotes that the thimble was made in Sweden, or in an oval-shape mark, in which case it was imported.

Collectors requiring more information about gold hallmarks should consult the latest edition of a good international reference book such as *Les Poinçons de garantie internationaux pour l'or et le platine,* published by Tardy, Paris.

Specially designed gold thimbles have often been made as souvenirs or gifts or to commemorate some occasion. Moreover, a thimble manufacturer making commemorative silver thimbles often made a few gold ones as well, which he might sell or else keep for distribution among his friends. At other times a gold thimble might be designed specially as a gift. A famous example was the one designed by Vernon and executed by Maison Duval in Paris in 1900 as President

Kruger's gift to Queen Wilhelmina. At the other extreme a thimble inscribed "Canary wins Ascot 1862" was evidently commissioned to celebrate some private occasion on the race course. Commemorative gold thimbles are few and far between and greatly prized by the fortunate owners.

Besides gold, thimbles are sometimes made of platinum which is another rare metal. Platinum is steel gray to silver-white in appearance and very similar to gold in many of its properties, notably its weight, because platinum is even heavier than gold. Platinum thimbles are known from Russia, which is perhaps not surprising because Russia is a large producer of the metal, and also from the United States (Simons Bros.).

NOTE

1. Therle Hughes, *English Domestic Needlework, 1660–1860* (London, 1961).

Mother-of-pearl Thimbles

THE IRIDESCENT INNER LAYER OF THE PEARL OYS-
ter shell and other molluscs is called mother-of-
pearl, or nacre, and has long been used for decorative purposes. Examples of mother-of-pearl
work possibly seven thousand years old have
been found in Babylon. An early Catalan text
dated 1365 associates thimbles with mother-of-
pearl but the interpretation is open to doubt,
and thimbles of mother-of-pearl did not come
into their own until the nineteenth century.

About 1810, it became the fashion in Paris for
small objects in everyday use to be made of
mother-of-pearl mounted or bound with gilded
bronze or similar material. Such objects were
manufactured in great variety, including snuffboxes, cases of various kinds, sewing items, and
even thimbles. This type of work was done by a
number of firms situated around the Palais
Royal and is now referred to under that name.
The fashion later spread to London, Vienna and
elsewhere. Palais Royal thimbles often have one
or more bands of gilded metal along the rim or
side of the thimble. They are quite distinctive
and a charming feature which may be found is a
single blue flower, possibly a pansy (Fr. *pensée* =
thought), inserted in the mother-of-pearl, approximately where a crest might otherwise be
situated. An Austrian firm, Jacob Schwarz,
showed a mother-of-pearl thimble at the Great
Exhibition.

Mother-of-pearl is sometimes used in the
place of cornelian or other stone and fitted into
the tip of a gold thimble where its purpose is to
take the wear of the needle. Thimbles made of
mother-of-pearl should be kept away from direct sunlight, as otherwise the mother-of-pearl
risks losing its iridescence and going "blind."

Abalone is a type of mother-of-pearl with a
strong green or red color. It is much prized for
jewelry and was sometimes used to decorate
thimble cases. It is not suitable for making thimbles, though occasionally silver thimbles have
been decorated with abalone.

Mother-of-pearl. Thimbles with rounded tops belong to the earlier part and those with square tops to the latter part of the nineteenth century. Probably French. *Private collection*

93

Ivory Thimbles

THE GREAT VIRTUE OF IVORY IS ITS STRENGTH AND homogeneous nature, which permits intricate and delicate carving without fear of running into unforeseen difficulties. Its working goes back to prehistoric times and it is not surprising therefore to find that ivory thimbles were used from an early date. The first written mention occurs about 1365 when a Catalan manuscript speaks of "un portador de didaleres de vori."[1] The first known example dates from the Renaissance and is carved with the design of a dog coursing after game, which was a favorite theme at that time. No doubt others have survived, but ivory thimbles are often plain without recognizable motif, dating them is difficult, and their shape provides little indication of their age. In time ivory assumes a yellow-brown patina, but even this depends very much on the conditions under which the object is kept. An ivory thimble may be discolored without necessarily being very old, or vice versa.

Ivory thimbles were sufficiently popular during the seventeenth century that the dictionary of Antoine Furetière, published in Paris in 1690, gives brass, silver, and ivory as the three materials from which thimbles were made. In the eighteenth century they were considered particularly suitable for embroidery, being light and convenient for delicate work. An ivory turner, Elizabeth Barton Stent, made ivory thimbles in London about 1740–50,[2] and in 1761 Parson Woodforde gave his sister Jenny an ivory thimble.[3] In the United States in 1767 Charles Shipman, "Ivory and Hardwood turner, lately from England," advertised "ivory thimbles" among a list of turners' articles.[4] In all likelihood these thimbles were mostly beehive shaped with the rim possibly strengthened or decorated with a gilt collar. In southern Germany at the end of the eighteenth or beginning of the nineteenth century ivory thimbles might be painted round the base with a polychrome floral motif, and the Städtdisches Museum at Schwäbisch-Gmünd owns a sewing case with a thimble of this kind dating from about 1820.

Ivory thimbles continued to be made during the nineteenth century and some beautiful designs were achieved, but being hand carved they were more in the nature of luxury articles. Some ivory thimbles were also imported which were smooth and without indentations. These came with workboxes from the Far East (see "Bone Thimbles") and were presumably intended for fine sewing, but so far no satisfactory explanation has been offered for their lack of indentations. Ivory thimbles may sometimes be found which are fitted with a steel top.

Ivory became increasingly scarce during the nineteenth century and its scarcity encouraged the use of another material known as vegetable ivory or corozo nut (see page 129). Vegetable ivory thimbles are possibly scarcer than thimbles made of bone or ivory but they are in many ways less attractive. The Colonial Williamsburg Foundation own a vegetable ivory thimble which is decorated in color round the base, but this is unusual because vegetable ivory, being oily, does not provide a suitable key for dyestuff and the

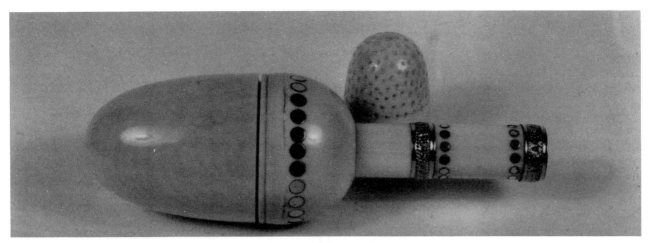

Ivory thimble and needle case combination. French circa 1800. *Private collection*

Ivory—delicately carved, probably English circa 1850. *Private collection*

attempts to decorate it have mostly resulted in failure. It was the increasing price and scarcity of ivory (and vegetable ivory) about 1860 which eventually led to the discovery of celluloid and with it the virtual disappearance of both ivory and vegetable ivory thimbles. Ivory thimbles with a peep-show view of the Pursall variety are of modern manufacture and not seriously intended for needlework.

NOTES

1. Antoni Rubió y Lluch, *Documents per l'Historia de la Cultura Catelana Mig-eval,* (Barcelona, 1908), 1 : 208.

2. Sir Ambrose Heal, *London Tradesmen Cards of the 18th century.*

3. *James Woodforde 1758–1781, The Diary of a Country Parson,* ed. John Beresford (London, 1924).

4. *The New-York Journal, or General Advertiser,* 6 August 1767.

Tortoise-shell Thimbles

THE TRUE LOGGERHEAD TURTLE *(CHELONIA IM-bricata)* has a domed shell or carapace on its back which consists of bone plates embedded in a leathery skin, covered on the outside with horny plates. It is the horny plates which are of ornamental value and form the material known as tortoise shell.

Tortoise shell is not really a suitable material for making thimbles, although some eighteenth-century thimbles were made from it and in 1816 John Piercy patented (English patent No. 4077) a process for making thimbles from tortoise shell, turtle shell, horn, or leather, to be lined, tipped, or decorated with iron, steel, silver, gold, or other metal. Thimbles made by Piercy's patent are scarce, and a fine example of tortoise shell tipped and decorated with gold is illustrated. This is the better known design. Another rarer design with the tortoise shell enclosed in a perforated pinchbeck surround is also illustrated.

Sewing items in gold or silver gilt decorated with tortoise shell or mounted with it were made during the nineteenth century and may include a thimble to match. Such thimbles often have a metal tip in order to help withstand the wear of a needle. Tortoise-shell thimbles may also feature a piqué type decoration.

Finger protectors which are intended to be used in the same way as finger guards may sometimes be found made of plastic imitation tortoise shell, but these are twentieth century appliances of little interest.

Tortoise shell should not be subjected to boil-

Tortoise-shell—English eighteenth century. *Private collection*

96

Piercy's patent—*left*, silver; *center*, gold; *right*, pinchbeck. English; circa 1816. *Private collection*

ing water or steam, which will distort it. Any dullness or scratches are easily treated with an oily polish. Genuine tortoise shell is distinguished from plastic imitations by wavy markings visible as small granular accumulations under magnification.

Silver Thimbles

IT IS NOT ALWAYS REALIZED THAT UNTIL THE SIX-teenth century silver was a much rarer metal relative to gold than it is today. For example, under the Egyptian code of Menes dating from about 3000 B.C. it was decreed that one part of gold was equal in value to two and a half parts of silver whereas nowadays a ratio of one to nineteen is often regarded as an appropriate yardstick. This scarcity of silver endured throughout the Middle Ages and is no doubt one of the reasons why goldsmiths continued to work in both gold and silver and why the trade of the silversmith did not emerge as a separate activity until later. Much of the silver produced in Christendom was mined in Germany so that not unnaturally it was the nearby German towns such as Cologne which became famous for their silver craftsmanship. However, silver being so scarce, it was reserved for coinage, for silver plate, and for church ornament. It was too valuable for use in domestic objects: a silver thimble might only weigh about 5 grams or say 3 dwts, but in the days when a pennyweight (dwt) was the same as the weight of a silver penny, it represented wealth untold. Possibly the odd silver (or gold) thimbles were made at this time but if so, they were exceptional and costly items of which no record has survived.

The sixteenth century was to witness a complete change of the situation. About 1530 the production of silver in Central Europe, notably Bohemia and Saxony, increased considerably, but more important, from the end of the fifteenth century the Spaniards began to ship precious metals back from the New World. During the first half of the sixteenth century gold became more plentiful, but it was silver which the Spaniards brought back in increasingly large quantities. Besides what they looted, the Spaniards found extensive and very rich deposits of silver in Mexico, Bolivia, and Peru, and following on the discovery of the Potosí deposits (1543) silver rapidly became a more commonplace material. Most of the gold and silver shipped from the New World was routed via the Spanish House of Trade (Casa de Contratación) in Seville, whose records of entry speak for themselves:

Total weight recorded

	Gold	Silver
	(kilograms)	
1503–1600	153,600	7,439,000
1601–1660	27,800	9,448,000

There was therefore a major readjustment in the relative value of gold and silver. The price of silver fell or, more accurately, the price of other commodities including gold increased with inflation, which is much the same thing, and silver became available for those purposes from which it was previously debarred on grounds of cost. One of the consequences of this readjustment is that the trade of the silversmith began to develop as a separate, if somewhat inferior, activity distinct from that of the goldsmith.

It is a common misconception that silver thimbles were originally made to gratify the demands

Silver, made in two parts: the right-hand portion fits over the left-hand portion to protect a letter seal. Round the rim the inscription "Mette Olles Dotter." Height when closed 2.6 cm. *National Museum, Copenhagen*

View from above. Seal inscribed IHS (*Jesus Hominum Salvator*) with initials MOD and date 1643. *National Museum, Copenhagen*

of fashion and luxury: in fact, nothing could be further from the truth. Obviously when the first silver thimbles were made in the early part of the sixteenth century only the more wealthy could afford them, but it was soon realized that silver was more serviceable than other materials. To start with, it does not tarnish or soil the thread so that it is cleaner than either brass which tarnishes and gets dirty or iron which rusts and is hard on the finger. Moreover brass, unlike silver, will readily infect a cut finger. There is a myth about silver that it keeps the wearer healthy and like most myths it has some vestige of truth. Silver nitrate, *lapis infernalis,* is antiseptic, a property which has undoubtedly encouraged the use of silver thimbles. Thus it is fair to say that in many ways a silver thimble was superior, and it follows that in a prosperous

country like Elizabethan England their use spread rapidly. The first known reference to a thimble made of silver comes appropriately enough from Spain, where the influx of silver was first felt and where an inventory dated 1517 mentions "Un aguller d'argent e hun didal d'argent."[1] The first mention in England dates from 1532, when a silver thimble was apparently still rare enough to be mentioned in the will of Dame Philippa Brudenell,[2] but such references are scarce, silver thimbles were soon taken for granted, and all we know for certain is that by the time of the English Civil War (1647) the ownership of a silver thimble was commonplace.

Silver in its pure form is extremely malleable and the addition of some copper is necessary to make it hard enough for practical use. Sterling silver was formerly described as 11oz 2dwt of pure silver to one pound (12oz) troy, i.e., 0.925 of pure silver. Nevertheless even alloyed with copper, silver remains relatively soft and a silver

Silver, German, eighteenth century. Note stylistic similarity to de Bry engravings. *Private collection*

99

thimble will wear out in use. In olden days it was customary for a holed thimble to be repaired, but eventually when a thimble reached a stage when it was beyond repair, it would be sold or part exchanged for the sake of its fine metal content. Early thimbles are therefore comparatively rare but, when they do occur, they are not difficult to recognize. Besides the more obvious differences of style and design, silver thimbles up to the middle of the eighteenth century were made in two pieces, namely the domed part of the thimble, which was hand raised or cast into the appropriate shape and thickness, and the sides of the thimble, consisting of a flat piece of silver rolled into a cylinder and vertically seamed. The two pieces were then joined together and the thimbles finished individually. The construction of later thimbles is quite different. During the second half of the eighteenth century silver thimbles began to be made in one piece and there is little room for confusion.

The modern technique for making a thimble is known as deep drawing and starts with a plain sheet of silver metal from which is cut out a circular disc the size of a large coin. The disc, which is referred to as a blank, is placed in a powerful press, which shapes it into the form of a small cup by a punch and die process. Blanks and dies of different sizes are used according to the size of the thimble which it is desired to make. The cup is then annealed, that is, it is heated to soften the metal and to release any stresses which may have built up during the pressing process. Several pressings are necessary to reach the desired shape. The next step is for the cup to be placed on a small spinning lathe where it is held in a solid boxwood female chuck and made to revolve. Hand tools are used to trim and clean the inside of the cup to the correct size and to burnish it. This process is known as insiding.

The thimble cup is then transferred to another lathe. It is fitted to a mandrel corresponding to the shape and internal size of the thimble, where it is cut to length and externally trimmed and burnished. The thimble cup is then ready for knurling, or grating as it is sometimes known. As the thimble revolves a series of knurled wheels and other tools carefully chosen for size are brought to bear with considerable force against the sides to impress the indentations. The pressure is applied physically by a

Early hallmark. Silver thimble by Francis Clarke, Birmingham 1834. Height 2.3 cm. *Private collection*

workman wearing a steel breastplate with a recess in the center to take the handle of the knurling tool. The end of the knurling tool is rested on the workbench and the working edge is levered against the revolving thimble, which immediately acquires its traditional appearance.

Lastly the thimble passes into the hands of the chasers, who apply the desired pattern either by hand or by machine. When the design is applied by hand any one of the traditional means of hand-decorating such as punch work, flat chasing, engraving, or bright cutting may be used, or indeed a combination of several, to achieve the required design. When it is applied by machine, it may be punched automatically and is referred to as bright cutting, or it may be rolled on, in which case the pattern is cut intaglio on the edge of a narrow steel roller and then pressed against the thimble as it revolves on the lathe. The design may also be engraved by engine turning with the help of a rose machine. Once the design is complete the thimble receives a final polish both inside and outside, following which it goes for final inspection and packaging.

Some consideration has already been given to the silver thimbles made in Germany, Britain, France, and the United States. These all evolved

Hallmarks with the Queen's head. *Left,* Henry Foskett, London 1872; *center,* George Unite, Birmingham 1897; *right,* Charles May, London 1869. *Private collection*

styles of their own, but of course other countries also developed their own styles. One of these is India, which has some very distinctive and attractive thimbles. Indian thimbles are invariably handmade and can be gloriously elaborate. They are often found in England, which has led to their being mistaken for English thimbles of the Georgian period. In fact they are imported and it may be relevant that in 1907 an Army and Navy Stores catalog was offering for sale thimbles made of Indian silver at one shilling each. Alternatively, they may have been brought back by expatriates and their families, but either way they date from about the turn of the century and the best source of supply remains the silver bazaars in India. Unfortunately Indian thimbles suffer from the defect that they were made by craftsmen who had no true understanding of their purpose. Their shape and size may therefore be odd and it is not unusual, for instance, to find a small shield designed for the initials of the owner located at the tip of the thimble instead of indentations. Nevertheless they can be most attractive.

Several countries in the Near East also make some interesting hand-worked thimbles, but few of these are marked and the collector must be guided by his own judgment. Here it is relevant to mention a device which is sometimes found, consisting of a silver thimble attached to a ring by a small chain. The ring is slipped on the finger and when the thimble is not used it is allowed to hang by the chain until required. No doubt this device saves a good deal of thimble hunting, and specimens have been found which originate from Greece, Southern Russia, Turkey, Turkistan, and Iran, which suggests that it is essentially a Near Eastern development. And while on the subject of the Near East it is timely to recall Doughty's observation among the Bedouins of Arabia that "commonly the housewife's key to her box is seen as a glittering pendant, upon her veil backward; and hangs,

Russian niello with ring and chain. The inscription stands for "Caucasus" in cyrillic characters. Circa 1900. *Private collection*

101

with her thimble and pincers, (to pluck the thorns out of their bare soles,) by a gay scarlet lace, from the circlet of the head-band. . . ."[3] Evidently some sort of eye would be required by which to hang the thimble.

Some countries, again mostly in the Near East, make silver thimbles which are distinctive by virtue of their being decorated with niello work. Niello is a type of ornamentation which consists of inlaying silver (or gold) with a mixture of metallic sulphide; the black of the niello contrasts well with the silver to give clarity and effect to the design. Grooves are cut in the silver with a graver and they are filled with a powder made of silver and copper, sulphur, lead or antimony, and some suitable flux like borax. When heated the powder melts and fills the grooves adhering to the metal. After the silver has cooled, the surface is ground and polished flat. Both the Russian town of Tula and the Caucasus were well-known manufacturing centers for niello decorated silverware in czarist times, and niello decorated thimbles which were sold as tourist souvenirs in the Caucasus are occasionally to be found. Niello decorated thimbles are also made in the Middle East, notably Iraq, where the silversmiths in the Amara region have evolved a type of thimble of their own. These have smooth sides and, as Amara is situated on the edge of a vast expanse of marshes, the thimbles are decorated with views of native boats and coracles, water fowl and reeds, *mudhifs* (barrel vaulted huts built of reeds and matting), and designs of Ezra's tomb, which is a well-known landmark on the Tigris. Thimbles of this kind were widely sold to tourists before the war.

It is not possible to comment individually on all the different types of silver thimbles, only some of which are referred to in these pages. Some fine silver thimbles were made in Austria and are still made there. Greece makes very distinctive silver thimbles decorated with wirework and so does Mexico, whose thimbles have found their way into many collections. Spain and Portugal have special styles of thimbles and so have countries in South America. Thailand has a style of its own and also countries in Southeast Asia. But besides all these there remain many interesting thimbles which are difficult to place, and there will always be room for research.

When examining a silver thimble, much help may be derived from the hallmarks, which for the present purpose may be defined as authenticating marks struck after testing to guarantee the silver content. Over the years the definition has been extended to include the maker's mark. Some countries have a system of hallmarking silver which helps to date the article but unfortunately thimbles are so small that they are often exempt from hallmarking regulations either because any duty payable would not be enough to justify the cost of marking or else because of the danger of damaging the design. In practice the older and more interesting silver thimbles are largely unmarked but nevertheless when a thimble is hallmarked this provides the means of determining its provenance and in some cases also its date of manufacture. It should be noted however that just because a thimble bears a country's hallmark it does not necessarily follow that it was produced in that country, as it may well have been imported. Some countries have special hallmarks to denote imported silver, but the rules vary. The interpretation of hallmarks is a specialized and somewhat complicated subject and it is not possible to give more than a few hints to help collectors place some of the more frequently occurring items:

Austro-Hungary. In early days the standard unit of purity in Central Europe was the loth which was equal to .0625 so that 12 lothige was .750 and 13 was .8125. The loth was discontinued about 1860 so that thimbles bearing a hallmark showing the numbers 12 or 13 are likely to date from the eighteenth or nineteenth century and to emanate from Central Europe.

England. The Lion Passant, sometimes called the Sterling mark, denotes that the silver is 92.5 percent pure. Provided the hallmarks are legible, the British system enables the collector to determine the place and year of manufacture. English thimbles normally carry the Birmingham mark (anchor) or Chester (dagger between three wheatsheaves) and only occasionally the Sheffield or London mark. English thimbles dating from before 1890 are mostly unmarked and those after 1910 mostly marked, so that an unmarked English thimble is almost certainly nineteenth century or earlier.

France. French hallmark regulations are com-

South American silver thimbles, mostly nineteenth century. *Private collection*

plicated, but as a general rule French thimbles manufactured after 1838 should carry firstly a maker's mark in a diamond shape outline and secondly a boar's head (Paris) or a crab (provinces) either at the rim or on that portion of the thimble between the border and the indentations. Imported thimbles or those of doubtful origin may carry a hallmark in the shape of a swan. Also since 1838 French silver hallmarks, like those for gold, are struck against an anvil bearing a design in relief. Only France makes use of this type of reverse marking and it is therefore an easy way of finding out whether a hallmark is French in the first place.

Germany. Since 1888 silver ought to bear the registered mark of the maker, the silver content and if over .800 a hallmark consisting of a crown and a moon. German thimbles mostly carry a figure denoting the silver content, usually .800 or .935, and nothing more.

Netherlands. A minute letter *Z* will sometimes be found impressed on the outside of modern thimbles at the top of the cap. This denotes an imported thimble (usually from Germany) the code being ZI for .925, ZII for .835 and Z only for .800. Older thimbles may be hallmarked.

Norway. Since 1891 the hallmark shows the purity of the silver which is a minimum of .830 and is followed by the letter *S*. There is also a title of ".925 S" which will be found on enameled thimbles. These marks will normally be found inside at the top of the thimble.

Portugal. Portuguese thimbles normally carry two marks, one a maker's mark and the other the official mark which from 1866 to 1938 was an eagle's head or a boar's head with a figure I denoting a purity of .916 or a figure II denoting a purity of .833. The outline of the mark varies depending on where it was struck, in Lisbon, Oporto, or elsewhere. Since 1938 the official hallmark has been the head of a cockerel with the title, whether .916 or .833, incorporated underneath.

Russia. Until 1925 the unit of purity was the solothnik, representing one-ninety-sixth of a Russian pound. Pure silver was therefore 96 solothniks. The most common title is 84 solothniks (.875) so that thimbles bearing a hallmark showing the number 84 (or since 1927 the number 875) are likely to come from Russia. Russian silver hallmarks are normally to be found on the rim. A woman's head facing left was used from 1896 to 1907 and a woman's head facing right from 1908 to 1917.

Sweden. The official state hallmark since 1912 consists of two marks, the first showing the three Swedish crowns and the second the letter *S*. In addition thimbles will normally show a maker's mark and a date code inside the top.

United States. American thimbles often carry the mark of the maker or distributor stamped inside the top. Since the 1860s American thimbles carry the mention "sterling" or "sterling silver," which denotes a purity of .925. American thimbles may also be marked "coin."

Deciphering hallmarks calls for considerable experience, and reference books such as the latest edition of the one published by Tardy,[4] or in

Niello decorated silver thimbles from Southern Iraq. *Private collection*

English silver, about 1895. Note the crispness of the chasing. *Private collection*

the case of maker's marks more specialized works such as Jackson,[5] are essential. In many cases however hallmarks merely serve to confirm what is otherwise obvious to an experienced collector. A collector of English thimbles, for instance, should have little difficulty in recognizing an English thimble without looking at the hallmark and with practice should even be able to guess at the marks with a fair degree of accuracy.

Finally, it is well to remember that silver thimbles are relatively commonplace and while there are many fine specimens and some very rare ones, there are a great many that are totally devoid of interest. Some dealers have the irritating habit of commenting that a thimble they offer for sale is made of "real silver" and to imply thereby that since silver is a precious metal, the thimble is something special. Nothing could be further from the truth. In the first place the value of the silver in a thimble is negligible—in 1928 Woolworths were selling silver thimbles at 6 pence each, equivalent to about 12½ cents at the time, and silver being one of the most common materials for thimble making, it follows that many silver thimbles are of little interest. What is much more important and distinguishes a good silver thimble from a bad one is age, condition, the nature of the decoration, and above all the quality of the workmanship. Many silver thimbles are quite magnificent—such as would grace any collection—but the fact that a thimble is made of silver is in itself of no consequence and the collector will be well advised to disregard it.

NOTES

1. "Inventaire dels bens d'en Eixarch, Valencia 1517. Ms de l'Arsciu del Comte de Sallent."

2. Joan Wake, *The Brudenells of Deane* (London, 1953).

3. Charles M. Doughty, *Travels in Arabia Deserta* (Cambridge: At the University Press, 1886).

4. *Les Poinçons de garantie internationaux pour l'argent* (Paris, Tardy).

5. Sir Charles James Jackson, *English Goldsmiths and their Marks* (London, 1949).

The Dorcas Thimble

THE PROBLEM OF MAKING A THIMBLE COMBINING the advantages of silver with the durability of iron is one which long exercised the ingenuity of thimble-makers. Already in the eighteenth century a small iron or steel cap was often fitted to the top of silver, brass, or even gold thimbles to make them less susceptible to the wear of the needle, but this device was not entirely satisfactory. For one thing, the steel cap was apt to work loose and for another the users did not necessarily sew with the tip of their thimbles, and indeed many needlewomen use the side of the thimble only. Thus one of the more commonplace tasks carried out by silversmiths was the repairing of thimbles, known as topping, and most collectors will have seen thimbles which have been repaired on this account. Other inventions were tried but none proved wholly satisfactory, and it was not until toward the end of the nineteenth century that Charles Horner, a retail jeweler who ran a business in Hebden Bridge, Yorkshire, found a solution which proved so successful that nearly a hundred years later many of his thimbles are still in use.

As mentioned previously, the preference for silver thimbles is not entirely a matter of prejudice but arose because silver keeps cleaner than brass, which gets unpleasantly dirty, or iron, which rusts, and because silver is also kinder to wear on the finger. In other words silver (or gold for that matter) is a better material for sewing purposes. Charles Horner therefore had the idea of constructing a thimble which would include a steel core to give it strength, but which in every other respect would appear as a normal silver thimble. In 1884 he patented his steel-lined thimble and he described it in the application for the patent as follows:

> The object of this my said invention is to manufacture a thimble of combined silver and steel which shall possess all the advantages of silver, be durable and free from danger of being pierced or punctured as a steel thimble.
>
> In the construction of thimbles, according to this my said invention, I employ an outer casing of silver and corresponding in form to an ordinary silver thimble but having a shoulder formed round its rim. Within the outer casing is received a steel cup or lining and within the latter is received an inner lining of silver forming the interior of the thimble and having a hollow flange which is received on and encloses the shoulder of the outer silver casing which is burnished over completing a thimble having a steel lining which cannot be pierced.

Needless to say that there is often a gap between the claims which an inventor makes for his brainchild and what is actually achieved in practice. There are literally scores of so-called inventions and improvements concerned with thimbles which were patented but never saw practical application. However, Charles Horner's invention proved different. Not only were his claims regarding resistance to wear and durability amply fulfilled, but because the steel lining was an integral part of the thimble, the latter achieved a

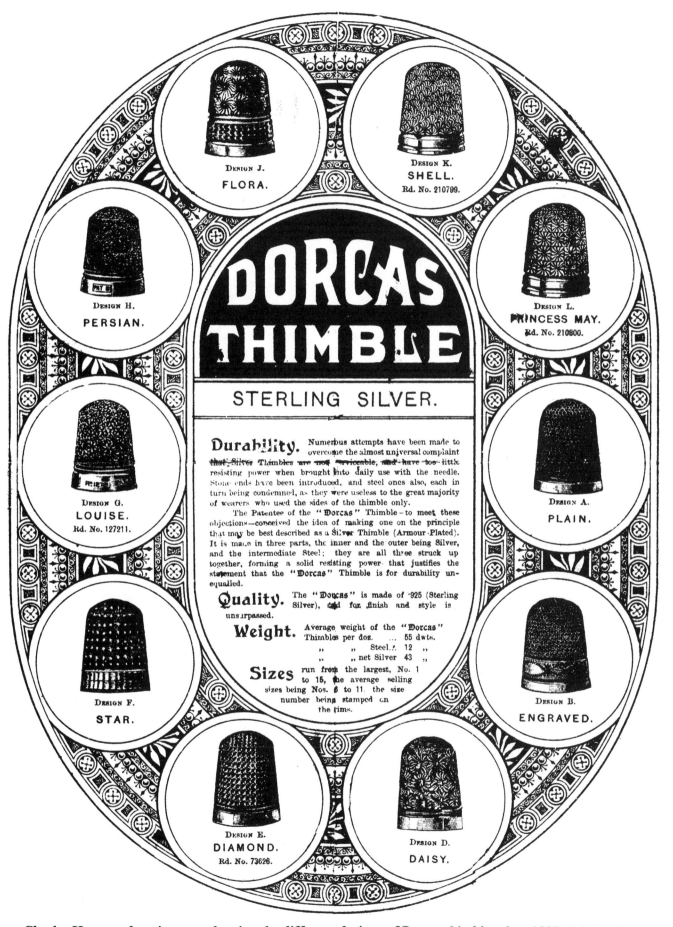

Charles Horner advertisement showing the different designs of Dorcas thimbles circa 1890. *Private collection*

more balanced construction than, for instance, a silver thimble with a steel top; also the added thickness and weight served to underline its quality. Thus the new thimble was ideal for anyone wanting a heavy-duty thimble for everyday household purposes.

The merits of the new thimble would no doubt have been sufficient in themselves to ensure its success, but it would never have been the outstandingly successful thimble it was if Charles Horner had been content to sell it in the same way that thimbles were normally sold at the time. Besides being an ingenious jeweler and a successful inventor, it appears that Charles Horner was also a gifted salesman who foresaw the advantages of advertising and widespread distribution of a standard product sold in a standard pack at a standard price. Certainly he set about promoting the sales of the new thimble with all the skill and energy associated with modern marketing techniques.

The first requirement for the launching of the new thimble was a suitable name, and Charles Horner chose to call his invention the Dorcas thimble, after the name of a woman mentioned in the Bible called Tabitha, which by translation from the Greek is Dorcas, referred to in Acts 9:36–42. Dorcas was a needlewoman living in Joppa (ancient Jaffa) who made coats and garments for the poor. In Victorian days many churches in England had a Dorcas Sewing Circle under whose auspices the ladies of the parish would devote themselves to sewing and charity. The name was therefore most suitable.

Next he provided a simple but attractive packaging. The new thimble came in a presentation box covered with dark blue paper and the name "The Dorcas" printed in gold script letters on the lid and lined inside with blue velvet. The label on the bottom of the box read "The DORCAS Thimble. Sterling Silver. Made in three parts, the inner and outer being silver and the intermediate steel, giving a resisting power not obtained in silver alone."

And lastly he arranged for the new thimble to be promoted vigorously on a nationwide scale. Charles Horner obtained his patent (No. 8954) on 14 June 1884, and it is surely no coincidence that in October 1884 he attended some celebrations held in Amsterdam to mark the two hundredth anniversary of the so-called invention of

the thimble by Nicolas van Benschoten. Charles Horner used the occasion to advertise the Dorcas thimble, and there must be some suspicion that the celebrations themselves may have been contrived as part of a successful publicity exercise. Thereafter advertisements appeared in numerous publications, both in London and the provinces. The weekly publication *The Queen,* which was the leading ladies' fashion magazine of the period, wrote on 8 May 1886: "The Dorcas thimble is more durable than the generality of these indispensable work table implements; it is made in three parts: the inner and the outer being silver and the intermediate being steel, forming a resisting power not obtained in silver only. What is more uncomfortable than sewing with a thimble that has seen service to such an extent that it has holes in its sides? With the Dorcas thimble this annoyance vanishes." Other publications copied these comments which were widely reported, and the Dorcas thimble became a household name.

The design of the Dorcas thimbles was carefully chosen to fit in with the image of solidity and reliability. In addition to thimbles with plain indentations, "The Plain," a new bright-cut design, "The Diamond," was registered in 1887 (Reg. No. 73626), another, "The Louise," was registered in 1889 (Reg. No. 127211) and another, "The Shell," was registered in 1893 (Reg. No. 210799). Other nonregistered designs included "The Engraved," "The Daisy," "The Persian," and "The Star," and there was also a design called "The Flora," which was a mixture of "The Daisy" and "The Diamond." Somewhat surprisingly, the original Dorcas thimbles did not carry a trademark, nor of course did they carry a hallmark since, although made from .925 (sterling) silver, they stood disqualified because of the steel lining. Thus, besides the registered design number (if applicable) the only mark was the abbreviation *Pat.* standing for patent (occasionally the word *patent* may be found spelled out in full) and a size number running from No. 1, the largest, down to 15, the average selling sizes being Nos. 6–11, stamped on the rim. There is not therefore a great deal by which to recognise the original Dorcas except for their sturdy construction, their weight (55 dwts per dozen on average), which is heavier than normal for thimbles of comparable size, and the fact that

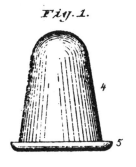

Fig. 1.

Fig. 2.

Fig. 3.

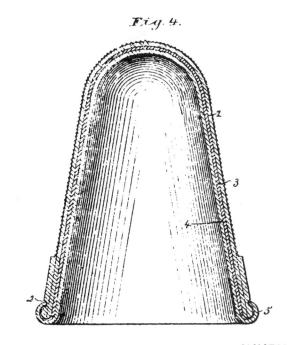

Fig. 4.

WITNESSES:
Joseph S. Latimer
Carleton E. Snell

INVENTOR:
Charles Horner,
By his Attorneys,
Arthur C. Fraser & Co.

United States Patent

CHARLES HORNER, OF HALIFAX, COUNTY OF YORK, ENGLAND.

THIMBLE

SPECIFICATION forming part of Letters Patent No. 404,910, dated June 11, 1889

Application filed June 21, 1886. Serial No. 205,824. (No model.) Patented in England June 14, 1884, No. 8,954.

To all whom it may concern:

Be it known that I, CHARLES HORNER, of Halifax, in the county of York, England, a subject of Her Majesty Queen Victoria, have invented new and useful Improvements in Thimbles, for which
5 I have obtained a patent in Great Britain, No. 8,954, bearing date June 14, 1884, of which the following is a description.

Thimbles have heretofore been made of gold or silver, which are objectionable because of not having sufficient rigidity or durability, so that they are liable after wear to be punctured by the needle; and they have also been made of steel, which is objectionable because of
10 its cheap appearance and liability to rust.

My invention aims to produce a thimble which shall have the appearance of being made of a precious metal, and shall be as durable and as free from danger of puncturing as though made of steel. I attain this object by the construction illustrated in the accompany-
15 ing drawings, in which—

Figure 1 is an elevation of the inside lining of the thimble, Fig. 2 is an elevation of an inside lining made of steel. Fig. 3 is an elevation of the outer covering. Figure 4 is a sectional elevation showing the three parts in position, one within the other, and drawn to enlarged
20 scale in order to clearly illustrate the invention.

Like letters refer to like parts throughout the several views.

In the construction of thimbles according to this invention, I

employ an outer casing of silver or precious metal and corresponding
25 in form to an ordinary silver thimble, but having a groove 2 formed around its rim. Within the outer casing 1 is placed a steel cup or lining 3, and within the latter is inserted an inner lining 4, of silver, forming the interior of the thimble, and having a hollow flange 5, which incloses the shoulder 2 of the outer silver casing 1, and is
30 burnished over the shoulder 2, thereby completing the thimble, which has a steel inner lining which cannot be pierced by the needle when the outer covering 1 becomes worn.

I am aware that prior to my invention thimbles having "ends" of steel have been made, and I therefore do not claim the combination
35 of steel and silver or precious metals, broadly; but

What I do claim as my invention, and desire to secure by Letters Patent is—

A thimble composed of an outer casing and an inner lining, both of precious metal, in combination with a steel core interposed be-
40 tween said casing and lining, substantially as set forth, whereby a thimble having the appearance of the precious metal and the durability of steel is formed.

CHARLES HORNER

Witnesses:
A.F. CHAPMAN
J. BIRERLEY HOWARD

Specification presented by Charles Horner in connection with the grant of his United States patent dated 11 June 1889. *Private collection*

Engraved Dorcas of unusual design. Circa 1890. *Private collection*

they readily respond to a magnet.

Over the years the price of Dorcas thimbles remained remarkably steady. At the time they were launched, Dorcas thimbles were advertised at two shillings and sixpence each, but two years later the price had been reduced to one shilling and ninepence plain and two shillings for fancy thimbles. By 1907 the Army and Navy Stores were selling them at one shilling and sixpence each plain and one shilling and ninepence fancy, but by then, as we shall see, a new and cheaper method of manufacturing Dorcas thimbles had been introduced and the prices were not necessarily comparable. During the 1930s, Dorcas thimbles were selling at around three shillings each. These prices may appear low but they were substantially higher than the price of ordinary silver thimbles at the time. No doubt Dorcas thimbles were more expensive to make but they were also a quality product with a nationwide reputation, and Charles Horner Limited were able to reap considerable advantage on that account.

Early in his career Charles Horner moved from Hebden Bridge to Halifax, where he took premises at 23 Northgate and where besides Dorcas thimbles he also made thimbles of plain silver and gold. The latter are readily recognizable because in addition to the C. H. maker's mark, they were normally assayed at Chester and therefore carry the three sheaves and dagger Chester hallmark. They were produced in a variety of designs and achieved considerable success in their own right so that, if Dorcas thimbles are included, the firm of Charles Horner was the largest producer of silver thimbles during the period 1900–1910. Subsequently under the weight of competition business in plain silver thimbles became less profitable, Charles Horner gradually lost interest, and by 1925 they were making Dorcas thimbles only.

Contrary to what might be expected of someone with such an enterprising turn of mind, Charles Horner does not appear to have paid much attention to the overseas market. He did apply for a patent in the United States on 28 June 1886, which was granted on 11 June 1889, but this was probably a defensive move. Dorcas thimbles were exported mostly to Commonwealth countries, including India, where they still turn up occasionally in the silver bazaars and serve to confuse the merchants, who cannot understand why what looks like a silver thimble proves to be attracted by a magnet. They were not, however, advertised on a sufficiently wide scale to become known outside Britain or to acquire an international reputation. Export sales were largely a function of a loyal British following and were based on their reputation in the home market.

Charles Horner's flair for publicity was well exemplified in 1893 on the occasion of the wedding of Princess Victoria Mary of Teck (Princess May as she was known throughout the country) to Prince George (Duke of York). No doubt the operative thimble-makers in his employ were happy to celebrate this popular occasion, but the hand of management is obviously to be seen behind the decision to present the Princess with a gold thimble embossed with a specially designed "Princess May" pattern (Reg. No. 210800) and engraved with wreaths of York roses and May blossom joined by a true lovers' knot. The Princess was pleased to accept the gift, which went to join the many treasures which, as Queen Mary, she was to amass during her lifetime as a dedicated collector.

Early Dorcas: *left,* **Daisy;** *center,* **Shell;** *right,* **Princess May. Late nineteenth century.** *Private collection*

Not surprisingly, the Northgate premises became too small, and in 1903 the company moved to extensive new buildings and premises at Mile Cross, Halifax, which were to become their headquarters and where they have remained ever since. The company also had a warehouse or showroom at 38 Frederick Street, Birmingham, which was referred to as their Birmingham branch. In 1905 they abandoned their retail activity to concentrate exclusively on the manufacturing side of the business. At first Charles Horner devoted themselves to all classes of bijouterie with special attention being placed on the output of enamel goods, but later they switched to jewelry in chrome plate, rolled gold, and gilt of medium cheapness and quality. The patent Dorcas thimble, however, remained their specialty.

Charles Horner, the founder of the firm, died in 1896, and the business was carried on by Messrs. J. D. Horner and C. H. Horner. It was turned into a limited company in 1909, and on the death of J. D. Horner in 1913, C. H. Horner became managing director assisted by Messrs. H. M. Horner and F. M. Horner as directors.

The original Dorcas thimble continued to be made until 1905, when a thimble of different construction was introduced. The method of drawing out each silver and steel shell separately and then assembling the three together was obviously cumbersome, and instead Charles Horner developed a new process and were granted a pa-

tent for "the manufacture of a thimble from a sheet of hardening steel coated on both sides with a thin sheet of gold, silver or other suitable metal from which a solid thimble could be drawn in one piece having a hardened or partially hardened steel lining."

The basis of the new process was to take two pieces of silver and one of steel, bonding them together like a sandwich, with the steel in the middle, and cold rolling it to the desired thickness. The rolled strip was then annealed, after which it was ready for cutting into blanks from which thimbles could then be made in the usual way. Thimbles manufactured by this new method were marketed under the name of "Improved" Dorcas and coincidentally there was a change in the markings. The *Pat.* abbreviation was dropped and instead the thimbles were stamped with the name Dorcas together with the mark C.H. and the size number. Registered numbers were also abandoned. The small cardboard boxes remained largely unaltered but the label underneath was changed to read: "Im-

Charles Horner label, circa 1930. *Private collection*

111

proved Dorcas thimble. Sterling Silver—steel lined, will be exchanged FREE OF CHARGE if rendered useless from ANY CAUSE. None genuine unless stamped Dorcas together with the initials C.H. and size number." A later variant read: "Guarantee. Exchanged free if rendered useless from any cause whatsoever. Made of Sterling Silver with interlining of hardened steel. None genuine without the name 'Dorcas' C.H. British made." Obviously this proud and unconditional guarantee did a great deal to enhance the prestige of Dorcas thimbles. It must also have helped to counter the activities of those manufacturers who sought to emulate Charles Horner Ltd.'s success by producing steel lined thimbles of their own. At various times Henry Griffith & Sons brought out a "Dreema" thimble, Walker & Hall of Sheffield a "Dura" thimble and another unknown manufacturer made a "Doris" thimble. Fred Griffith had a daughter called Dreena, and it is popularly supposed that "Dreema" thimbles were called after her. It will be noticed however that all three brand names are alliterations of the name Dorcas, and Walker & Hall went so far as to use a *Pat.* symbol with their size numbers. In the event these efforts proved unavailing and although as late as 1935 Henry Griffith were advertising their "Dreema" thimble, "The beauty of silver with strength of steel, plain, halfchased, fullchased designs, all one price 2/6d," nevertheless it never achieved the success of their solid silver models and the Dorcas thimble retained its supremacy.

As the wording of the patent for the improved Dorcas thimble suggests, Dorcas thimbles were also made in gold. Gold Dorcas thimbles are inscribed "9 ct. gold steel lined," and they carry the C.H. mark and size number. They were packed in a small velvet-lined presentation box with the usual Dorcas guarantee underneath and the words "9 ct. Gold Dorcas" inscribed on the silk facing inside the lid. Gold Dorcas are relatively rare which suggests that only a few were made and that they were never very popular. This is not altogether surprising because in a sense a gold Dorcas was an anachronism. The Dorcas reputation was acquired on the strength of hardwearing thimbles for everyday use and these are hardly the attributes normally sought after in a gold thimble. Moreover because of the steel core

there were limitations on the design of Dorcas thimbles: they could never achieve the elegance of the better quality 18 carat gold thimbles and inevitably suffered by comparison. Indeed, gold Dorcas are very similar to silver Dorcas except that their construction is somewhat lighter. Collectors should beware that silver Dorcas are sometimes gold plated and offered as gold Dorcas, but the fraud is easy to detect because of the different markings.

Another attempt to broaden the range of Dorcas thimbles was the development of the Little Dorcas. The improved Dorcas thimble, being a quality item, appealed to those who could afford it, but it obviously failed to reach the lower end of the market. Charles Horner Limited therefore developed the Little Dorcas, which was designed to have the same general characteristics as the improved Dorcas but which could be sold at a cheaper price without compromising the latter's standing or reputation. It was advertised as: "The Little Dorcas . . . made on the same principles as the 'Improved Dorcas' but a little shorter with a slightly flatter top . . . allowing exceptional freedom of the finger joint, a feature highly ap-

Cross section of Dorcas thimble with box. The steel lining shows as a thin black line. *Private collection*

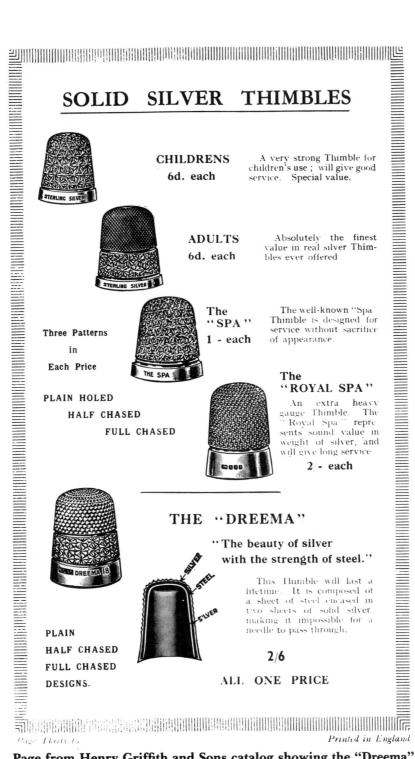

SOLID SILVER THIMBLES

CHILDRENS
6d. each

A very strong Thimble for children's use ; will give good service. Special value.

ADULTS
6d. each

Absolutely the finest value in real silver Thimbles ever offered

Three Patterns
in
Each Price

PLAIN HOLED
HALF CHASED
FULL CHASED

The **"SPA"**
1 - each

The well-known "Spa" Thimble is designed for service without sacrifice of appearance.

The **"ROYAL SPA"**

An extra heavy gauge Thimble. The "Royal Spa" represents sound value in weight of silver, and will give long service

2 - each

THE "DREEMA"

"The beauty of silver with the strength of steel."

This Thimble will last a lifetime. It is composed of a sheet of steel encased in two sheets of solid silver making it impossible for a needle to pass through.

PLAIN
HALF CHASED
FULL CHASED
DESIGNS.

2/6

ALL ONE PRICE

Printed in England

Page from Henry Griffith and Sons catalog showing the "Dreema" thimble. *Private collection*

preciated by needlewomen. Although lighter in construction it is practically equal in durability to the 'Improved Dorcas.'" Surviving specimens of Little Dorcas are scarce, but the intriguing feature is that at some stage the Improved Dorcas was modified to have the same characteristics as its lesser brethren. The early improved Dorcas are heavy, relatively long and with a rounded top, but the later improved Dorcas were lighter, shorter and with a flatter top. Whether the characteristics of the Dorcas thimble were modified to reduce the costs of production or whether they were modified in response to change in customer demand, or both, is obscure but it is possi-

113

ble that the Little Dorcas was brought out to test the market. Some weight is given to this suggestion by the fact that when advertising the Little Dorcas, Charles Horner Limited spoke of its advantages as pointing to its "rapidly becoming the thimble of the future." This wording may have arisen by coincidence but equally it may have been chosen by design, as an indication of changes to come. Unfortunately the timing of the change remains unknown beyond the fact that it took place after 1905, but whatever the date, the later Dorcas thimbles are quite distinctive, and regrettably some of the quality of the earlier Dorcas came to be sacrificed in the process.

By the time of the First World War it must have been evident that the market for thimbles was contracting, and some leading manufacturers such as James Fenton and Samuel Foskett ceased production. Wisely, Charles Horner Limited continued to broaden the range of their activities and in particular they became manufacturers of casein plastics in the form of rods, blanks for buttons, and so on, in a variety of colors and sizes. They also supplied the standard gauge of rods suitable for knitting needles, but unfortunately it is not clear whether they supplied thimbles in this material. In the event, however, the full extent of the loss of market for silver thimbles was not felt until the trade depression in the thirties, when under the combined weight of reduced demand due to the inroads of the sewing machine, the growing production of plastic thimbles and above all the weight of the depression itself, more thimble manufacturers were compelled to cease production. Charles Horner Limited, with the advantage of the Dorcas name and reputation, were able to continue and the strength of their position is well illustrated by the fact that Dorcas thimbles were advertised at three shillings each plain or fancy when Woolworth were selling ordinary silver thimbles down to sixpence each. Nevertheless, this was but a reprieve, the market continued to decline, and they finally ceased to manufacture Dorcas thimbles about 1948, by which time the demand for better quality thimbles had fallen to the point that it was no longer profitable to make them. Indeed one cannot escape the thought that the very durability of the Dorcas thimble may have contributed to its extinction.

Charles Horner Limited remain in existence as manufacturing jewelers but they no longer make thimbles and there are few written records or surviving employees from this period of their activity. It appears that even the trade name Dorcas has passed out of their control, being used nowadays by a company marketing dressmakers' steel pins. Nevertheless in their time Dorcas thimbles were a household name and it is a tribute to their quality that there are still so many left in good and serviceable condition.

Bone Thimbles

THE TYPE OF BONE WHICH IS NORMALLY USED FOR carving comes from the legs of the larger animals and consists therefore of a cylinder of compact bone with a central cavity which held the marrow. Thimbles are occasionally carved from solid bone, but more usually long bones are selected for size and cut into short lengths. In the case of the latter, the problem of the dome is solved by fitting a piece of bone at one end of the cylinder with a screw thread to keep it in place. The thimble is then ready except for the indentations and for any decoration which it may be desired to add.

Bone being somewhat brittle, the main disadvantage of bone thimbles is that they need to be made relatively thick and heavy in order to achieve sufficient strength. If they are carved down too much they become delicate. Thérèse de Dillmont made the point succinctly: "Bone are very liable to break."[1] For this reason bone thimbles tend to be larger and clumsier than those made of ivory.

It is not always easy to distinguish bone from ivory, but the former generally contains minute tubes so that where the surface cuts across the grain the tubes become filled with dirt and they show as little black specks or as a thin dark line. Ivory, on the other hand, is smoother and the grain shows as silky stripes of slightly varying intensity. Moreover ivory thimbles are more often made in one piece, so that a thimble made in two or more pieces is likely to be a bone thimble.

Toward the end of the eighteenth century and the beginning of the nineteenth, large quantities of bone thimbles were imported into Britain as part of the furnishings of the needlework boxes which became fashionable about that time. These needlework boxes were imported mostly from India, which already had a well-established reputation for caskets made of precious woods, and from China, which was well known for its lacquerware boxes. They contained a wide range of sewing tools such as cotton reels, clamps, bodkins and of course a thimble which was usually made of bone. Unfortunately the artisans who made these furnishings had little idea of the purpose for which they were used, which led to some strange results, not least with thimbles which were sometimes made in totally impracti-

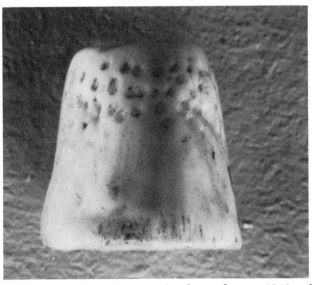

Eskimo sewing ring made from bone. *National Museum, Copenhagen*

115

Bone thimble case inscribed "A Trifle from a Friend." Probably prisoner-of-war work, circa 1810. *Private collection*

at the time of the Napoleonic Wars,[2] but this remains unconfirmed and in all probability there is some confusion with the Far Eastern thimbles, which being handmade could lend themselves to a false attribution.

The Eskimos and other races dwelling in the extreme north, having few resources, made extensive use of bone and have used it to make bone thimbles. Genuine Eskimo thimbles may be seen in specialized museums such as the National Museum in Copenhagen. They are roughly made and have little appeal.

During the nineteenth century, sailors on whaling vessels took up whalebone carving, or scrimshaw as it is known in the United States. Some genuine scrimshaw thimbles have no doubt survived from this period but more recently scrimshaw has become fashionable, all types of scrimshaw objects have been produced including thimbles in great profusion, and regrettably there is little to differentiate the old and the new.

Bone thimbles will occasionally be found which have a metal waffle-indented cap fitted into the tip to take the wear of the needle and which are decorated with a design, for example, the head of a reindeer burnt round the sides with a red hot needle. These are believed to have originated from Lapland and were designed for the tourist trade.

cal shapes. Moreover, since the thimbles were not chosen for size, they did not necessarily fit the finger of the recipient. Thus quantities of bone thimbles came to be left unused in workboxes, which accounts for the large number that have survived. It is sometimes stated that bone thimbles were made by French prisoners of war

NOTES

1. Thérèse de Dillmont, *Encyclopédie des ouvrages de dames* (Paris, 1886).
2. James Toller, "French Prisoners-of-War Work," *Collector's Guide* (July 1971).

Horn Thimbles

THE OXHORN HAD A SPECIAL PLACE IN EGYPTIAN and Greek mythology, and the cornucopia, or horn of plenty, was the Roman symbol for the Goddess of Good Fortune. Oxhorn ranges from transparent white to dark brown. It is a relatively soft, fibrous, and flexible material and consequently not altogether suitable for thimble making.

Horn thimbles are known to have been made in France about 1700,[1] but no surviving specimen has so far been identified. The accompanying illustration shows an example of a ring-type thimble made of horn and originating from an outlying village in India.

A type of horn thimble will be found which is smooth and without indentations. This is believed to date from the nineteenth century and is similar to ivory thimbles of the same design.

NOTE

1. Jacques Savary des Bruslons, *Dictionnaire universel du commerce* (Paris, 1723/30).

Horn ring-type thimble, India, nineteenth century. Height 2.1 cm. *Private collection*

117

Glass Thimbles

GLASS HAS OCCASIONALLY BEEN USED TO MAKE thimbles but authentic specimens are rare. The British Museum possesses a fine example made of cut glass decorated with cross hatchings and there is another in the collection of the Colonial Williamsburg Foundation in the United States which has a crenellated rim. There are also a few known examples in private collections. The origin of these thimbles is obscure, and the best that can be said is that they probably date back to the nineteenth century.

Tradition has it that thimbles were made of Venetian glass, and this would seem to be correct. An example is illustrated inscribed "Venezia 1884," but this is more in the nature of a thimble shape.

During the Second World War the Corning Glass Works, Corning, New York, decided that because of the scarcity of some metals which were required for strategic purposes they should attempt to develop the manufacture of glass thimbles. Sundry trials were made, but these were unsuccessful and the project did not proceed beyond the prototype stage. As the company has pointed out, a direct substitution of materials presents technical problems which do not always yield to economic solution. Nevertheless some of the prototypes have found their way into the hands of collectors, and Corning

Nineteenth-century cut glass, probably English. Height 3.0 cm. *Private collection*

118

Spun glass, inscribed "Venezia 1884." Italian. Height 2.5 cm. *Private collection*

glass thimbles are reported in plain glass marked "Pyrex" or "Corning glass" and others in a light blue shade.

In recent years rudimentary glass thimbles have appeared for sale, but these are modern items made to delude collectors and of no conceivable interest.

Stone Thimbles

PRECIOUS AND SEMIPRECIOUS STONES HAVE OFTEN been used to decorate thimbles or to protect the top from the wear of the needle, but stone thimbles as such are a comparative rarity. The reason is that a stone thimble is necessarily heavy, it is not particularly pleasant to the touch, and it tends to look clumsy and unattractive. Indeed stone thimbles are so unsuitable for needlework that there must be some doubt whether they were ever intended for workaday purposes. It is known that A. Ruppenthal of Idar-Oberstein in Germany made agate thimbles about the turn of the century. These were dyed in shades of rusty red, emerald green, or a kind of sapphire blue, but few have survived and they were probably made largely as curiosities. Similarly, thimbles are known made of jade, though in all likelihood this is not true jade, which is a highly prized material of exceptional hardness, but one of the many imitations such as the bowenite variety of serpentine which is commonly worked in the Far East. Thimbles are also known made of onyx, which is an agate formed of layers of chalcedony of different colors and which is the same stone often used to make cameos. Undoubtedly thimbles have been made of other kinds of stone but these are mostly modern and were designed for little purpose save as an article for sale to collectors.

According to a report dating from the late nineteenth century, very pretty thimbles composed of lava from Mount Vesuvius were occasionally sold in Naples but rather as curiosities than for real utility, being, from the extreme brittleness of the lava, very easily broken.[1] Some credence may be given to this report since it appears that there was a vogue in Italy about this time for thimble novelties such as those produced in Venetian glass (see page 119).

More interesting and certainly more practical are thimbles with a stone top. The working of semiprecious stones is an industry which has roots in Germany, and when at the end of the eighteenth century German thimble-makers adopted deep-drawing techniques, with the consequent problems of wear and quality, they were influenced by it. Broadly stated, the problem was that to make a good strong silver (or gold) thimble was costly because of the heavy weight of the metal required and because it was more difficult to process it, but that if on the other hand the thimble-maker used lighter gauge metal plate the thimble was less resistant and wore out more rapidly. English thimble-makers sought a solution on the lines of protecting the thimble with a steel cap, which was widely adopted but did not prove entirely successful. For one thing iron tends to rust and for another some English needlewomen used the side of the thimble instead of the top, so that the steel cap offered them no protection. Later the Dorcas style thimble was developed and this proved the perfect answer under English conditions. In Germany, however, where needlewomen tend to use the top of their thimble more than in England, thimble-makers found that the stone top thimble provided a better solution. Stone tops have the double advantage that they do not rust and that they

Gold thimbles with cornelian tops. Scandinavian, nineteenth century. *Private collection*

look attractive. The only drawback is that the needle may eventually wear a hole in the metal where the stone meets the metal seating, but this is a minor inconvenience and need not occur if the thimble is used correctly. As a result, stone top thimbles proved very popular in Germany and neighboring countries such as Norway and Sweden; they were made in large quantities and they continue to be made to this day.

Stone top thimbles have also been produced in Britain, though as explained they are less popular than on the Continent. Moreover, for some unaccountable reason, the method of manufacture of stone top thimbles in Britain is usually different. In Germany thimbles are made in such a way that the stones rest on a base of metal but in Britain there is no base as such; the stone is mounted in a recess and gripped round the edge so that it appears translucent if the thimble is held up to the light. Such thimbles are some-

times referred to as "Scottish" or "pebble" thimbles, though there is little evidence linking them with Scotland. On the contrary, one popular model in vogue shortly after the turn of the century bore a shamrock and harp design and had a green stone top said to be made of Connemara marble. But whether "Scottish" or "Irish," the manufacture of this type of thimble was held firmly in the hands of the Birmingham silversmiths who produced most of the stone top thimbles made in Britain. The stones were bought ready cut and with the necessary indentations from manufacturing silversmiths' suppliers, and it remained for the thimble manufacturer to fit each thimble with a stone and to knurl the stone firmly into position.

There are many types of stones used for making stone top thimbles and the following are the more commonplace:

Silver with applied ornamental skirting set with stones. German, made for Italian market circa 1920. *Private collection*

Agate. Brazil, Germany, and India are the main suppliers and Scotland also has a species of agate called Scotch pebble which has presumably given its name to the so-called pebble thimbles. Agate is a variety of chalcedony with differently colored layers. Transparent chalcedony with green mosslike inclusions is called moss agate. As indicated above, agate can be dyed and the center of the agate industry is Idar-Oberstein.

Amethyst. A purple or bluish violet variety of quartz, also worked in Idar-Oberstein.

Bloodstone. A dark green variety of chalcedony with small red patches of jasper.

Chalcedony. A mixture of crystalline silica and amorphous hydrated silica, i.e., of quartz and opal. It has a waxy lustre and is commonly white or cream. Agate, cornelian, and chrysoprase are varieties of chalcedony.

Chrysoprase. A variety of chalcedony of yellowish-green appearance. An imitation chrysoprase can be produced by staining agate with chromium salts.

Cornelian. Also called carnelian from the Latin *carnis,* flesh. A variety of chalcedony which varies in color from yellowish-red to reddish-brown. The red color is due to iron and can be evened and intensified by heating. Cornelian is found in Saxony and is much used for thimble-making purposes in Germany.

Moonstone. Notable for the play of light, called adularescence, which occurs when light falls on the stone. Moonstone began to be imported in large quantities from Ceylon about 1900, when it cost next to nothing. Essentially moonstone is a variety of feldspar.

Other stones may sometimes be used besides the above, and also mother-of-pearl, which is not strictly a stone but which is nevertheless occasionally used in place of a stone top.

In modern times the pressure of competition and the need to cut down costs has led thimble-makers to replace the traditional stone by a piece of glass of similar shape. The tip of a glass rod of appropriate color is heated to melting point and placed under a stamp, where it is moulded into shape. As soon as it is released from the stamp the glass hardens and it only remains to trim any excess glass which may have formed around the edges. Glass tops of this kind are colorful but they look what they are, namely, a cheap substitute for a natural product, and on the whole are best avoided.

Finally, stones of various kinds have been used to ornament thimbles, the more precious stones such as diamonds and rubies tending to be seen on gold thimbles and the cheaper kind on silver. Here it is necessary to introduce a note of caution: some of the most outstanding thimbles are decorated with precious stones and are valuable and rare objects, but there are others, usually dating from around 1900, for which ostentation on the one hand and mass production on the other combined to produce thimbles of somewhat doubtful taste. In this connection may be mentioned a thimble which the king of Siam is reputed to have commissioned as a present for his bride and which succeeded in outdoing all competition.[2] Having seen European and American ladies accompanying diplomats and naval officers at his court sewing with thimbles, he was struck by their usefulness and ordered a thimble in the shape of a lotus, which was the royal flower of India at the time. The young queen therefore received, as a wedding gift, a gold thimble made like a lotus bud, of exquisite workmanship and heavily decorated with diamonds, arranged to spell out her name and the date of the wedding. There were so many diamonds, however, that it is doubtful if the thimble was ever of any practical value.

More sensible and better balanced are the many gold thimbles which were produced during the nineteenth century decorated with coral, garnet, pearl, and above all turquoise which was a great favorite for the purpose. The English thimble-makers produced some particularly fine examples in multicolored gold inset with posies of turquoise or other lesser gems. Turquoise is a blue-green or pale blue stone with a somewhat waxy luster and has been used extensively to decorate thimbles. Unfortunately it has the defect that the blue color may fade in time or assume a greenish tint which is thought to be due to dehydration. All blue stones are not necessarily turquoise, there are similar stones which have a marked resemblance to it, glass has been used

Silver with stone tops. German, late nineteenth and early twentieth century. *Private collection*

Silver with ornamental rim set with multi-colored stones by James Fenton. *Left,* pepper pot; *right,* thimble. **Registered design No. 202313, circa 1892.** *Private collection*

to imitate turquoise, and there are even modern plastic imitations. However, turquoise is not so valuable as to encourage falsification. It is an attractive stone and the combination of gold and turquoise is capable of producing some very fine thimbles.

Lastly, this account would not be complete without mention of the garnet .decorated thim-bles which were made in Austria at the end of the nineteenth century. Garnet, which gets its name from the French for pomegranate *(grenat),* is a generic name for a group of minerals with the same crystalline characteristics and of similar chemical composition. One of these is almandine, which is purplish-red, an iron-aluminum silicate somewhat resembling a ruby. Bohemian garnet-studded jewelry was popular in Victorian times and thimbles of this kind, encrusted with small garnets and with a garnet stone top, are known to exist.

NOTES

1. *Dorcas Magazine* (New York), August 1884.
2. *The Watchmaker, Jeweller and Silversmith* (London), 1 July 1887.

Leather Thimbles

THERE IS GOOD REASON TO BELIEVE THAT UNTIL the thirteenth or fourteenth century many thimbles in England were made of leather, but regrettably none of these early leather thimbles appear to have survived and we cannot even be sure what they looked like. Some would have it that they consisted of a band of leather sewn into a cylinder with a stitched-on cap, similar to one of the thimbles illustrated which is believed to date back to the eighteenth century. Others suggest that, because our forebears tended to sew with the side of the finger, these early thimbles were ring-type thimbles like the other two thimbles in the illustration. The latter are relatively modern and come from Outer Mongolia, but since the Mongols, in common with other Eastern peoples, tend to sew with the side of the finger it is not unreasonable to think that they may be similar to the thimbles which were used in England prior to the introduction of metal thimbles. However, as we shall see, some of the references to thimbles which are to be found in early medieval texts are associated with thumb- or fingerstalls and this would seem to suggest that leather thimbles covered the whole finger rather than the side only.

As is well known, the word for a thimble originates from the Old English *thūma*, a thumb, from which is derived the word *thȳmel* and from that *thimble*. It is relevant therefore that the first recorded use of the word *thȳmel*, which dates from about A.D. 1000—"Wyrc (th)onne (th)ýmel tó"[1]—was in the sense of a thumbstall to protect an injured thumb nail. This same interpretation arises again in A.D. 1180 but in a Latin text: "Tecam habeat corrigialem acus insidiis obvian-

Leather. *Left,* **eighteenth-century thimble with closed end;** *right,* **contemporary sewing rings from Outer Mongolia.** *Private collection*

125

Eskimo leather sewing ring. *National Museum, Copenhagen*

tem que vulgariter polliceum dicitur."[2] *Theca (Teca)* is Latin for a sheath, and we are told therefore that a leather sheath to prevent the needle from causing injury was called a *polliceum.* The word *polliceum* is derived from the Latin *pollex,* a thumb, and was sometimes used in low Latin to denote a thimble. Moreover there is another reference to a sheath to be found in the Dictionary of Jean de Garlande, which is dated about 1200: "Haec sunt instrumenta mulieribus convenientia . . . fusus et theca."[3]

In other words the spindle figures with the sheath among women's implements, and if there was any doubt whether *theca* really designated a thimble, then the point is surely resolved by the *Glossarium Latino-Gallicum,* dated about 1348, which includes the following entry:

Digitarium: Theca, Gallice deis et deaul, id quod mulier habet in digito[4]

This may be interpreted to mean that the Low Latin word *digitarium* denotes a sheath and that the latter in French corresponds to the words for a thimble, i.e., that which a woman wears on her finger.

The number of different words for a thimble which may be found in Low Latin, such as *polliceum, digitarium* and others, is at first puzzling but it is less so if we assume that there was no word for a thimble in classical Latin and that the leather thumb- or fingerstall was in the process

of being replaced by a metal thimble. This seems to be what happened during the thirteenth century and while there would obviously be no shortage of names in the vernacular, the task of finding a suitable equivalent in Latin would lend itself to different solutions. Certainly by the fourteenth century the metal thimble was currently used, but it would be wrong to assume that the leather *thymel* was displaced overnight. In England during the early fifteenth century Thomas Occleve wrote:

> Come hider to me, sone and look whedir
> In this purs ther be any croyse or crouche,
> Sauf nedl and threde and themel of leather.[5]

It is said that leather thimbles were still used in Southern Ireland and remote parts of England as late as the nineteenth century, and a specimen used in County Cork up to about 1820 is described in the records of the British Archaeological Association and may be seen at the Cuming Museum in South London. It is very similar to the one illustrated. Another interesting item which arose in London at a sale of antiques and bygones was a ring-type leather thimble attached to a leather bracelet. The thimble consisted essentially of a band of leather to fit round the finger and the attachment was intended to keep the thimble hanging close at hand when not in use. In all probability this was a home-made article designed by an artisan such as a leather worker or sailmaker accustomed to doing a great

Fishskin thimble as used by eskimos of Canada and Alaska. *National Museum, Copenhagen*

126

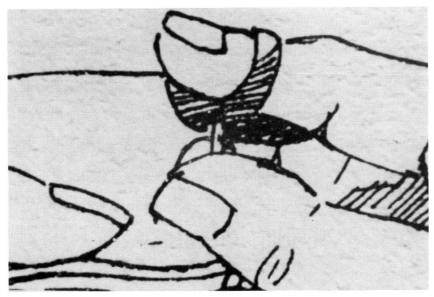

Eskimo sewing method. *National Museum, Copenhagen*

deal of heavy stitching. The item was said to be Elizabethan but no great reliance can be placed on this, as leather is impossible to date with any accuracy.

Leather is seldom used for thimble making nowadays except that a sophisticated kind of ring-type leather thimble is made in Japan. Leather thimbles are also used in Korea. Leather is sometimes used to line brass or plastic ring-type thimbles, and there is an interesting specimen of this kind in the Colonial Williamsburg collection.

Finally, in the Arctic regions fishskin sometimes serves to make thimbles. An example of fishskin thimble is illustrated. It will be noted that the method of use is different, as appears in the illustration.

NOTES

1. *Leechdoms, Wortcunning and Starcraft of Old England* (ed. Cockayne), Rolls series, 1844.
2. Alexander Neckam, *De Utensilibus: Glossaire archéologique du Moyen Age et de la Renaissance* (Paris: Victor Gay, 1887).
3. Johannes de Garlandia, *Diccionario Scolástico*, 63.
4. *Glossarium Latino-Gallicum*, ex cod. reg. 4120.
5. Thomas Occleve, *De Regimine Principium*, ed. Thomas Wright (London: Roxburgh Club, 1860).

Wooden Thimbles

WOOD WAS NEVER POPULAR FOR MAKING THIMBLES because it tends to be too soft and splits easily. Nevertheless it can have a beautiful grain and occurs in many different colors ranging from almost white (sycamore) to black (ebony). The vogue for small articles made of wood in England at the end of the eighteenth century led to the manufacture of wooden thimbles, sometimes with matching cases. Mulberry wood and boxwood were used among others. Wooden thimbles are difficult to date, but early Tunbridge thimbles with circular rings instead of indentations and with painted lines round the base are unmistakable. Many of these thimbles were beautifully turned, but wood could never offer the same advantages as metal and consequently wooden thimbles were never produced in any quantity.

More workmanlike are the Irish bog oak thimbles, which are hard and resistant. Bog oak, which was popular about the middle of the nineteenth century, is semipetrified wood (not necessarily oak) obtained from the Irish swamps; it is black and resembles ebony.[1] Care must be taken, however, when buying bog oak thimbles because of imitations made of bakelite. Genuine bog oak thimbles tend to be heavier and with a coarser grain.

During the latter part of the nineteenth century thimbles made of ebony were recommended for embroidery, and these were known by the name of Nuns' thimbles.[2]

Possibly the most attractive and delicate wooden thimbles were made in France at the

Wood with faceted steel rim and cut nail decoration. French circa 1800. *Private collection*

end of the eighteenth century. These were turned and carved from close grained wood and decorated round the rim with a cut steel border and with minute cut steel nails. Some thimbles of this kind are said to be made of sandalwood, whose odor when kept in work boxes was reputed to keep out moths. During the latter part of the nineteenth century wooden thimbles were

Mrs. Richard Yates by Gilbert Stuart (1755–1828). Courtesy of the National Gallery of Art, Washington, D.C. (Andrew Mellon Collection)

(Below left) The thimble-maker Fingerling, after a miniature in the registers of the Mendelschen Foundation, Nuremberg, late fourteenth century. Courtesy of the City Library of Nuremberg

Sixteenth-century brass thimbles. Private collection

The thimble-maker, after a miniature in the registers of the Landauer Foundation, Nuremberg, 1621. Courtesy of the City Library of Nuremberg

(Above right) Silver thimbles from the seventeenth and eighteenth centuries. Private collection

Gold thimble with two matching finger guards in leather case, seven gold thimbles, and one ivory thimble with gold band mostly eighteenth century. Private collection

Rare and important Meissen thimbles. Private collection

Meissen thimbles. Private collection

Eighteenth century ormolu thimbles and thimble holders from chatelaines. Private collection

Porcelain thimble from the Royal Naples factory about 1810—View of the Bay of Sorrento. Courtesy of the Colonial Williamsburg Foundation

Silver toys from the eighteenth century—the head of the fish (a pike) separates from the body to reveal a thimble inside; the egg unscrews and contains a small thimble to match. Private collection

English silver and silver gilt filigree toys from the eighteenth or early nineteenth century. Private collection

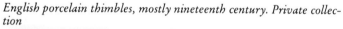

English porcelain thimbles, mostly nineteenth century. Private collection

English gold thimbles from the nineteenth century. Private collection

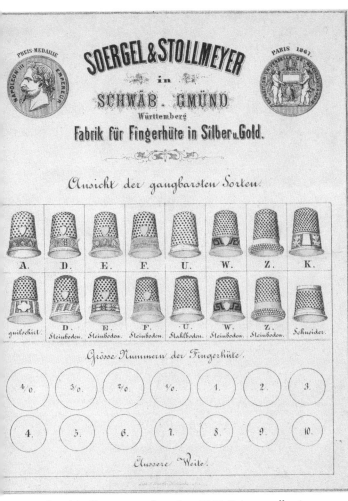

Soergel and Stollmeyer catalog, circa 1867. Private collection

Wood block print of Japanese lady sewing by Mizuno Toshikata (1866–1908). Courtesy of the Tokyo National Museum

...rcester porcelain thimbles from the late nineteenth century. Private ...ection

Silver thimbles from India, circa 1900. Private collection

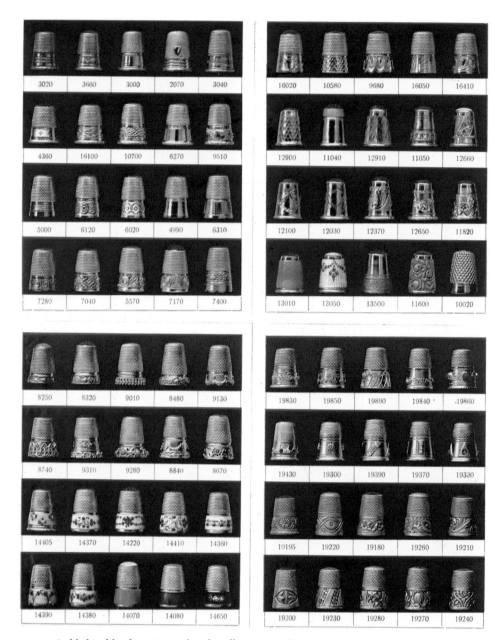

Gold thimbles from Soergel and Stollmeyer catalog, circa 1922. Private collection

Title page from Wm. Lotthammer catalog, circa 1930. Private collection

Title page from Gebrüder Gabler catalog, circa 1930. Private collection

produced in Germany and Austria, where they were sold as souvenirs to tourists. Some of these were made of boxwood. Occasionally the wood is capped with a cornelian or other stone for added strength.

In recent years the popularity of thimble collecting has led to the manufacture of a large number of wooden thimbles of all kinds. Unless, therefore, a wooden thimble can be clearly authenticated or else is bought with a matching and authentic thimble case, wooden thimbles are best avoided. Collectors may come across large white painted wooden thimbles or similar thimbles made of plastic. These are not intended for sewing but are stage properties designed for the purpose of conjuring tricks.

Thimbles have also been made from several substances which are not strictly wood but which, being of vegetable origin are conveniently mentioned under the same heading. The first is papier-mâché, a material consisting either of paper-pulp or of sheets of paper pasted together so treated that it is made to resemble varnished or lacquered wood. It is believed that papier-mâché thimbles were made during the latter part of the nineteenth century.

Another is the substance known as vegetable ivory, or corozo nut. Vegetable ivory, which is often confused with bone, horn, or real ivory but which can be distinguished by its somewhat oily feel and by its obvious vegetable appearance where it is unpolished, comes from a South American tree (*Phytelephas macrocarpa*) which is allied to the palm. The hardened albumen of the seed, called corozo nut or ivory nut, was turned and carved, and in Victorian times millions of nuts were imported every year from Colombia. This was used to make small objects such as buttons and it was also used for sewing tools, including thimbles and thimble cases. The color varies from light cream to brown. The vogue for vegetable ivory was relatively short-lived and most vegetable ivory thimbles were made between 1840 and 1880. In 1863 the world shortage of ivory, coupled to rapidly rising demand, forced the price up dramatically and led an American company, Phelane and Collander, manufacturers of billiard balls, to offer a prize of $10,000 to anyone who could produce a satisfactory substitute. This resulted in the development of celluloid in 1871 and the formation of the Celanese-Celluloid Corporation, after which plastics

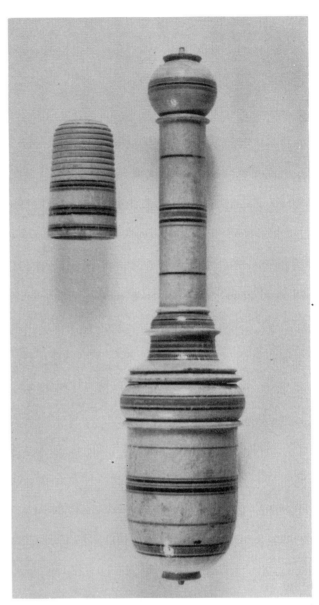

Thimble and needlecase combined. Decorated with polychrome painted rings. Early Tunbridge ware, circa 1800. *Private collection*

came into their own and the use of vegetable ivory fell away. Vegetable ivory thimbles are now only made in Ecuador, where the corozo nut is known as tagua and where tagua thimbles are sold to tourists as gifts or souvenirs.

Yet another substance from which thimbles have occasionally been made is the coquilla nut, which comes from a Brazilian palm tree known locally as the Piassaba (*Attalea finifera*). Like corozo, coquilla is the hardened albumen of a seed but it differs from corozo in being altogether harder and much darker in color. At the end of the eighteenth century some coquilla thimbles were made in France which have the

Child's wooden thimble and thimble case. English, nineteenth century. *Private collection*

characteristic French beehive shape, together with a gilded band round the rim and a gold shield. More recently some elaborately carved coquilla thimbles with ornate gold decoration have been made in Brazil, but their precise source or origin is unknown.

Finally, amber is included under this heading even though being a fossilized resin it is arguable whether it is a vegetable or a mineral substance. True amber is largely derived from the resin of a now extinct species of pine, *Pinus succinifera,* and comes mainly from the Baltic coasts. Thimbles made of amber are known which presumably date from the latter part of the nineteenth century, but their purpose is obscure and they are hardly practical, being too soft and brittle for real wear. The main characteristics of an amber thimble are that it is warm to the touch, light in weight, and if rubbed against fur or similar material, will, like all amber, develop a negative electric charge and attract small, light particles.

NOTES

1. See *Illustrated London News,* 4 June 1853.
2. Caulfield & Saward, *Dictionary of Needlework* (London, 1882), s.v. "thimbles."

Fabric Thimbles

THE SHAPE AND MATERIAL OF THE THIMBLES USED in parts of the far East are unlike those in Europe, most probably because they are intended to serve a different purpose. On account of the extremes of heat and cold in countries such as Northern China or Japan, and because of great poverty, it was customary for clothes to be made of thin textile fabric, which was ripped apart for washing and sewn together again with some padding inserted as a lining for the colder season. Small running stitches were used to seam garments together, and a special method of sewing known as speed stitching came into being.

In speed stitching a Japanese thimble, called a *yubi-nuki*, is worn between the first and second joints of the middle finger of the right hand, with its working surface or indentations turned outward. The threaded needle is held between thumb and index finger of the right hand, which also grips the fabric, with the head of the needle pressing against the thimble. The left hand holds the material a short distance to the left and as the right hand weaves the needle in and out gathering evenly spaced folds, the left hand assists this process by a slight forward and backward movement which has the effect of varying the tautness of the material as the needle moves along the seam. When there are sufficient stitches on the needle, the left index finger and thumb grasp the tip of the needle and the material, holding them fast, and the right hand is then used to pull the material to the right along the thread to reveal the stitches. In this method of sewing the fingers remain folded and the thimble stays in contact with the head of the needle except when drawing through the material. In a sense the main difference between speed stitching and the more customary form of sewing is that here it is the material which is pulled along the thread, whereas in normal sewing it is the thread which is pulled through the material.

Besides the modern *yubi-nuki*, which is a ring-type expandable band about half an inch wide made of metal, plastic, or leather, the Japanese also have a plate shaped thimble which is worn round the middle finger with the plate on the palm side. Alternatively they may also use Western style thimbles, but the latter are essentially a modern development. Traditionally a Japanese lady made her own thimble from silks and cardboard and the following instructions are translated from an unknown Japanese author:

How to make a sewing thimble

Prepare some thin cardboard and cut it into a strip one centimetre wide. Make it into a double circle to fit your finger. Cover this double ring cross-ways with a band of floss-silk winding evenly. Stitch it down with gaily col-

Silk and cardboard sewing rings. *Tokyo National Museum*

131

Japanese lady sewing. After Ito Shinsui (1898–1972). *Private collection*

and so on. After completing the stitching one way come back the other in order to achieve a lozenge shaped pattern round the ring. You can then stitch a flower pattern in the lozenges or sub-divide them by sewing smaller lozenges as desired.

This thimble is soft and at the same time the needle will find it difficult to penetrate so that it can be used for a long time and will prove very useful when speed stitching with folded fingers.[1]

Some thimbles made in this way from silk on a base of cardboard are illustrated. It is hardly necessary to add that such thimbles were not expected to last indefinitely and it is pointless expecting to find antique thimbles in Japan, even though the art of needlework was practiced there from ancient times.

Somewhat different thimbles made of textile fabric hand-stitched over a padded cardboard framework are used in Korea. Because of their shape, collectors sometimes refer to them as tea-cozy thimbles.

Contemporary base metal thimbles surrounded with a band of petit point (or sometimes hand embroidery) are made in Austria and Hungary.

oured silk thread starting near the edge to make a feather stitch round it. Proceed to the next stitch diagonally across to the other edge

NOTE

1. Translation provided by the Tokyo National Museum.

132

Brass Thimbles

THE PRINCIPAL INGREDIENT OF BRASS IS COPPER, which was one of the first metals known to man, who used it long before iron, either pure or as an alloy in the form of bronze. Rich mines on the island of Cyprus (Greek *Kupros,* copper) were of great importance in antiquity and copper was sacred to the island's goddess Aphrodite. The mines of Tharsis in southern Spain were also exploited. There was, however, little understanding of the metallurgy involved: for instance, no distinction was made between pure copper, bronze (copper alloyed with tin), and brass (copper alloyed with zinc) until at least the third century A.D. Nevertheless new deposits were gradually discovered, methods of working copper with calamine (zinc carbonate) were developed, and brass (or yellow metal as it was often called) came to the forefront. By the Middle Ages copper was obtained primarily from the Spanish mines, from Bohemia, from Thuringia (Mansfeld), from Saxony, from Hanover, and from Sweden. Brass became more widely used and it is likely that the growth of thimble making, which appears to have taken place at this time, was associated with the improved availability of the metal. As we have seen, thimble making developed into a trade of its own which was recognized as such in France, Germany, and elsewhere. Other metals may have been used, but iron was scarce and difficult to work and silver was too valuable, so that most thimbles were made of brass or like material.

Before considering the various methods of making brass thimbles, it is necessary to say something about the physical properties of the metal itself. Cast brass is a reasonably soft metal and can therefore be hammered and drawn with relative ease. As hammering is continued, the brass becomes progressively harder and more brittle until it eventually cracks. Stated briefly, the hammering distorts the crystalline structure of the metal and a point is reached when the distortion is so great that the crystals break away. Thus before reaching this point, the thimble-maker will need to anneal the metal by reheating it gently to a dull red heat and allowing it to cool slowly. A fresh crystalline structure is formed as a result (although different from the original cast structure), which leaves the metal soft, malleable, and ductile again. Where much hammering or shaping is required, the process of annealing may need to be repeated at intervals.

The above will serve to explain the principles underlying the processes illustrated in the Jost Amman and Christopher Weigel engravings and outlined earlier when discussing the subject of German thimbles. As the sheet metal was gradually hammered into shape it would be heated from time to time until the final shape was achieved. The difficulty was that the sheet metal was seldom uniform either in substance or in quality, with the result that instead of slowly compressing and shaping the metal, the hammering might cause it to bulge over and settle into folds. Folds of this kind may sometimes be seen on the inside of medieval thimbles and are a

the top which was the more usual way. Small notches might be cut in the rim to hold the thimbles steady when cleaning or finishing on a lathe. A thimble with four small notches of this kind is also illustrated. Casting as a means of making thimbles was not entirely satisfactory during the Middle Ages because the technique was insufficiently advanced and cast thimbles tended to be unduly squat and heavy. It was not until later when casting techniques improved and better machinery, capable of "insiding" the thimbles and of applying the indentations mechanically, became available, that casting came into its own.

Arising from the above, the term *latten* will often be found mentioned in the same context as brass, and collectors may well inquire about the difference. Latten was synonymous with brightness, and Chaucer compares it with the sun:

Phebus waxed old,
And hewed like laton
That in his hote declination,
Shone as the burned gold.

In earlier times the term *latten* was used to denote different kinds of brass, though frequently used for brass generally, and it can be the cause of much confusion. The confusion is worse confounded because the French language does not have a separate word for brass, which is called *cuivre jaune* as distinct from *cuivre rouge,* which is copper, and because the French often used *laiton* for the same purpose. Thus certain types of brass imported from Flanders came to be designated as latten, but the precise meaning of the word changed over the centuries and it can also vary according to the context. A Parliamentary Commission of the early eighteenth century found itself recording that "Black Lattin is round Bottoms, and Folds of thin Brass," which is hardly enlightening but serves to illustrate the difficulties of the subject.[1] It follows that the wise collector, who does not wish to spend years researching the different meanings of the word *latten* as it evolved according to time and place, will do well to forget the differences and assume that for thimble-making purposes brass and latten were nearly enough the same thing.

The importance of Nuremberg as a cradle of the thimble-making industry has already been explained, and during the fourteenth and

Hispano-Moresque thimbles from the tenth to the twelfth century. Made by lost-wax process. *Museo Arqueologico Nacional, Madrid*

sure sign that the thimble was made by a battery process. Another technique which was sometimes employed was casting. The problem with casting was to secure the core which had to be held in place inside the mold in order that the molten metal might run in between to form the thimble. This core could be supported from the bottom of the mold as if spiked on a nail, in which case the molten metal would run around the support and the casting would show a small hole at the apex of the thimble. A thimble made in this way and with a small hole at the top is illustrated. Or else the core could be held from

Medieval brass thimbles. *Left*, **cast with notches on the rim;** *center*, **hammered, note fold in the metal;** *right*, **cast with hole at top.** *Private collection*

fifteenth centuries Nuremberg thimbles were exported far and wide. Nevertheless this did not prevent some artisan thimble-makers from plying their trade elsewhere, and at some stage it appears that the thimble making in the Low Countries began to gain in importance. When this happened is uncertain and the reasons are not entirely clear. It has been said that the decline of Nuremberg thimble making was due to an inordinately conservative outlook, which may well be true but there may have been some more fundamental reason such as, for instance, a change from the earlier technique of hammering to the later technique of brass founding. Here again it is not known when this change took place, but by the end of the seventeenth century the Dutch thimble-making industry was based on brass founding and this could be the reason why Nuremberg found itself unable to compete.

Surprisingly little is known about the origins of the Dutch thimble-making industry. Dinant on the Meuse river dominated bronze and brassware production from the time of Charlemagne until Philip the Good, Duke of Burgundy, besieged and destroyed the town in 1466. Those bronze casters who survived moved elsewhere and settled mostly in the Low Countries including Tournai, about whose thimble-making activities nothing is known save that according to an anonymous poem entitled the *Dict des Pays*, published about 1597, Tournai was well known for its large thimbles. Possibly the Dutch thimble-making industry emerged from the upheaval, but all that is known for certain comes from two deeds in the archives of the city of Amsterdam, one dated 14 March 1609 and the other dated 23 July 1609, concerning one Babtista van Regemorter, living in Haarlem. The deeds, which relate to the secrets of making thimbles belonging to Geraerdt van Slagenborch of Amsterdam, suggest that already by the end of the sixteenth century the thimble industry was well established. In another deed, dated 28

Sixteenth-century brass thimbles. Very similar to those seen in the color illustration but with black finish. The reason for the latter is still undecided but may be due to the thimbles being finished with a coating of linseed oil. Probably made in Nuremberg. *Private collection*

135

English seventeenth-century brass thimbles. *Left,* **with chevron pattern, height 3.0 cm;** *center,* **with chevrons and copper top inscribed "Be true my hart" and with initials IH on crown, height 3.9 cm;** *right,* **inscribed "Love" and with clock dial at top, height 2.8 cm.** *Private collection*

March 1613, the same Babtista van Regemorter, now living in Schoonhoven, bought from Jacob Seyne an invention for making thimbles. Then in 1628 Marichger Petersdochter, a female thimble-maker, asked the Burgermeister and Town Council of Utrecht for permission to install a water mill next to her house to use the power to make thimbles. This request was granted, and she later married Jan Claess Schot, also a thimble-maker from Schoonhoven. The business was extended and consolidated, potential competitors being bought out or merged with the Schot family. By 1700 the Schots and their associates were making 26,000 gross of brass thimbles, i.e., about 3.7 million thimbles per annum, and were exporting large quantities abroad. Some went to the Dutch colonists in North America and some to France, which was an important market. Thimbles are specifically mentioned in a French tariff dated 1641 and entitled the "Subvention du vingtième sur les marchandises entrant en France." The entry reads: "Déaux, le cent pesant estimé trente livres." some also went to England, which had not yet succeeded in establishing a brass-founding in-

dustry of its own and still depended on imports. However, by the end of the seventeenth century the Dutch thimble-making industry had reached a turning point. Competition from the newly established thimble-making industry in England began to make itself felt, and in Germany new mills were installed near Iserlohn in the region of South Westphalia. The Dutch thimble-makers continued the struggle during the early part of the eighteenth century. For instance, when marine archaeologists investigated the remains of the *De Liefde (The Love),* a vessel belonging to the Dutch United East India Company which was wrecked on the Out Skerries (Shetlands) in 1711 on a voyage from Amsterdam to the Cape, Ceylon, and Batavia, they found that the cargo included thimbles among a wide range of small objects. It appears, however, that the competition became too great, and by the end of the eighteenth century the Dutch thimble industry had fallen into oblivion.

The growth of thimble making in England was a direct consequence of the development of an indigenous brass-founding industry. Copper mining had been practiced intermittently in En-

136

Seventeenth-century brass thimbles. Made by casting, probably in the Netherlands. *Private collection*

gland during the Middle Ages, but it was not until the reign of Elizabeth I that serious efforts were made to develop copper resources or to start a brass-founding industry such as already existed in Germany. The initial progress was slow and during the sixteenth and seventeenth centuries most copper and brass manufactures, including thimbles, continued to be imported from abroad. Obviously some brass thimbles were made locally: during the seventeenth century some strikingly tall but ungainly English brass thimbles were made by rolling and seaming plate metal, but there is little information about them. One report is of a mill at Marlow where it is said that the manufacture of thimbles had been carried on since the reign of Henry VIII, but this is now known to have been mistaken.[2] Another is that a privileged company of

Seventeenth-century brass thimbles made in two parts, the top being held in place by the body of the thimble, which is seamed into a cylinder. Probably made in the Netherlands. *Private collection*

which Prince Rupert was governor produced thimbles among a wide range of other manufactures.[3] Regarding the latter it is tempting to think that the thimble made of Prince's metal which was described by Syer Cuming to the British Archaeological Association in March 1879 was made on that account, but be that as it may, the brass-founding industry in England was growing and by the end of the eighteenth century it had become large enough to supply the country's requirements. Inevitably many brass manufactures which had formerly been imported began to be made at home, and it is in this context that John Lofting brought the technique of making thimbles across from Holland and that thimble making in England became an industrial activity.

John Lofting was a native of Holland who in 1693 obtained a patent for making thimbles (see "Patent Thimbles") and set up works at Islington. The material used was battery brass or shruff metal (i.e., old hammered brass) and the molten metal was poured into molds prepared with red ocher and sand, which was said to be obtainable only at Highgate in Middlesex. Hollow castings, necessary for the making of thimbles, required a center of sand, known as a corè, which had to be supported in the mold so that the metal could be poured round it. At the Islington works about six or seven such castings were made each day. When the castings were cold they were taken out and separated from one another and boys were employed to remove the cores from the thimbles. The castings were next put into a drum, which was revolved by horse power, in order to remove all traces of sand (barrel tumbling). Once this was done the thimbles were taken to the mill to be turned, after which the finished articles were packed up ready for sale. All these various operations were carried out by specialized workers. In the foundry six persons were employed; first of all there was the founder, then two men who prepared the molds, and two boys who made the cores and one who worked the bellows. At first horse power was used to drive the mill but subsequently John Lofting moved to Great Marlow where, with a water mill, he was able to produce twice as many thimbles.

There is no record of the reasons which prompted John Lofting to remove to Marlow, but the availability of water power and adequate supplies of raw material, notably suitable sand for casting, must have figured largely in his calculations. The mill had an installed capacity of about two million thimbles per annum, so that it is obvious that with the total population of England and Wales being only five or six millions, the capacity was greatly in excess of domestic requirements. It follows that Lofting's plans must have envisaged not only the capture of the home market but also the building up of an extensive foreign trade. Regarding the latter, in about 1700 Lord Bellomont, governor of New York, when referring in a dispatch to the seizure of the *Hester,* a vessel belonging to Lofting's brother-in-law, mentioned that the ship had brought from England some cargo which belonged to John Lofting to the value of eight hundred pounds. He did not state the nature of the cargo, but it is likely that John Lofting exported thimbles to the American colonies and that he took over much of the business which had previously belonged to the Dutch. Little more is

known about Lofting's thimble-making activities except that his mill operated with "profit and success for the proprietors." Lofting died in 1742 and there is reason to believe that the mill was still producing thimbles in 1748.[4] A thimble mill is shown on a Thames Conservancy map drawn in 1815, but by then the mill had probably ceased production and the date it closed remains uncertain.

Inevitably other manufacturers sought to copy John Lofting and emulate his success. The artisans of Birmingham, which was then a small country town, had an established reputation for working metals (mostly iron and steel) when the demands of fashion and luxury after the Restoration on the one hand, and the war with France, which disrupted trade at the end of the seventeenth century, on the other, created favorable conditions for the manufacture of a multiplicity of small luxury articles including buckles and buttons, such as came to be known under the name of the Birmingham "toy" trade. The growth of an indigenous brass and copper industry contributed enormously to this development. Many Birmingham artisans turned to brass founding, and from the beginning of the eighteenth century a vast quantity of small brass articles were made using essentially the same method employed by John Lofting, namely, casting in molds and then working by hand or else machining to a finish. Although thimble making had obviously started well before, there is no record of any thimble-makers in Birmingham until 1767, when according to an early trades directory, there were two registered as such, namely, Joseph Ashwell in Temple

Eighteenth-century brass thimbles. A type of thimble found both in England and in the Netherlands, which suggests that John Lofting may have made thimbles like it. *Private collection*

138

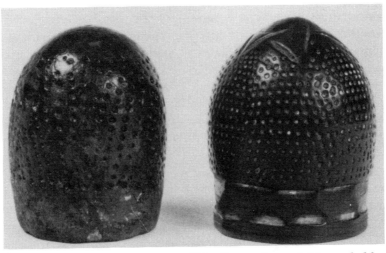

From Asia Minor. *Left,* **possibly Byzantine;** *right,* **probably eighteenth or nineteenth century.** *Private collection*

Street and Walter Davenport in Cannon Street.[5] Significantly, William Hall in the Dale End, a button-maker, also made thimbles, thus giving the first hint that thimble making was ceasing to be an activity which fell exclusively within the province of the specialized thimble-maker.

The event which revolutionized the making of thimbles and led Birmingham to emerge ahead of its competitors was the introduction of the deep-drawing process. In the early part of the eighteenth century the quality of English brass was poor: "So hard, flawy and scurvy that it won't make several Sorts of Goods particularly Buttons." Obviously so long as brass continued to be made by adding calamine to the molten copper, the quality was difficult to control. The development of a satisfactory method of obtaining the metal (zinc) from the ore (calamine) in 1738 did not greatly alter the situation because calamine continued to be used to a large extent, but it did lead to a better understanding of the processes involved, with the result that the end product gradually improved. Similarly, as long as sheet metal continued to be produced by a battery process it was ill-suited for pressing, but the development of rolling mills, coupled with the better quality brass, opened the way for the introduction of more sophisticated techniques. In 1769 John Pickering, a toy-maker from London, invented a simple device for raising ornaments on sheet metal surfaces, and a few months later Richard Ford of Birmingham showed how Pickering's invention could be adapted to a more

fundamental use, namely, the shaping of hollow ware. Ford's patent (No. 935) dated 1769 provided that "two implements called dyes placed under the hammer of a stamp or screw of a press, the one being concave, the other convex, which by the pressure of the hammer or press forced into the dye, the shape or the form of the thing designed is accomplished." The new process was an immediate success. Until Ford's invention hollow ware could only be produced by casting, as in the case of thimbles, or else by hammering by hand. Thereafter a wide variety of goods, including thimbles, could be pressed into shape quickly and simply and the new method (known as deep-drawing) gave an immense impetus to trade. Sundry patents followed, including that of William Bell (No. 1242) in 1779, who patented a new way "of affixing impressions from dies upon gold, silver or metals by means of rolling cylinders, on which such dies are engraved, which would be to the great benefit of trade, particularly the buckle, button and toy manufactories." It will be seen therefore that by about 1780 at the latest the Birmingham thimble manufacturers possessed all the elements of modern thimble-making technique.

But before proceeding with this account of the development of the brass thimble industry in Britain it is necessary to go back in time and to examine the situation in Germany. It will be recalled that Nuremberg had lost its position as the chief supplier of thimbles to the Dutch and that the latter in turn had lost it to the British.

139

Throughout the seventeenth century the German industry remained in a state of comparative decline and it was not until the eighteenth century that it sprang up again in South Westphalia in the region of Iserlohn, Hemer, Sundwig, and Altena in the valley of the river Lenne and its tributaries. It is recorded that next to the wire-drawing industry the thimble-making industry was the first to settle in the region,[7] and it thereby helped to lead the way for the many important industries which subsequently developed in the area. In 1712 Bernhard von der Becke, who had amassed considerable experience traveling in Holland, where he is supposed to have studied the thimble industry in Utrecht, erected a thimble factory at Sundwig. The King of Prussia, Friedrich Wilhelm I, lent his patronage to the enterprise, which in its early days concentrated on the production of iron sewing rings. Bernhard von der Becke's successors developed the business by making thimbles, first of steel and also in 1760 of brass, and thus prepared the ground for a series of enterprises which were started both by members of the family and by others anxious to emulate their success. The following list of thimble-making factories established in the Iserlohn region illustrates the growth of the industry during the latter part of the eighteenth century and the important part which the von der Becke family played in its development.

Thimble factory	Founded 1712	Sundwig	Bernhard v.d. Becke
Factory for needles, thimbles, military buttons	Founded 1756	Hemer	v.d. Becke & Cie
Thimble mill	Acquired 1796	Hemer	Heinrich & Johann Adolf v.d. Becke
Thimble and button mill	Founded 1774	Westing	Schlieper
Thimble factory	Founded 1775	Hemer	Johann Diedrich v.d. Becke son of Heinrich v.d. Becke
Thimble mill	Founded 1780	Sundwig	Heinrich v.d. Becke
Brass thimble factory	Founded 1782	Hemer	Anton Pauli
Brass thimble factory	Started 1786	Iserlohn	L. Lecke
Thimble mill	Founded 1797	Sundwig	Christian v.d. Becke
Thimble factory	Founded about 1800	Iserlohn	Wilhelm Faber
Thimble and brass casting factory	Founded 1815	Iserlohn	Casp. Diedr. Piepenstock

Following on the above, several new businesses were opened during the nineteenth century whose principal product was thimbles but which were located in Altena.

Thimble mill	Founded about 1800	Altena	Joh. Caspar Rumpe
Thimble mill	Founded 1827	Altena	F. W. Rump
Thimble factory	Branched off from above, 1863	Altena	Joh. Henrik Rump
Metal haberdashery factory	Founded 1869	Eringsen zone of Altena	Gustav Adolf Kayser

Brass filigree of unknown origin. Height 3.2 cm. There is an identical thimble in the Colonial Williamsburg Foundation collection. *Private collection*

needle workers) were exempted from military service. This was a rare privilege in those days and demonstrates the importance attached to the industry.

The method of production originally employed in the Rumpe works was based on casting. After casting, the edges of the thimbles were trimmed smooth, then followed the processing of the inner and outer surfaces on a lathe, and lastly the knurling of the indentations on the dome, which was achieved by forcing the thimble against an engraved roller. Finally, after the turning came the finishing, such as polishing and rounding off the inside of the edges.

The key figure in the development of thimble making in Altena was Johann Caspar Rumpe. Like van der Becke, Rumpe was one of the prominent entrepreneurs of his time and an account of his career has been published.[8] He knew how to make the most of water power and so that the river Lenne should better supply his works, he arranged for channels to be excavated out of the solid rock to improve the head of water and to increase the available power. In order to facilitate the realization of what was for those days a daring project, he secured the support and patronage of Frederick the Great, King of Prussia, who, following a personal visit, was so impressed that he gave Rumpe a special dispensation whereby his thimble workers (as well as his

From about 1817 the Rumpe works introduced a punch and die process (deep-drawing) which revolutionized the manufacture of thimbles as it had done in England forty years earlier. It was now possible to make full use of the available water power to drive the presses, whose rapidity and accuracy of operation resulted in a considerable increase in production. Unfortunately there are no available figures to show how casting compared with the new pressing method. It is reported however that in 1845 the Rumpe works were producing 12,000 gross thimbles per annum, besides a large quantity of other products such as curtain-rings and saddlers' rings, with a work force of forty to fifty people. Voye states that production in 1833 was around 2 million. The Rumpe works at Altena still exist and continue to make thimbles for sale in Germany and abroad.

Having followed the changes in the thimble-making process so far, no great effort is required to understand its later developments. In particular since the introduction of pressing methods, the same technique has been adopted all over the world, there has been no further change save

Brass thimbles from the nineteenth century. *Private collection*

141

in matters of detail, and it will be sufficient to give but one description. For the more technically minded an article complete with machine drawings, which was published in an English publication entitled *Machinery*, is reproduced as an appendix. It will be noted that the article is signed "F. H.," which presumably stands for Fingerhüter and suggests that the author was a thimble-maker from Germany.

The modern method of making a brass thimble, which is known as deep drawing, starts with a strip of brass sheeting selected with regard to quality and strength according to the type of thimble which it is desired to make. This strip is made to run through a press which acts on a sharp-edged punch and serves to cut out a series of round discs the size of a large coin. The diameter of the discs is carefully chosen according to the size of the finished thimble. The strip of brass passes through the press and the discs, which are known as blanks, emerge in two continuous rows.

The next operation is to shape the blank into the form of a small cup by a punch and die action. At this stage the width of the cup is still considerably larger than that of the finished thimble. The operating tool is again a press, which cold punches the brass into a suitably shaped die with the stamp just sufficiently smaller than the die to allow for the thickness of the brass to fit in between. This operation is sometimes included as part of the blank-cutting process. In this case the press stamp is situated inside the cutting stamp and after the blank is cut from the original brass strip, the press stamp descends and passes through the cutting stamp to shape the cup. This telescoping of two operations into one was evolved as the result of practi-

cal experience and has the advantage that it enables the operations that follow to be carried out with a single piece of machinery known as a graduated press.

In the subsequent operations the cup is first shaped by stamp and die to become both taller and narrower and the base is made to assume a rounded form. Next comes the so-called conical pressing, which is frequently followed by a roller pressing. The conical pressing stretches the shaped sides into their final form. The next stage is usually to impress the indentations on the cap of the thimble. This and the following operations are not always conducted in the same order. Inevitably at some stage there must be an annealing process so that the hardened metal can be softened and again become malleable. Depending on the quality of the brass, more than one annealing operation may be necessary. It is essential that after annealing, the metal should be allowed to cool gradually, as otherwise it may again harden. Also, as a result of the various pressing operations, the edges of the thimble will have become irregular and they must be trimmed straight. This process, which is carried out on a small spinning lathe, is known as edging. The thimble is placed on a rotating mandrel which is chosen to fit the inside dimension of the thimble accurately. A light pressure on the cap ensures that the thimble is held firm. The apparatus for applying pressure is often lined with leather to protect the thimble from damage. A cutting tool or wheel is pressed against the thimble and cuts the surplus metal away. The shape of the spigot inside the thimble serves to determine the line of cut.

Most good quality thimbles have a rounded rim to protect the finger and the rounding is

Stages in the manufacture of a brass thimble. *Private collection*

142

again carried out on a lathe by a process known as "curling" or as "turning over." The thimble on its rotating die spigot is brought up against small toothed wheels which grasp the thimble and bend the metal forward until it curls over itself. The indentations or holes designed to hold the head of the needle are then applied by means of a process known as "grating," whereby the thimble is forced against an engraved roller. Any grooves to be applied round the thimble or any decoration is worked in the same way with the above-mentioned tools. Needless to say that this lathe work calls for considerable skill and experience on the part of the operator, who can easily spoil the work by, for instance, selecting too large or too small a grating hub to produce the indentations. Then follows the cleaning of the oxidized metal with sulphuric or nitric acid and lastly the polishing with a rotating cloth, which completes the process and yields the finished article.

An immediate consequence of the new method was a change in the shape and appearance of thimbles. Prior to 1770 English brass thimbles, being cast, tended to be short and dumpy. Moreover, since they were turned after casting, small parallel lines caused by the edges of the cutting tool may be seen on the inside, they are generally of thicker and more rigid construction than pressed work, and quite often, though by no means always, cast thimbles bear the mark of the lathe center on the inside. Pressed thimbles, on the other hand, tend to be longer and thinner, and instead of a solid rim it became a simple matter to turn over a rim round

Sewing ring as sometimes used in Japan. The plate is worn on the palm side. *Private collection*

the edge of the thimble. Thus a new style of thimble emerged, easily distinguishable from the older and inevitably rarer cast thimbles.

The introduction of deep drawing had another important consequence, namely, that thimble making ceased to be the highly specialized business which it had been ever since the Middle Ages. The juxtaposition of thimble making with other activities is well illustrated in a Birmingham trade directory for 1800 which names fourteen thimble-makers, of whom at least half made some other articles as well.[9] For instance, Joseph Ashwell, mentioned as a thimble-maker in 1767, made ferrules as well as thimbles; Thomas Bartleet made gilt, plated, and metal buttons, sleeve links, and shoulder clasps; Thomas Iliffe made buttons and spoons; Abraham Ireland made buttons; William Pratt made scabbards; William Robbins made gilt bottle stands; and John Rose was a plater, thimble-maker, and roller of metals. In the course of the nineteenth century many firms would come to manufacture brass thimbles and some might regard thimble making as their principal activity, but none would flourish on thimbles only.

With the second half of the nineteenth century there was a gradual reversal toward more concentration. Thimble making continued to be dovetailed into other activities but with better, and above all more uniform, quality brass sheeting, and with the development of more sophisticated machinery, more efficient methods of production became possible. Production capacity increased and the result was that those firms which were less skilled or which were not prepared to invest the necessary capital to keep themselves up to date began to drop out from

Knurling wheel (also known as a grating hub). *Private collection*

what was becoming an increasingly specialized and competitive activity. By the end of the century only a handful of thimble-making firms were left in each of the main producing countries to face the challenge of aluminum and plastic thimbles. However, the trend toward more powerful and specialized machinery continued, several more firms faced with the choice of having to buy expensive specialized presses or to drop thimbles from their range of products chose the latter, and when after the Second World War plastic thimbles left the orbit of the thimble manufacturers there was only one brass thimble manufacturer left operating in each of the main producing countries, namely, Rumpe in Germany, Iles in England, and Scovill Manufacturing in the United States. It is interesting to note that these firms share common characteristics, namely, that they are all long-established thimble manufacturers with a history stretching back a century or more. Rumpe was established about 1800, Scovill Manufacturing in 1802, and Iles about 1840. All three have a long tradition of thimble making and it is unfortunate that so much attention tends to focus on the activities of silver thimble manufacturers. Historically brass thimbles are in many ways more important than silver, and it is necessary to bear this in mind if the subject is to be kept in its right perspective.

NOTES

1. *Journal of Parliament* 17.
2. Leland, *Itinerary*, 2d (1744) edition where the editor (Hearne) printed a letter from Rev. Francis Brookesby dated 1711. Contrary to what is stated in the Victoria County History of Buckingham, the reference does not carry the foundation of the mill back beyond the late seventeenth century, and the author of the Victoria History account was guilty of inaccuracy in attributing the statement to Leland himself.
3. Stringer, *Opera Mineralia Explicata*, 221–22.
4. Daniel Defoe, *Tour through Great Britain* (1748).
5. *Sketchley's Birmingham Wolverhampton and Walsall Directory, 1767* (3d edition).
6. *Journal of the House of Commons* 17:162.
7. Dr. Ernst Voye, *Geschichte der Industrie in Märkischen Sauerland* (Hagen, 1908), 3:119.
8. Wilhelm Claas, "Johann Caspar Rumpe und sein Werk," in *Beiträgen zur Geschichte der Technik und Industrie*, vol. 22 (V.D.I. Verlag, 1933).
9. *Chapman's Birmingham Directory, 1800*.

Iron and Steel Thimbles

IRON IS ONE OF THE OLDEST AND MOST IMPORTANT metals known to mankind. Tubalcain is mentioned in the Old Testament as being a worker in bronze and iron (Genesis 4:22) and by about 1200 B.C. the Hittites were making iron weapons whose edges were hardened by quenching, but there was little understanding of the processes involved, iron was largely reserved for military purposes, and it is not until the Middle Ages that the use of iron began to overtake the use of bronze and copper. Thus, although it is possible that some early thimbles were made of iron, in practice early thimbles were more probably made of bronze, and it is unlikely that iron was used to any great extent before the thirteenth or fourteenth century at the earliest.

One of the serious disadvantages of iron is that it rusts easily, and so does steel, which is iron combined with a small proportion of carbon to change the molecular structure and make it harder and more brittle. Small objects are particularly vulnerable to rust and unless iron (or steel) thimbles are kept in a dry atmosphere or protected from dampness by a layer of grease, they soon oxidize and rust away. It follows that few (if any) really old iron thimbles have survived, and although iron thimbles were undoubtedly used in large numbers, there must be

Italian cut steel thimble decorated with a hunting scene, probably eighteenth century. *Colonial Williamsburg Foundation*

145

some doubt as to what they looked like. The earliest iron thimbles known to exist are some fine specimens made in Italy at the end of the seventeenth and the beginning of the eighteenth centuries. They are decorated with flowers, leaves, birds, and animals and sometimes with gold inlay. In all probability they were made in Brescia in Northern Italy, which was then well known for small objects worked in chiseled iron, and there is a fine collection located in the Musée Le Secq des Tournelles at Rouen. These tend to be rather heavy, weighing up to 17 grams instead of 3 or 4 grams, which is the average weight for an ordinary thimble, and possibly it is because they are heavier and larger that they have survived in good condition. There is of course no difficulty in knowing whether a thimble is made of iron, if only because the thimble will respond to a magnet.

It is unlikely that iron thimbles made for ordinary domestic purposes were decorated to any great extent, but there is little evidence available. The first known reference to thimbles made of iron is an indirect one in a Book of Rates of the London Customs House dated 1690, where there is mention of a subsidy (or duty) which was imposed on the wrought iron content of imported merchandise, including thimbles. There was no subsidy on brass, so that under the heading of thimbles two separate rates of duty and also two separate rates of repayment of duty (duty drawback) are shown, one for iron and the other for brass thimbles respectively. Clearly if there had been no iron thimbles it would not have been necessary to distinguish between the two metals, and it is possible to deduce that both types were imported.

More precise evidence is available from Germany, where in 1712 Bernhard von der Becke established a thimble mill at Sundwig in South Westphalia. In its early days this was a relatively unimportant enterprise confined to the production of iron sewing rings, but later Bernhard von der Becke's heirs and successors extended the business to the production of thimbles, first of iron and also in 1760 of brass. They thereby laid the foundations for a series of enterprises which have led to the name of von der Becke becoming closely associated with the development of the thimble industry in Germany.

Some evidence is also available from France, where a French commercial dictionary published in 1723–30 states:

> Les Dés et Deaux de cuivre et de fer font partie du négoce des Marchands Merciers et des Maîtres Aiguillers et Epingliers. Ils se vendent en gros par assortiments de douzaines et en détail à la pièce.[1]

Elsewhere the dictionary wrongly equates *Des* with thimbles and *Deaux* with sewing rings, so that it may be the latter only which were made of iron, but either way they belonged to the trade of the mercers and of the master needle-makers and pin-makers. It will be noted that thimbles were sold wholesale in assorted sizes by the dozen and that they were retailed individually. The corporations and guilds occasionally used thimbles as an attribute: for instance, the banner of the needle-makers and pin-makers of Douai consisted of thimbles interspersed with silver needles on a blue ground.

Coming back to England, it appears that iron thimbles like brass thimbles, which were imported at the end of the seventeenth century, also began to be manufactured locally and that in turn, like brass, they came to be exported abroad and notably to the United States. For instance, Mary Jackson & Son advertised in the *Boston News-Letter*, dated 15 May 1760, that they

Steel sewing rings lined with brass, mostly eighteenth century. *Private collection*

French steel thimbles from the nineteenth century. *Private collection*

had for sale "brass and iron thimbles" among a variety of London, Birmingham, and Sheffield made merchandise. This confirms that iron thimbles were being made in England and lends credence to the belief, which is otherwise unsupported by factual evidence, that Matthew Boulton, the well-known industrialist and silversmith, may have made iron thimbles at his Soho works in Birmingham.

By the beginning of the nineteenth century, Britain and Germany were the leading thimble-producing countries and were exporting thimbles to many parts of the world. On the continent Germany dominated the market to such an extent that in 1819 France was importing thimbles to the value of 800,000 francs, or the equivalent of two hundred kilos of gold. In the face of these imports, a French firm, Messrs. Rouy et Berthier, sought to revive the ailing domestic thimble industry by developing the production of a high-quality steel thimble. At the exhibition held in Paris at the Palais du Louvre in 1819 they showed steel thimbles which the judges reported were well made, well designed, and free of the disadvantages attaching to thimbles of copper, gold, ivory, mother-of-pearl, and wood. The list is interesting since it names several materials such as mother-of-pearl and wood which were then fashionable, but ignores silver, which given a steel top would have been equally resistant. Similarly, in 1823 another French firm, Messrs. Delaporte Frères exhibited some tailors' thimbles known as *"verges de fer"* and received an hon-orable mention for steel and copper (brass) thimbles. However, more unusual, the authorities of the central prison at Melun established a workshop where the inmates produced plain steel thimbles as well as thimbles inlaid with gold[2]. This was about 1840 and the process is described as follows:

Strips of iron sheeting of suitable thickness are placed under a punch which is used to cut round discs of a given diameter. Each disc is then made to go through a succession of stamp and die operations whereby the disc is formed by stages into the shape of a thimble. The thimble is then held on a lathe and by means of an engraved roller which is forced unto its surface the small indentations destined to receive the heads of the needles are quickly imprinted. The thimbles thus prepared are placed a batch at a time on a steel plate with a suitable preparation for case hardening and for drenching. They are finished after being brought to a blue state by lining them with the help of a lathe either with a leaf of fine tin or else sometimes with a leaf of gold. Should it be desired to decorate the thimble by adding a band of gold, a cavity is cut on the lathe, with the sides of the cavity undercut in such a way that the cavity is wider at the bottom than it is at the surface. A small strip of gold is prepared, chosen of exactly the right length to encircle the thimble, and is pressed into the cavity with an engraved roller and with sufficient force that the gold spreads toward the bottom, dovetailing into the undercut position. The design imprinted on the gold by the roller serves to hide the join.

The reference to temper blueing evidences a practice which was widely used for steel thimbles. If clean steel is heated in an oxidizing atmosphere to around 300°C–400°C, the surface oxides formed will be blue in color and besides being more attractive, will provide a degree of corrosion resistance. Presumably the French authorities knew what they were doing in introducing such a valuable commodity as gold within the confines of a prison, but in any event the above account serves to underline that there was apparently a market for better quality steel thimbles. This is confirmed independently by a noted authority. Thérèse de Dillmont, who in her *Encyclopédie des ouvrages de dames,* published in Paris in 1886, stated unreservedly:

> Thimble—Steel thimbles are the best; bone are very liable to break, and silver ones are not deeply enough pitted, to hold the needle. A thimble should be light with a rounded top and a flat rim.

Thérèse de Dillmont's encyclopedia was translated into several languages (the above is reproduced from the English edition published in 1892 under the name of *Encyclopedia of Needlework*) and it did a great deal to raise the standards of technique and design for needlework. It is doubtful, however, if her preference for steel thimbles was entirely justified. It may possibly be explained by the fact that silver thimbles

Rudimentary iron sewing ring as used by Eskimos.
National Museum, Copenhagen

with a steel top were never popular on the Continent, where thimbles with a stone top were preferred. In Britain, on the other hand, steel top thimbles being readily available, the use of iron and steel thimbles was confined to heavier work such as saddlery and upholstery. In due course the steel top thimble was replaced by the Dorcas, which proved a great success in Britain but which was never copied on the Continent, where evidently tastes were different.

The great advantage of iron and steel thimbles is that they combine strength with low cost, so that they were normally most popular in poor countries. For instance, between the wars Russia, while still recovering from the revolution, imported large quantities from Germany. On the other hand, because they rust, iron and steel thimbles are not really suitable for the finer types of needlework. They can also be very hard on the fingers, and in England they were normally lined with a softer metal such as silver, brass, or tin in order to make them more comfortable. The steel thimble with a silver lining was of course a distant cousin of the silver thimble with a steel top. Both sought to offset the disadvantages of one metal by the advantages of the other, but for heavy-duty purposes a plain iron thimble or sewing ring lined with brass or with white metal remains preferable. Iron thimbles inscribed Iles, OA&S, or Abel Morrall are of English manufacture.

It will serve to establish the relative value of steel thimbles to quote an extract from Harrod's catalog for 1895. Gold and silver thimbles were available from the jewelry department on the first floor, while the haberdashery department on the ground floor offered the following:

Steel per dozen 0/10¾
Plated per dozen 0/10¾
Silver plated each 0/4¾
Silver lined each 0/6¾
Sterling silver each 1/3½
Plated, enamel lined 0/10¾

It will be noted that Harrod's offered steel thimbles in two qualities, plain and plated. The explanation is that steel thimbles may be plated with nickel to inhibit rust and may also be plated with chromium. Unfortunately the plating soon wears off in use and the end result is very much the same.

Iron with gold inlay, German made by Gebrüder Gabler and decorated in Spain. Early twentieth century. Height 2.4 cm. *Private collection*

Collectors may come across iron thimbles made of cheap sheeting or tin plate pressed or stamped into shape in a rudimentary way. Such thimbles are easily damaged and hurtful to wear, and despite various finishes designed to render them more attractive, they tend to deteriorate and become unsightly. One of the more common designs consists of a somewhat elongated thimble with a plain rim and two or three tiers rising round the sides and often plated in yellow metal. Besides being used as thimbles, these were intended to act as the caps for small tubular containers enclosing needle and thread—or in other words, small emergency sewing kits.

This account would not be complete without some reference to damascene work, that is, the decoration of steel by etching and by inlaying it with gold and other metals. Eighteenth-century Spain was celebrated for this kind of work done by the craftsmen of Toledo, whose skill in decorating swords was handed down from generation to generation. Presumably thimbles came to be decorated in this manner, but if so there is no record. What is known however is that the German thimble manufacturers Gebrüder Gabler made iron thimbles which were sent to Toledo for decoration and were then returned for sale as German-made damascene thimbles. It is believed that this practice came to an end when Gebrüder Gabler ceased production. Thimbles are still made with so-called Toledo designs on them, but these are tourist items made of brass and of little artistic value.

Plain iron thimbles lined with brass or white metal continue to be used for heavy sewing, mostly of a nondomestic nature, and are made in several countries. From a thimble collector's point of view however they are of little interest and can well be ignored.

NOTES

1. Jacques Savary des Bruslons, *Dictionnaire universel du commerce* (Paris, 1723-30).
2. *Encyclopédie du XIX siècle*, edited by Laurentie, (Paris, 1842–54).

Nickel Thimbles

NICKEL IN ITS PURE STATE IS A GRAYISH-WHITE metal which is very malleable and ductile and is seldom used except in combination with other metals. It gained its name because early copper miners in Saxony would extract it thinking it was copper ore but when processed it would yield nothing but a slaglike material. They therefore associated the ore with "Old Nick," the devil, and it became known as *Kupfernickel* (Old Nick's copper). Subsequently this ore was shown to be comprised of copper, nickel, and zinc, that is, the same composition as so-called nickel silver or, as it is also known, German silver. These names are misleading however, and it is important to realize that there is no silver content in either nickel silver or German silver. The presence of nickel hardens the alloy and because the latter does not easily tarnish, it is also known as "white metal" among the Spanish-speaking countries. Nickel silver is marketed sometimes with other additives under a great many names, including alpacca (or alpaca) silver. Alternatively nickel may be combined with copper only, in which case it is known as cupronickel, an alloy not unlike nickel silver. Or again nickel may be used on its own account as a plating agent for base metal thimbles, either as a very thin coating (known as "flash") which is little more than surface coloring, or as a layer of appreciable thickness which is more fairly described as plating.

Nickel silver came into general use from about 1830 and it seems that thimble-makers were quick to recognize its merits, because already in 1834 the *Lady's Shopping Manual and Mercery album* by E. E. Perkins recorded as follows:

> Thimbles are made in the several sizes of girls', maids', slender women's, women's and outsize women's, of every quality.
>
> In Yellow Metal, with or without Steel Tops
> In White Metal, with or without Steel Tops
> All Steel, fine or coarse
> All Silver, or Silver with Steel Tops.

The reference to yellow metal is obviously to brass and since aluminum was still unknown, the reference to white metal is presumably to some form of nickel alloy, though it is puzzling to know why anyone should want to make a nickel thimble with a steel top. Nickel alloys are sufficiently resistant that a steel top should be unnecessary, and no nickel alloy thimble with a steel top is known to have survived.

A more positive reference to nickel thimbles may be found in Wrightson's *Dictionary of Birmingham* for 1839, where Stephen Brown of 85 Bartholomew Street is mentioned as making thimbles of German silver. Other manufacturers who are known to have made thimbles of German silver include William Beynon (1843), Joseph Lunn (1847–56), Joseph Addis (1861 or earlier), so that contrary to what might otherwise be expected, the manufacture of thimbles from nickel alloys dates well back into the nineteenth century and was obviously well established by 1840 at the latest.

150

Stages in the manufacture of a cupronickel thimble. *Private collection*

The principal advantage of a nickel thimble is its wear resistance, and a well-made nickel thimble is almost indestructible. Another advantage is that it is resistant to corrosion. The main disadvantage is that it is less pleasant to wear than a silver thimble and that as with brass a cut finger may become infected. Nickel thimbles are made in the same way as brass or silver thimbles, starting from sheet metal and following the same sequence of operations. The shape and style tend to follow those of the plainer silver thimbles. Nickel thimbles may be left unmarked except for a size number, or else they may be marked "Solid nickel silver," "nickel silver sterling silver plated," "nickel plated nickel silver," or "electro plated nickel silver" (EPNS), and other variations denoting the composition and method of manufacture. The principal use for nickel silver is as a base for silver plating, but since it can be plated with either nickel or silver it follows that the mention of "nickel plated nickel silver" is not a fancy designation intended to mislead, except possibly in so far that there is no silver content in

nickel silver. As already mentioned, nickel may also be used in its own right to plate brass and copper. Brass thimbles may be finished with a light coating of nickel, which has the effect of preventing tarnishing and looks more attractive. This is not intended to last and soon rubs off. On the other hand the brass may be given a heavier coating of a more permanent nature. This serves to give the thimble added strength as well as preventing tarnishing, but unfortunately once the coating is pierced the softer brass wears off, leaving a hole, and the thimble is soon useless. Charles Horner of Halifax made thimbles of nickel-plated copper which bear the initials CH, but this type of thimble presumably failed to find favor with customers because the number which have survived is small.

The main producing countries for nickel thimbles were England, Germany, and the United States. Specimens may be found marked England or Germany, indicating that they were made for export. In England the principal manufacturer was Charles Iles, whose

151

trademark, a small shield bearing three thimbles, may occasionally be found, as for instance on thimbles inscribed "Queen's Record Thimble." The mark being so small and sometimes ill-defined, the three thimbles can be difficult to distinguish. Nor should the mark be confused with the Chester hallmark, which in any event should be accompanied by the sterling mark and a date shield. Charles Iles had a wide range of products, and besides plain thimbles they also sought to reproduce in nickel some of the more elegant silver designs. Furthermore, not content with English designs, they made nickel silver thimbles in imitation of American styles and in American sizes for export to the United States and, at least on one occasion, they imitated a French design complete with fancy border and a garland of rosettes round it. All was not imitation however, and they also developed their own models such as a design registered in 1888 (No. 108544) with a dodecagonal skirting.

Other British firms which made nickel thimbles include Abel Morrall, who in their early days operated from Studley Mills, Manchester. Both they and Charles Iles participated in the 1862 International Exhibition in London, where Abel Morrall showed their needles and their thimbles. Abel Morrall subsequently discontinued the production of thimbles, but they remain well known as needle and general smallware manufacturers as part of the Aero Needles Group. Nickel silver thimbles marked Morrall or "OA&S" (also "OA&Co.") are of English manufacture. Other markings which have been noted include Coroza Silver with a maker's mark of four pellets in a triangle. Presumably *Coroza* is derived from the name of the corozo nut, or vegetable ivory, which was widely used for thimble making in the mid-nineteenth century.

Whereas English silver thimble manufacturers did not normally touch base metals, there was no such compunction in Germany, where the

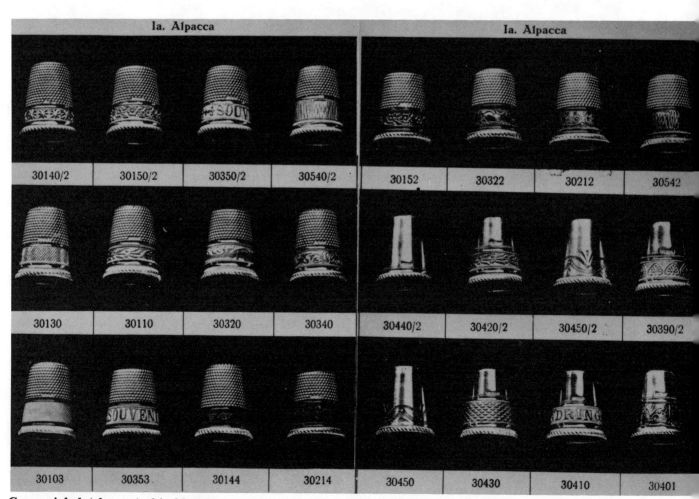

Cupronickel (alpacca) thimbles from a Soergel und Stollmeyer catalog circa 1922. *Private collection*

Iles cupronickel thimbles. *Left to right:* patent celluloid lining; daisy pattern; registered design No. 108544; French pattern; patent ventilated with lining. Early twentieth century. *Private collection*

manufacturers also produced thimbles of nickel silver, or alpacca as they usually called it, which were available in very much the same designs but at a suitably lower price. The brand "Alpacca prima" is believed to have been the property of Gebrüder Gabler. Alpacca was used extensively for souvenir thimbles, very often in the form of a plain nickel silver thimble with an appropriate badge added to it, and also for thimbles with a religious motif. Similarly in the United States, besides silver thimbles, an American thimble manufacturer might make nickel silver thimbles, and Simons, for instance, made nickel thimbles which were not marked with the familiar Simons "S" in a shield but instead bear the letters SBC in a differently shaped shield. The shape and style of American nickel thimbles generally follow those of plain silver thimbles and are therefore easy to recognize on that account. Most of the thimbles manufactured in the United States were sold in the home market, and in addition the United States imported substantial quantities of nickel thimbles from Britain and from Germany between the two world wars.

Thimbles made of nickel alloys have often been used for souvenirs. Among the oldest are a thimble commemorating the accession of Queen Victoria and another issued on 26 July 1843 to mark Queen Victoria's visit to the tunnel which Brunel was then constructing under the Thames. Charles Iles made a "Victoria Jubilee" thimble decorated with a crown, and more recently nickel thimbles were made to commemorate the Silver Jubilee of King George V in 1935, the Coronation of King George VI in May 1937, and that of Queen Elizabeth II in June 1953. Other souvenir thimbles include a nickel silver

version of the silver railway thimble, which dates back to Victorian times. In England thimbles made of nickel alloys have also been used for advertising, notably by the Prudential Insurance Company. The Prudential Insurance Company in the United States issued a large number of brass thimbles in 1904 and it seems likely that the English company followed its lead by issuing nickel thimbles on their own account. Another advertising thimble was made by Abel Morrall themselves, which urged the recipients to "Use Morrall's needles."

Finally, nickel and nickel alloys were the preferred material for many gadget thimbles. Besides the many specialty thimbles which Charles Iles made at various times, there have been other items such as for instance a nickel version of the finger shaped thimble patented by H. Bourne in 1904 (No. 19157) and a thimble lined with silk or other fabric or soft leather, as patented in 1892 (No. 20188) by T. Johnson trading as W. and S. Freeman. A popular thimble was "the Threader Thimble" made of nickel-plated nickel silver with a hook-type attachment to pull the thread through the eye of the needle, which retailed together with a thimble case and instructions at 2/3d. In Germany nickel was also used for gadget thimbles, notably a collapsible thimble and a thimble with a magnet serving as a steel top. There are many others, and the subject is dealt with separately elsewhere (see "Patent Thimbles").

Attempts have been made to print or ink a colored band round the base of plain nickel thimbles, either as a means of decoration or for possible use in advertising, but the color wears off and it has never proved much of a success.

Aluminum Thimbles

ALUMINUM (OR ALUMINIUM AS IT IS KNOWN IN Great Britain) is the most modern of the common metals. Its name is derived from *alumen,* the Latin name for alum, which is a naturally occurring aluminous sulphate. Pliny refers to alum which was widely used in the ancient and medieval world as a mordant for dyeing textiles. But although the crude salts of aluminum were used as early as the fifth century B.C. the metal itself was not isolated until 1825 and it was not produced commercially on any scale until 1888.

Besides its well-known property of being a very light metal, aluminum is also very ductile. It can be cold worked without intermediate annealing and it is therefore highly suitable for making thimbles, which can be produced quickly and in large quantities at relatively low cost. As in the case of nickel, thimble manufacturers were quick to realize the advantages of the new metal, and as early as 1897, the Sears Roebuck catalog featured aluminum thimbles as follows:

> Aluminium thimbles 1 cent each, German silver thimbles 3 cents, solid silver 20 cents, with border 30 cents, engraved 45 cents, hand engraved 55 cents; gold filled 75 cents, engraved warranted $1.15; solid gold 10 carat $1.90.

At the end of the nineteenth century Charles Iles, who made aluminum thimbles under the name of "Alurine," sold them through the Hudson's Bay Company, which shipped the thimbles to North America, and Sears Roebuck distributed them from Chicago to the Far West by mail order. It is probable therefore that the aluminum thimbles mentioned in the Sears Roebuck catalog above were of Charles Iles manufacture.

Thimbles made of aluminum have the advantage of being both inexpensive and light to wear on the finger. Also they do not oxidize. The disadvantage is that aluminum being comparatively soft the thimbles are easily damaged and wear out quickly. Thimble manufacturers have sought to remedy these defects by making thimbles from aluminum alloys but this presents difficulties. Alloying aluminum with other elements causes it to become stronger, but in the process it also becomes harder and less ductile. In other words it becomes more difficult to process and what is gained in strength tends to be lost because of the greater expense of the raw material and the higher production costs. For this reason other alternatives have been sought such as fitting an iron, or more commonly a glass or plastic, top designed to take the wear of the needle. The glass tops are normally red, green, or blue, but amber is also occasionally used.

Another disadvantage of aluminum is that it tends to look somewhat dull and lifeless. Manufacturers have therefore sought to embellish their aluminum thimbles to hide this characteristic, and this has been achieved in one of two ways. The first is to design the thimble in imitation of brass or silver thimbles, and Charles Iles for instance made several models of this kind. Similarly, Ketcham & McDougall decorated some aluminum thimbles to good effect. This

Aluminum. *Left to right:* **Iles aluminum bronze; blue anodized with magnet inside; Stratnoid; Japanese finger ring; advertising with glass top.** *Private collection*

solution, however, has the disadvantage that it seeks to give individuality to what is essentially a mass-produced article and it fails on that account. Another solution has therefore been followed which is to color anodize the thimbles. Under this process the thimbles are anodized by electrochemical action in the normal way but before completion they are immersed in an appropriate dye to achieve a tinted metallic finish. A color anodized thimble is not only more resistant to corrosion than a nonanodized thimble but it is impossible to remove the color from the aluminum surface without mechanically stripping the metal. Unfortunately the play of the needle soon wears out the surface and the final result is the same.

In practice it has been found that the best method of decorating aluminum thimbles for advertisement and like purposes is to have a painted band round the base, usually in red, green, blue, or black. It is then a simple matter to arrange for the advertisement to stand out against the color. The wording of the advertisement is first stamped on the thimble, it is painted all over, and a cutting tool is then used to scrape off the paint from the raised portion, which leaves the paint as background to offset the advertisement. Occasionally advertising thimbles may have the advertisement printed direct on the aluminum with a special type of ink. In such cases the skirting of the thimble is left plain, but this is not a very satisfactory solution because the ink tends to rub off. Aluminum thimbles being so cheap, they were used extensively for advertising until the advent of the polystyrene injection molded thimble which has taken their place.

In England Charles Iles made large quantities of aluminum thimbles throughout the period 1920–40, which was the heyday of the advertising thimble. Thimbles would be ordered in enormous quantities, as much as half a million or a million at a time, and supplied in bulk to shopkeepers who would distribute them to their customers; similarly in the United States and on the Continent (see "Advertising Thimbles"). Since the Second World War plastic thimbles have taken over much of the market for aluminum thimbles, but nevertheless they continue to be made, and in Britain the brand name "Stratnoid," belonging to Laughton & Sons, occurs frequently.

Aluminum thimbles being so plain and vulnerable, they are seldom used for keepsakes or souvenirs, though there are exceptions. An aluminum thimble with a dainty rolled border inscribed "Mother 1907" has been recorded, and they are occasionally found with "Forget me not" or "Remember me" inscribed round the sides. There are also various items decorated with horseshoes and the like, but none of these embellishments are very convincing. In the United States aluminum thimbles are known with religious slogans inscribed round the sides. Aluminum thimbles can also be made with needle-threading attachment of the type with a wire loop. During the Second World War some tailors' thimbles were made of aluminum alloy.

Thimbles may also be made of aluminum bronze, an alloy of aluminum and copper which is very much lighter in weight than gold but somewhat the same color. These are easy to recognize because the abnormally light weight leaves no room for doubt.

155

Plastic Thimbles

AN AMUSING CONCEIT OF THE AGE IS THAT PLAS-
tics are a twentieth-century development. It is
therefore appropriate to quote a French author
writing in 1886 on the subject of ivory thimbles.

Les dés en celluloïde leur sont supérieurs; on
en fait de toutes nuances.[1]

Given the above it is obviously desirable to re-
view the history of the plastics industry and see
how the manufacture of plastic thimbles has
evolved.

The first plastic to be produced on a commercial scale was cellulose nitrate (celluloid) invented by an Englishman, Alexander Parkes, in
1855 and named by him Parkesine. In 1865 Alexander Parkes read a paper to the Society of
Arts about his invention, examples of which had
won prizes at the Kensington Exhibition of 1862.
One passage should be noted:

He succeeded in producing a substance par-
taking in a large degree of the properties of
ivory, tortoise-shell, horn, hardwood, india
rubber, gutta percha etc. and which will, he
believes, to a considerable extent, replace such
materials. . . .

Unfortunately this was somewhat overoptimis-
tic. Parkesine was produced commercially from
1862 to 1868, but technical difficulties with the
production of cellulose nitrate led to the collapse
of the enterprise and the initiative passed to the
United States.

The stimulus for the development of plastics
in the United States arose from a world shortage
of ivory, which, coupled with rapidly increasing
demand, had forced up the price dramatically.
In 1863 a manufacturer of billiard balls sponsored a competition for the development of an
acceptable substitute, following which John Wes-
ley Hyatt, a printer, and his brother Isaiah eventually resolved the problems associated with cellulose nitrate in about 1869 and the American
Celanese Corporation was formed to exploit
their invention. The new product, under the
trade name "Celluloid," was used universally
from the 1870s until about 1930. The chief advantages of celluloid were its flexibility and resistance to wear. The main disadvantages were
that it was highly inflammable and deteriorated
in sunlight. A feature of celluloid was that a wide
range of colors could be achieved by the addition
of suitable fillers.

Celluloid was successfully employed for a
large variety of small articles, notably thimbles,
but because the early manufacturers were concerned to imitate ivory many early celluloid
thimbles were cream-colored and collectors can
easily be misled by so-called ivory thimbles. The
characteristic features of celluloid thimbles are
that they normally (but not always) have a squarish thin-walled cross section and that they may
be marked with a size number either round the
rim or inside at the top. They are also relatively
light in weight and have a shiny appearance. If
still in doubt, the sure way to find out whether a
thimble is made of celluloid is to touch it with a

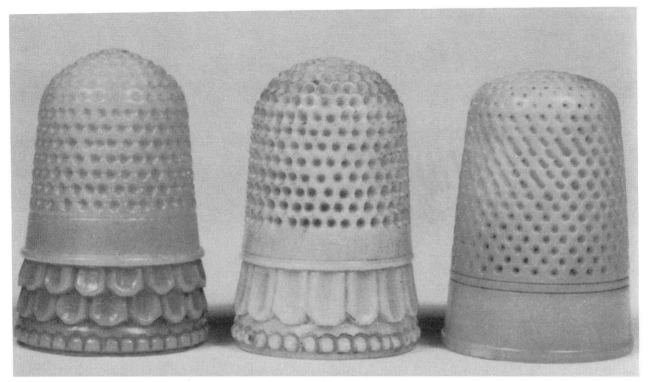

Left and center, **ivory;** *right,* **early plastic.** *Private collection*

red-hot needle. Care must be taken because celluloid, as already mentioned, is highly inflammable and of course the thimble will be marked, but celluloid gives off camphor fumes and the smell of camphor is unmistakable. Two of the earlier companies concerned with the development of celluloid thimbles were the Celluloid Fancy Goods Co. of Newark, N.J., which took out a patent dated 17 February 1880 concerning apparatus for and process of forming thimble blanks of celluloid and other materials, and the Lignoid Fancy Article Manufacturing Co., also of Newark, N.J., which took out another patent dated 2 November 1880 covering dies for moulding thimbles from celluloid or other materials.

About the same time attempts were made to develop thimbles made of rubber-based and like materials, including gutta-percha, which is a substance similar to rubber but somewhat harder and is derived from the juice of trees found in Malaysia. Already by 1857, C. Iles had patented the use of gutta-percha for lining thimbles, and it is claimed that gutta-percha was also used to make thimbles themselves, but if so they were not successful and failed to command accept-

ance. More practical was vulcanite, a plastic type substance derived from the vulcanization process discovered by Charles Goodyear whereby rubber mixed with sulphur is hardened under heat. Thimbles were made of vulcanite and it was reported that embroiderers "usually prefer ivory or vulcanite thimbles."[2] Moreover, in 1905 H. M. Arparian patented (No. 21630) the manufacture of thimbles made of vulcanite or vulcanized rubber of such thickness that while giving sufficient protection, they would after a short time become bedded to the finger of the user. Nevertheless it seems that vulcanite thimbles were never really popular and never challenged the position of celluloid.

Following the introduction of celluloid, two other plastics were developed which attracted the interest of thimble manufacturers. One was bakelite, a thermo-setting molding product pioneered by Leo Hendrick Baekeland, a Belgian-born American chemist whose discovery led to the foundation of the Bakelite Corporation in 1910. Bakelite is based on phenolic resins which are made by reacting phenol and formaldehyde together with heat in the presence of a suitable catalyst. An appropriate filler such as

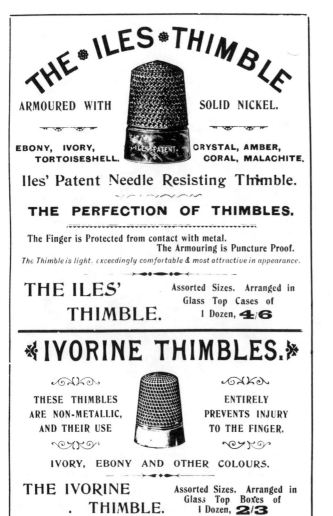

Iles advertisement mentioning Ivorine plastic thimbles. *Private collection*

wood flour is added to the ground resin and the resulting powder is molded into shape under pressure. Thimbles made of bakelite are likely to have the same weight and density as heavy wood and to be either dark brown or black. They can be mistaken for closegrained wood except that the grain is too close, the finish is too regular and the walls too thin to be anything else but plastic. At least one series of bakelite thimbles was made to simulate Irish bog oak and the thimbles bear Irish town designations.

The other plastic to challenge celluloid for the making of thimbles was casein, which is made by reacting casein from milk with formaldehyde. It was used mostly from 1920 to 1940. Casein is a generic term covering a range of different products which in England have included Dorcasine, Erinoid, Keronyx, and Lactoid; in the United

States, Ameroid and Galorn; and in Germany, Galalite. All caseins are distinguished by their wide and brilliant color range and by their susceptibility to high polish. They were produced as an imitation of both ivory and tortoise shell but their use was limited to small articles such as thimbles because of poor water resistance limits. Thimbles made of Erinoid and Galalite are known to exist.

Because plastic thimbles do not have the same appeal for collectors as thimbles made from some of the more traditional materials, it is tempting to regard them as a cheap substitute, but this is not entirely correct. Plastic thimbles have certain advantages of their own such as, for instance, the fact that they are light and clean and do not oxidize. They are also pleasant to the touch. A plastic thimble feels smooth and warm and is preferred by those users who suffer from arthritis or rheumatism and who may find metal thimbles unpleasantly cold. The main disadvantage is that the resistance to puncture and the break strength is limited. Additionally, the early celluloid thimbles suffered from the drawback that they were highly inflammable, but this was overcome with the development of nonflam celluloid which was to prove an important step forward.

The Cupid thimble with heart-shaped celluloid thimble case. *Private collection*

158

Cellulose acetate, or nonflam celluloid, was first produced in 1894 for certain specialized purposes but it was not until 1926 that American Celanese developed a form of cellulose acetate which could be given a wider application. Celluloid, being cellulose nitrate, is related to cellulose acetate: both are based on cellulose, but whereas celluloid has the characteristics of nitric acid, that is, nitrocellulose or guncotton, which is a well-known explosive, its close relative cellulose acetate is based on acetic acid which is nonflammable.

The introduction of cellulose acetate powder in 1929 coincided with the development of the injection molding machine, and these together came to provide the foundation of the modern thermoplastic industry. Thimble-makers were quick to seize on the advantages of injection molding and used it extensively during the 1930s and 1940s. The raw material was cellulose acetate in the form of granules, which was heated electrically and forced under pressure through narrow nozzles into a cold injection mold. The granulated material would become plastic at about 80°C but it was heated to 140°C. It solidified immediately in the steel molds and the molding was ejected automatically by an ejection device operating vertically from under the mold. In a typical molding machine the thimbles would be produced eight at a time and would come out of the mold attached to each other. They would therefore need to be separated either mechanically or by hand. The thimbles were then placed individually on the end of a rotating spigot and the indentations were applied to the sides in the same manner as with a metal thimble. There was no need to apply indentations to the top of the thimbles, as these were embossed as part of the molding process. They were not, however, applied to the sides, as this would have prevented the thimbles from sliding out of the mold, and it was necessary therefore that each thimble should be finished individually. The thimbles were then subjected to a first check, after which they were polished with the help of a rotating cloth polisher and then passed on to a final control, thus completing the production process. The hourly production of an injection molding machine working on the above principle was about three to seven gross thimbles, depending on the size, which assuming a

working day of seven hours implied a capacity of between one and two million thimbles per annum.

It will be evident from the above that thimble manufacturers were not slow to take advantage of the possibilities which the use of plastics could offer them, and they even developed techniques and practices of their own. Charles Iles, for instance, took out patents covering molded thimbles in casein and celluloid under the name of Ivorene. Similarly, Charles Horner became involved in the manufacture of casein products. Later, with the development of nonflammable celluloid acetate, some firms, including again Charles Iles, switched to buying moldings in bulk which they finished on their own account, while others, such as Gebrüder Gabler, chose to purchase a molding machine and to make their own moldings. Gebrüder Gabler sold their cellulose-acetate thimbles under the brand name of Rillo. Either way, so long as the indentations needed to be applied separately, the manufacture of plastic thimbles continued to fall within the province of the specialized thimble manufacturers, but with the emergence of polystyrene this situation was to change completely.

Polystyrene was originally discovered in England in the early 1820s, but it never gained commercial application, and it was left to chemists in the United States to recognize its possibilities and to develop its full potential. The Dow Chemical Company and the Bakelite Company were responsible for bringing it on the market just before the Second World War, and it has grown from strength to strength ever since. It has been used for thimble making for at least twenty years on a regular basis. Polystyrene thimbles are made in special 8 or 16 capacity molds, using a screw-top injection barrel with several tons of pressure applied to force the hot mixture into the molds. Water is used for the cooling process. The thimbles are then ejected from the molds and the telltale nipples and any flaring is cut off at the top or at the side rim of the thimbles, depending on the design of the mold. The main departure from the prewar injection molding machine is that the molds have been improved and the design of the thimbles simplified so that it is now possible to produce a thimble complete with all necessary indentations which does not require any further processing

Plastic thimbles of the mid-twentieth century. *Private collection*

on the lathe. Polystyrene thimbles are usually, made in shades of pink, blue, yellow, white, cream, etcetera, which are chosen so that any printing which it may be desired to add will stand out clearly round the rim. A special rounded roller printing stamp is made to print such lettering as may be required.

The introduction of a process capable of producing thimbles complete with all necessary indentations resulted in the manufacture of plastic thimbles, moving from the traditional thimble-makers to specialized plastics manufacturers, who produce thimbles much as they do any other object made of plastics. Quite obviously a traditional thimble-maker making only thimbles cannot compete with the specialized plastics manufacturers, who are able to spread the cost of their expensive molding machines over a wide range of products. In the United States there are perhaps a half dozen or more firms capable of making polystyrene thimbles, and the only limiting factor is the cost of designing and building suitable molds. What applies to the United States goes for other countries, and notably the Far East, where plastic thimbles are made in large quantities and exported to Europe and elsewhere. It is understood that other plastics may also be used nowadays for thimble making, including phenol furfural resins, urea formal-

dehyde resins, melamine formaldehyde resins, acrylic resins, and polyamide resins, but from the point of view of thimble collectors it is hardly necessary to distinguish between them and they are only mentioned for the sake of completeness.

The early plastics manufacturers were chiefly concerned to emulate the properties of bone and ivory and were therefore happy to produce plain, cream-colored thimbles with little or no decoration. Thus celluloid and casein thimbles were normally left undecorated save possibly for an odd circle round the base in red or black or the name Iles or Abel Morrall, which appears occasionally. It was not until the interwar years that more positive efforts were made to make plastic thimbles look more attractive, and one solution was to paint them round the rim with posies of flowers and other floral embellishments. Halex is a brand name sometimes encountered on thimbles decorated in this way: one thimble is decorated with a rudimentary landscape scene in black and white and another with a sedan chair and liveried porters in polychrome. But hand-painting plastic thimbles was an extravagance, and not surprisingly thimbles were also decorated with transfer designs. The more common are "Forget me not" with a garland of the flowers of that name and "The

160

Contemporary plastic thimbles. Note nature of indentations. *Private collection*

Cupid" with cherubs and garlands of roses. "The Cupid" was a particularly popular thimble, the best examples of which are to be found in their own small heart-shaped celluloid thimble cases lined with red satin. The design has persisted and may be found on some contemporary polysterene thimbles, but the latter are usually made in such bright and vivid colors that it is pointless to attempt any decoration and they are usually left plain and unadorned.

Various attempts have been made to improve the designs of plastic thimbles. They may embody special features, such as stepped rings or helical spirals inside the thimble to give a better grip on the finger, or they may have some ribs placed vertically down the sides to prevent the thimble from rolling about. The design of plastic thimbles, however, is dominated by the requirements of the molding process, so that they tend to have a flattened top and a squarish cross section. Moreover, in order that the molding should come out of the mold more easily, the indentations featured on the side of thimbles up to and including the Second World War have been replaced by stepped vertical grooves or equivalent pattern. There is therefore little originality, and apart from color most plastic thimbles are depressingly similar.

Because polystyrene thimbles can be mass-produced at very lost cost, they are ideal for advertising and are widely used for this purpose in the United States. Not only are they used for straightforward commercial advertising but also to promote political candidates and even as a means to raise funds for charities. There is also a class of polystyrene thimbles known as "personal" thimbles, which bear the name and address of the owner and which American lady thimble collectors use in the nature of a small gift or as a visiting card.

In Japan where it is customary to work the needle forward with the back of the finger, there are specially designed plastic ring-type thimbles known as Yubi-Nuki. These are made in two parts, consisting of an adjustable band of leather or plastic which fits round the second joint of the finger and holds in place a small shield of hardened plastic, which is the part that actually protects the finger. Alternatively, they consist more simply of an expandable ring of some metal such as aluminum with overlapping ends and an indented front section.

One of the few novelty thimbles made of plastic is that old-established favourite, the thimble in the shape of the top of a finger. As if it was not of sufficiently bad taste already, some of the colors—bright pinks and greens— have to be seen to be believed. One specimen is inscribed inside "Betterwear—free gift" and was made to be given away by door-to-door salesmen peddling brushes and household goods. Another is vivid pink with a bright red nail. The Germans also have their finger-shaped thimbles including the so-called Atomic thimble, which was made in Germany immediately after the Second World War and which has "Ato 17 DBP" embossed on the rim. DBP stands for Deutsches Bundesland Patent and indicates that the design is registered with the German patents office. Various rough and ill-finished plastic thimbles are sometimes made in the Far East (Hong Kong) as tokens or cheap gifts for Christmas crackers and the like.

To sum up, plastic thimbles have a long and respectable history which stretches back further than many collectors realize. Because of the circumstances at the time they started, they were originally produced to look very much like ivory or bone, but it would be wrong to succumb to the prejudice that a plastic thimble represents a cheap replacement or ersatz copy of a more valuable article. Plastic thimbles have evolved on their own account and are strictly functional. Unfortunately they are also a mass-produced article and as such have only a limited appeal, but they cannot be ignored.

NOTES

1. Mme P. W. Cocheris, *Histoires sérieuses sur une pointe d'aiguille* (Paris, 1886).
2. C. W. Paulson Townsend, *Embroidery; or, The Crafts of the Needle* (London, 1907).

Tailors' Thimbles

HISTORICAL EVIDENCE SUGGESTS THAT THE RING-type thimble with an open top such as is used by tailors may have predated the domed type thimble. Certainly most of the early Byzantine thimbles excavated at Corinth have open ends, but that is not to say that they were necessarily used by tailors. What it does suggest, however, and what is confirmed by the fact that metal thimbles during the Middle Ages had a bare crown free of indentations, is that sewing with the side of the finger was more widespread. Subsequently, it seems that with the introduction of better and finer needles a growing number of needle-workers found it more convenient to sew with the tip of the thimble, but nevertheless a minority, including tailors because they used larger needles or for some other reason, preferred to continue in the traditional fashion. That there is a fine dividing line between the two methods of sewing is proved by the many silver thimbles which are to be found with signs of wear round the sides. There are obviously some needlewomen who, while employing a domed type silver thimble, prefer nevertheless to use it sideways, and there is therefore nothing strange in certain classes of needle-workers choosing to sew the same way.

A careful examination of the thimbles pictured in the Mendelschen Institute illustration (see color plate) reveals that two of the seven thimbles illustrated have an open top, which confirms that during the fourteenth century there was a demand for open top thimbles. It is possible that these were intended for tailors and

it is equally possible that in the sixteenth century, the Spaniards who differentiated between tailors' thimbles and thimbles for women (see "Thimbles in America") did so because tailors' thimbles had an open top. On the other hand, when the tailors' guild of Nuremberg commissioned some goblets in 1586, these were designed in the shape of domed type thimbles and the fact is that despite the many references to tailors' thimbles—and there are many, because the thimble was the attribute of the tailor—we have little idea what kind of thimble a tailor normally used. We may assume that in accordance with tradition tailors used open top thimbles but it is not until 1804 that the question stands resolved:

> The Tools requisite in the business of the taylor are very few and inexpensive, the shears for the foreman, who stands to his work, for the others a pair of scissars, a thimble, and needles of different sizes. In the thimble there is this peculiarity that it is open at both ends.[1]

Tailors, however, are not the only ones to use a sewing ring in preference to a domed type thimble. They are used by all those trades in whose method of sewing it is the side of the finger which serves to exert pressure on the needle. During the early part of the eighteenth century, according to Savary des Bruslons, these included harness makers, saddlers, upholsterers, shoemakers and the like.[2] Some of these trades have lost their importance and others are now

Silver-gilt cup commissioned by Tailors' Guild of Nuremberg and made by Elias Lenker in 1586. *Germanisches Landesmuseum, Nuremberg*

almost wholly mechanized, but where hand-sewing is still practiced, a ring-type thimble continues to be used. For obvious reasons thimbles of this kind need to be strong and hard wearing and they are usually made of base metal and without decoration.

The early sewing rings that have survived are made of bronze and may be of various designs ranging from a narrow ring, with at most three or four rows of indentations, to a broad tapering cylinder somewhat resembling a topless thimble. Later, bronze appears to have given way to brass and iron, and by the seventeenth century the design had become more consistent. There is reason to believe that John Lofting made sewing rings, because under a deed dated 20 July 1693, which is to be found in the archives of the city of Amsterdam, Laurens Borger, maker of thimbles

Brass sewing rings, mostly sixteenth century or earlier. *Private collection*

in Utrecht, undertook that his eighteen-year-old son Pieter Borger should go to London to work for Lofting making sewing rings *(naairingen)* and brass thimbles. Otherwise the first manufacturer to be recorded as making sewing rings is Bernhard von der Becke, who in 1712 set up a mill at Sundwig for the purpose. There is no record of how they were made, but a hundred years later there is an account of the method of manufacture of iron sewing rings as practiced at the Joh. Caspar Rumpe Works at Altena to be found in an anonymous travel journal dated 1845. The starting point was sheet metal, and it seems that Rumpe were fortunate in obtaining a special type of iron sheeting in rolls, which gave them an advantage over the competition. The thimble rings were cut from the rolls, presumably mechanically by means of a punch, and bent into shape by boys. The joints were then soldered by girls with so-called hard solder, which was a copper-zinc alloy looking somewhat like brass but which could be used to solder brass or iron. The rings were then turned on a lathe and a ring of fine brass sheet, which had also been cut from a roll, was added by pressure. The indentations were impressed by forcing the sewing ring against an engraved roller and finally, after turning, came the finishing, such as polishing and the rounding off of the inside edge.

Because iron rusts, not many of these older iron sewing rings have survived. From the few which are available, however, it is obvious that they closely resembled the modern sewing ring and that the design has remained largely unchanged for the last three hundred years. Nowadays tailors normally use an iron sewing ring with a zinc lining, whereas shoemakers prefer an iron sewing ring with a brass lining. In both cases the lining is rolled round the rim at one end and the indentations are necessarily large on account of the thickness of the material being sewn,

which necessitates large needles. Sewing rings may also be lined with a pewterlike material. Lesser quality sewing rings are sometimes made of aluminum alloy.

The use of sewing rings is not necessarily confined to those engaged in heavy work. Whereas in Britain and in Germany sewing rings are usually made of base metal, in the United States they may be made of silver or even of gold. They may also be decorated with some design or motto round the base. Obviously sewing rings of this kind are intended for needlewomen preferring to stitch with the side of the finger.

In the Far East, where sewing techniques differ, sewing rings of one kind or another are commonly used for household purposes. The Chinese use ring-type thimbles which are usually made of base metal but which may also be made of silver. The Japanese also use ring-type thimbles. Nowadays these are usually made of leather, plastic, or base metal, but in earlier times they were made of padded cardboard (see "Fabric Thimbles").

At the other extreme, for really heavy sewing

Expandable silver sewing ring with design of a bird, Chinese, nineteenth century. Height 1.2 cm. *Bethnal Green Museum*

165

such as sailmaking or leather work, a palm-protector may be used in preference to a thimble. It will be recalled that in Rudyard Kipling's *Captains Courageous,* "Harvey spent his leisure hours . . . learning to use a needle and palm." The sailor's palm (*Handplatte der Segelmacher* in German) was already well known in the eighteenth century when it even featured in a naval dictionary: "The palm is formed of a piece of leather or canvas, on the middle of which is fixed a round plate of iron of an inch in diameter, whose surface is pierced with a number of small holes to catch the head of the sail needle. The leather is formed so as to encircle the hand and button on the back thereof, while the iron remains in the palm."[3] The modern palm-protector remains substantially unchanged except that nowadays there is a surprising variety of styles and makes. There are adjustable or nonadjustable models and there are models for the right or left hand. A nonadjustable palm is usually soaked thoroughly and then allowed to dry to the shape of the hand. To sew with a palm, the needle is held firmly seated on the palm save when it is being pulled through the material being sewn. The wrist is held rigid and the pressure comes from the arm.

NOTES

1. *The Book of Trades; or, Library of the Useful Arts,* ed. Tabart & Co. (London, 1804), pt. 2, "The Taylor."
2. Jacques Savary des Bruslons, *Dictionnaire universel du commerce* (Paris, 1723-30).
3. William Falconer, *An Universal Dictionary of the Marine* (London, 1769).

Children's Thimbles

A WELL-KNOWN THIMBLE, "DIE FLEISSIGE FAMILIE" (The industrious family), which was produced by Gebrüder Gabler after the design of a Professor Christaller of Stuttgart, depicts a little girl helping a lady to wind wool, a small boy playing with the household cat, and a third child watching her mother at her needlework. It was justifiably popular and serves as a reminder that a generation or two ago the members of a family lived more closely together. Children were brought up alongside domestic activities to a much greater extent than they are today and they relied more on household resources for their entertainment. In particular because of the large amount of sewing which had to be done, a child might spend much of its time watching its mother at work. Its attention would focus on the thimble, partly because it was a small object in constant use and partly because of its added attraction as a maternal possession. From an early age small children would reach out for their mother's thimble and the wise mother would take care that when not in use it was put away safely. One of the earliest recorded mentions of a thimble concerns a miracle worked by Saint Hyacinth, a Polish saint of the early thirteenth century, who is reputed to have saved the life of a four-year-old child who had swallowed a thimble.

Puer quator annorum . . . casu Digitarium, alias naperstek, deglutivit.[1]

As the child grew a little older the thimble would continue as a familiar object. It would feature in fairy tales such as Hans Andersen's "Thimbelina," about a child who was so small that she had a walnut shell for a cradle, or in stories such as the Grimm brothers' "Thumbling," about a tailor's son, who was also so small that on one occasion he hid under a thimble. It would also feature in nursery rhymes such as that of Mother Goose:

Cushy cow bonny, let down thy milk,
And I will give thee a gown of silk;
A gown of silk and a silver tee,
If thou wilt let down thy milk for me.

Moreover the thimble, being always ready at hand, was a convenient object to use as a token or otherwise serve in nursery games. The game of hunt-the-thimble was already played in the eighteenth century and remains popular to this day.

As a girl became a little older she would start with sewing lessons. Small fingers need small thimbles and a pretty thimble might be given as an encouragement or else as a reward for good work. Sewing ranked with the three R's and because most little girls had a thimble, and not a few might mislay it, the subject might come up again when learning to read:

A place for everything

Mary: I wish you would lend me your thimble, I can never find my own.
Sarah: Why is it, Mary, you can never find it.

167

Design for Gebrüder Gabler's thimble "Die fleissige Familie," circa 1920. *Private collection*

I have a place for everything and I put everything in its place when I have done with it.

Mary: I am ashamed. Before tonight I will have a place for everything. You have taught me a lesson.[2]

Moral tales of this kind were a feature of early nineteenth-century education and the thimble features in another tale called "The Silver Thimble,"[3] which was written for somewhat older children. The thimble is the narrator at the opening of the story:

Myself and a numerous progeny were the offspring of a union founded on rational principles; our parents, on one side renowned for worth and beauty, on the other for stability and firmness. At a famous manufacturing town in Yorkshire we were first ushered into the world; and from the hands of labour, more than high descent, derive that reputation which we have since acquired among mankind.

One fine summer's morning I found myself, with many others of a similar species, though of different parentage, enclosed within the narrow limits of a small travelling box. . . .

The thimble thus starts its journey in a peddler's pack. Three ladies appear:

. . . Miss Clara Steady, wishing to buy something, said she did not recollect any thing she wanted, unless it was a thimble. Several were shown to her, some of silver fillagree, others of highly polished silver, with blue enamelled edges, inlaid with curious mottos, but none of them seemed to please her. . . .
Just as my master was closing his box, almost angry at the trouble she had given him without buying any thing that was shown her, she espied me, and my companions in our obscure station, and reaching out her delicate little hand begged he would show her "Those thim-

"Die fleissige Familie" thimble. Height 2.2 cm. *Private collection*

bles in the corner"; adding "she had not till that minute observed them."

"What the steel-topped ones!" said Miss Careless, "I hope you are not going to buy one of those clumsy awkward things." "Why not?" returned Miss Steady; "I think they look quite as well as the others, and I like them best because they are more durable." "What signifies the strength of a thimble; it will last only till it is lost, and so will any other; I believe I have had a half a dozen within these twelve months."

"You are very heedless then, I think, my dear," said Miss Prudentia Colville, who had listened attentively to their discourse. "Clara is, I believe, more careful, and I daresay she is also aware of another advantage which a steel top has over a silver one."

"Yes, Madam" replied Miss Steady. "I have observed that they do not soil the thread nearly so much as those that are all silver, and that is the reason why I prefer them."

The thimble leaves the peddler's pack; "to become the property of a young lady, who, at ten years of age, possessed more solidity of judgment than many who have attained twice that number."

The action then develops with high drama. The thimble gets lost in a field. It is found by Little Patty, daughter of Dame Primrose. Little Patty seeks to find the rightful owner but Miss Smallwits wrongfully claims it as her own. The thimble is seen in the possession of Miss Smallwits by Miss Steady, who disputes its ownership. Miss Smallwits is confounded, Little Patty is praised for her honesty, and right in the person of Miss Steady prevails over wrongdoing, thus concluding the tale of the silver thimble.

There are several features of interest in the above story, notably the reference to silver filigree and to blue enameled silver thimbles, which must obviously have been fairly common at the end of the eighteenth century if they could be found in a peddler's pack. The reference to a famous manufacturing town in Yorkshire is puzzling. Presumably this would be a town in the West Riding and the most obvious would be Sheffield, but no thimble-maker is known from that area. Thimble collectors who might wish to own a copy of "The Silver Thimble" may be dis-

Eighteenth century children's thimbles made of brass. *At left,* **adult size for comparison, height 2.0 cm.** *Private collection*

Children's thimbles. *Left to right:* eighteenth-century English silver; eighteenth-century ivory; eighteenth-century brass; early-nineteenth-century English silver; early-nineteenth-century English silver with steel top; adult size English silver with steel top circa 1820 for comparison, height 2.4 cm; nineteenth-century bone; nineteenth century with steel top and Russian hallmark; nineteenth-century brass with steel top; nineteenth-century Dutch silver; doll's silver thimble by James Fenton hallmarked 1907; nineteenth-century silver early railway design. *Private collection*

appointed. The Newbery series of children's books is greatly sought after by book collectors, and although a second edition of "The Silver Thimble" was published in 1803, copies are rare and expensive.

The high moral tone of these stories and the appeal to the finer feelings of the youthful readers could easily lead one to overlook the fact that if exhortation failed, the alternative was severe punishment. Discipline was strictly enforced and in this connection the thimble might assume a different significance. On the occasion of milder transgressions the rapping of a thimble-covered finger on the sewing table might serve to denote impatience but it could also serve as a painful mode of emphasis, as happened to Pip, who, it will be recalled, went upstairs "with his head still tingling from Mrs. Joe's thimble having played the tambourine upon it to accompany her last words."[4] In more extreme cases it could become a form of punishment and during the eighteenth century it became the practice in small boys' or girls' village schools, which were known as dame-schools, for the teacher or dame to rap naughty or inattentive children on the head with a thimble-covered finger. This punishment was known as "thimel-pie" or "thimmy-pie" making, and the thimble itself was referred to as "dame's thimmel." "Missus pullin me ears, broddin me with knittin needle and giving me sa mich thimal-pie."[5] The practice was not confined to Britain: "And God forgive me, I cracked Tom's head with my thimble, poor boy . . . " lamented Aunt Polly after Tom Sawyer had run away—which, if we are to believe Mark Twain,

confirms that about 1840 it was also current in the United States.

Coming down to more recent times, older children might graduate to the delights of Lewis Carroll's *Alice in Wonderland.* They would read of the episode when having handed out the prizes for the race that never was, Alice finds herself without a prize:

> "But she must have a prize herself, you know," said the Mouse.

The Dodo presenting Alice with a thimble. After an illustration by Sir John Tenniel (1820–1914). *Private collection*

170

"Of course," the Dodo replied very gravely.

"What else have you got in your pocket" he went on, turning to Alice.

"Only a thimble," said Alice sadly.

"Hand it over here," said the Dodo.

Then they all crowded round her once more, while the Dodo solemnly presented the thimble, saying "We beg your acceptance of this elegant thimble"; and, when he finished this short speech, they all cheered.

Or else they might read about Sir James Barrie's Peter Pan and learn of the misunderstanding which arose between Peter and Wendy. Peter did not know about kisses, so that when Wendy said she would give Peter a kiss if he liked, he held out his hand expectantly.

"Surely you know what a kiss is?" she asked, aghast.

"I shall know when you give it to me," he replied stiffly; and not to hurt his feelings she gave him a thimble.

"And I know you meant to be kind," she said, relenting, "so you may give me a kiss."

"For the moment she had forgotten his ignorance about kisses.

"I thought you would want it back," he said a little bitterly, and offered to return the thimble.

"Oh dear," said the nice Wendy. "I didn't mean a kiss. I meant a thimble."

"What's that?"

"And so she kissed him and Peter said "How nice!" and he began to give thimbles in return and ever afterwards he called a kiss a thimble and a thimble a kiss.[6]

The Peter Pan story was made into a play which ran with great success in the United States. The American actress Maude Adams starred in more than 1,500 performances, and Simons Bros. made a thimble inscribed "A thimble from Maude Adams," which was intended for her fans.

This same incident from *Peter and Wendy* no doubt also provided the idea behind a traveler's sample case which was sold in March 1977 at Christie's Auction Rooms in South Kensington which contained seven silver thimbles with the names of the Lost Boys. Peter Pan enthusiasts will recall the Lost Boys, who, in their fur coats, looked more like bears than boys and were anxiously awaiting Peter's return. There were six of them: Slightly Soiled, the eldest, then came Tootles, and Nibs, and Curly, and the twins who were so much alike that one name did for both

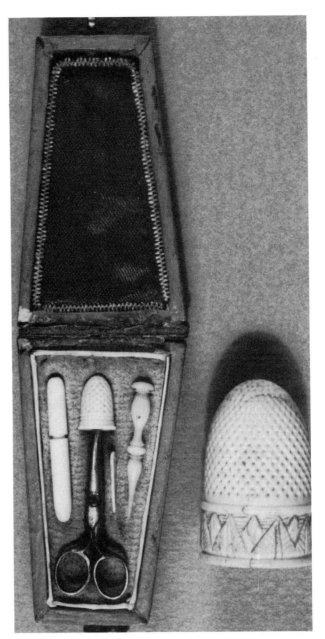

Miniature sewing compendium. Alongside eighteenth-century ivory thimble for scale, height 2.8 cm. *Private collection*

Design for "Der Jugend" by Soergel und Stollmeyer circa 1920. This was Soergel und Stollmeyer's answer to Gebrüder Gabler's "Die fleissige Familie." *Private collection*

of them, so each was called Twin. Six, that is, plus Peter, and each represented by a different thimble.

All small thimbles are not necessarily children's thimbles. Very small thimbles, far too small to fit even a child's finger, were made as charms to hang on bracelets; others were made for use in the dolls' house, and a third category served as tokens for children's games, the latter usually made of base metal and inscribed "For a good girl." These should not be confused with genuine children's thimbles, which normally resemble the thimbles worn by grown-ups and like them are often engraved or otherwise decorated around the base. Small silver thimbles of a size suitable for children may be mixed into a pudding as pudding charms.

NOTES

1. *Mirac S. Hyacinthi,* tom. 3 Aug., p. 370, col. 2. *Naperstek* is Polish for a thimble.
2. *McGuffey's Second Reader* (1836).
3. "The Silver Thimble," by the author of *Instructive Tales,* etc., (London: E. Newbery, 1801).
4. Charles Dickens, *Great Expectations* (1860–61).
5. Tom Treddlehoyle (Charles Rodgers), *The Barinsla Folk's Annual, 1847.*
6. J. M. Barrie, *Peter and Wendy* (London, 1911).

Commemorative Thimbles

ENGLISHMEN HAVE LONG COMMEMORATED THEIR history by decorating household objects with appropriate designs or inscriptions, and ever since the seventeenth century and possibly before, royal events have inspired the production of commemorative thimbles. If we disregard Elizabethan thimbles inscribed "God save the Queene" as more likely to be inspired by patriotism than to commemorate any special event, it is likely that the earliest recorded examples are some silver thimbles with medallion portraits of Charles II and Queen Catherine of Braganza which were presumably made to commemorate the royal wedding in 1662. The British Museum have one and also the Museum of London, and there is at least one other in a private collection. However, it was not until the nineteenth century that the commemorative thimble really came into its own. The reasons are fairly obvious: until the nineteenth century the population of England was still relatively small, it was widely spread in rural areas, and it had little money to spare. Means of communication were still rudimentary, news traveled slowly, and the mass of the people could hardly be expected to celebrate events about which they were inadequately informed.

By 1840 this situation had changed completely. The population was increasing and becoming more wealthy. The railways were revolutionizing communications, newspapers were reaching a wider public, and improved methods of manufacture based on the steam engine made it possible to envisage the production of large

Silver—decorated with two struck oval profile busts of Charles II and Queen Catherine of Braganza. Bears maker's mark. Probably made to commemorate royal wedding in 1662. *Private collection*

numbers of specially designed items such as thimbles at a relatively low price. Whereas Sketchley's and Adams's *Tradesman's True Guide,* dated 1770, included the names of only five thimble-makers, Wrighton's *Dictionary of Birmingham* for 1839 recorded no less than twenty-four. Competition was evidently growing and means of increasing sales were no doubt welcome. In these circumstances the climate for

173

Silver—birth of Prince of Wales, 1841. *Private collection*

commemorative thimbles was favorable and the early trickle soon became a flood.

The first recorded thimble which was actively commemorative as opposed to simply carrying the image of king and queen was a silver thimble engraved "Long Live King William, Long Live Queen Adelaide," which presumably dates from the coronation of King William IV in 1831. Thereafter during the reign of Queen Victoria royal weddings, royal births, and other royal occasions inspired countless designs. Among the chief events commemorated in this way are the following:

—Coronation of Queen Victoria 1837
—Wedding of Queen Victoria and Prince Albert 1840
—Birth of Prince of Wales 1841
—Queen Victoria's Visit to Ireland 1849
—Wedding of Prince of Wales 1863
—Queen Victoria's Golden Jubilee 1887
—Queen Victoria's Diamond Jubilee 1897

So popular did commemorative thimbles become during the reign of Queen Victoria that they were produced to mark the openings of new enterprises such as Brunel's Thames Tunnel (1843), the Great Exhibition (1851), the Dublin Exhibition (1853), the transfer of the Crystal Palace to Sydenham (1854), and the Kensington Exhibition (1862). In a more somber mood, the death of the Duke of Wellington (1852) was commemorated by a thimble.

The tradition of commemorating royal events by means of a special thimble continued into the twentieth century with the Coronation of King Edward VII and Queen Alexandra in 1902. This was followed by the Coronation of King George V in 1911, the Silver Jubilee of King George V in

Silver—death of the Duke of Wellington, 1852. *Private collection*

174

1935, the Coronation of King George VI in 1937, and the Coronation of Queen Elizabeth II in 1953. Special thimbles were also made to mark the investiture of the Prince of Wales in 1969, the wedding of HRH Princess Anne in 1973 and the Jubilee of Queen Elizabeth II in 1978.

The most recent is that of the wedding of HRH the Prince of Wales to Lady Diana Spencer in 1981. A great variety of thimbles were produced on this occasion, among which the most noteworthy featured as part of a collection of silver objects specially designed by Gerald Benney for the London jewelers Mappin and Webb. One side shows the Prince of Wales's badge of ostrich feathers and the other side, the crest of the Spencer family with a continuous band of decorative strap-work joining the two. As will be seen from the illustration on the next page, it is original while retaining a functional character.

British commemorative thimbles being usually made of silver, it is relevant to mention that on occasion special hallmarks have been authorized to commemorate some special event. For instance, from 1933 to 1935, a Jubilee Mark, showing the profile heads of King George V and Queen Mary, commemorates their silver jubilee, and the profile of Queen Elizabeth II was struck on all silver in 1952 and 1953 to mark her coronation. A special hallmark was also struck to mark her silver jubilee. Silver bearing these hallmarks is greatly prized, and of course so are

Silver—Liberty Bell, commemorating Anniversary of American Independence, Simons Bros. Height 2.0 cm. *Private collection*

commemorative thimbles which bear the special marks in question.

Besides silver thimbles, commemorative thimbles of a cheaper kind were also made in brass, nickel, or other base metal, and in this category must be included a cupronickel thimble made to commemorate the Great Exhibition (1851) and a brass thimble made to commemorate the British Empire Exhibition at Wembley (1924). Gold commemorative thimbles have also been made, but these are rare and correspondingly more valuable.

For obvious reasons commemorative thimbles never enjoyed the same popularity in the United States, though the Liberty Bell thimble is in many ways the most attractive of them all. In 1892 Simons Brothers patented a thimble designed as a replica of the Liberty Bell, inscribed "Proclaim Liberty in the Land to All Inhabitants. By order of the Assembly of Pennsy. in Phila 1752" (patent No. 21844). This was sold on the occasion of the Columbian Exposition and the design was brought back into use during the First World War to help the sales of Liberty Bonds and the like. It is said that when the Liberty Bell thimble was issued, Simons sent one to the second Mrs. Woodrow Wilson, who accepted it, explaining that she almost never accepted

Coronation of H.M. Queen Elizabeth II, 1953. Souvenir thimble resting on emery needle cleaner made from the silk velvet used for the purple robe of state and embroidered at the Royal School of Needlework. *Private collection*

Silver—Wedding of Prince of Wales, 1982. The crest of the Spencer family is shown in front and the Prince of Wales badge of ostrich feathers features on the reverse. *Private collection*

ternational Exposition of 1939, and appropriately enough another thimble issued to commemorate the Simons Brothers Company's 100th anniversary (1939). The only American manufacturers known to have made commemorative thimbles besides Simons Brothers are Ketcham & McDougall and Goldsmith Stern.

France is another country where commemorative thimbles have been made in this century. Two different designs were engraved to commemorate the canonization of Joan of Arc in 1920, one depicting Joan of Arc as a shepherdess standing among her sheep and the other Joan of Arc with an Angel conveying the message of Saint Michael. These thimbles were originally made in both silver and gold. Collectors should beware, however, because as happened with several other designs engraved in France, the original dies have since been used again for the purpose of making silver thimbles for sale to collectors. Commemorative thimbles are also known to have been designed on the occasion of the Paris Universal Exposition (1889) when the Eiffel Tower was built, for the Paris Universal Exposition (1900), and for the Lyons Exposition (1914).

In Holland the wedding of Queen Wilhelmina to Prince Heinrich of Mecklenburg-Schnerin in 1901 was commemorated by two separate thimbles, one, which was made in France, depicting the queen as a little girl playing with a doll, as a young woman doing embroidery, and as a queen together with the Royal Coat of Arms. A 22 carat version was presented to the queen as a wedding present, and a total of thirty-five 18 carat and one hundred silver thimbles were also made. The other was commissioned by President Paul Kruger of South Africa and made by Gebrüder Gabler based on a design engraved by F. de Vernon. It depicts six young Dutch women busy at their needlework. A gold version was given by President Kruger to Queen Wilhelmina as a wedding present and several thousand silver copies were sold in Holland. In 1909 the birth of Princess (later Queen) Juliana was commemorated with a silver thimble bearing an enamel portrait of a baby with tiny blue bows on the shoulders of its dress. In 1967, a German thimble-maker, Herr Helmut Greif, used the original die to make a copy in silver with an amethyst top, which he presented to Princess Beatrix and Prince Claus on the occasion of the birth of Prince Willem-Alexander.

gifts but would make an exception. The thimble was reissued in 1926 to mark the 150th Anniversary of American Independence. The thimbles in this issue may be recognized because the design includes a cluster of thirteen stars in a circle, absent from the first issue. A further issue was made in 1976 including gold, silver, and pewter, and on this occasion the design also included two asterisks, which did not feature in the original. Besides the Liberty Bell thimble, Simons produced thimbles in two different designs to mark the opening of the Chicago "World's Columbian Exposition 1492–1892," which was held on the occasion of the 400th anniversary of the discovery of America, and in 1904 they produced a thimble to mark the St. Louis World's Fair of that year, depicting men on horseback, a covered wagon, and a steam engine commemorating the hammering of the Golden Spike. A few lesser designs followed, including a thimble commemorating the San Francisco Golden Gate In-

In Spain the wedding of King Alfonso XIII and Princess Eugenia Victoria of Battenberg, which took place in 1906, was also commemorated by a thimble, which depicts the king and the princess surrounded by cupids and with the Royal Coat of Arms. Twenty-five gold thimbles were made, one of which in a gold thimble case engraved with the Spanish Royal Coat of Arms was presented to the royal bride. It is believed that no silver copies were made on this occasion and collectors should beware that silver thimbles in this design are likely to be modern reproductions made in France from the original dies.

Since the Second World War the fashion for thimble collecting has led to the manufacture of a wide range of commemorative thimbles, some of which may be justified but the bulk of which are merely intended to exploit collectors. As in all forms of collecting—porcelain is a good example—some commemorative items are well worth acquiring and may in time become sought-after rarities, but regrettably much of the material which is on offer to thimble collectors falls well below the desirable standards of true worth and quality.

Keepsake Thimbles

THERE IS EVERY REASON TO BELIEVE THAT FROM the time they were first introduced during the sixteenth century, silver thimbles were regarded as an ideal gift to make to a lady. The earliest keepsake thimble on record is dated 1587 and is inscribed in German "To this gift is joined my kindest thoughts," but no doubt the practice of presenting a thimble as a gift must have started earlier. Indeed it was such a popular gift that already by the end of the sixteenth century it was losing much of its novelty, or so we would judge from the following account dated 1616:

> It was a happy age when a man might have wooed his wench with a pair of kid leather gloves, a silver thimble or with a tawdry lace; but now a velvet gown, a chain of pearl, or a coach with four horses will scarcely serve the turn.[1]

Obviously these lines contain some exaggeration, but during the seventeenth century the use of silver thimbles was spreading to a wider range of the population and even if the more wealthy might take a silver thimble for granted, there were those who would be glad to welcome one as a gift. Moreover the appeal of the gift could be enhanced by adding a suitable inscription. Thimbles of this period may be found "cunningly inscribed and writ upon," as for instance one with the motto "A frendes gift" in the Museum of London and another "The gift be small, goodwill to all" in the Greg Collection of Handicrafts in the Manchester Museum. A gift of thimbles is recorded in 1663 when James Dillon, later to become Lord Roscommon, returned from a visit to the Verney family at Claydon and sent two thimbles to Mary Verney and her cousin Doll Leeke "that one should not hurt a fine finger by the making of handkerchiefs, nor the other receive a prick in working my lady's buttons." It would not have been considered seemly for a gentleman to make ladies a gift which was too personal, such as perfume or jewelry, and the thimble served admirably to bridge the rules of etiquette. By the end of the seventeenth century mottoes became less frequent and instead it became the practice for thimbles to be decorated round the rim with two hearts joined together, which were intended to bear initials, and with attendant cupids supporting them. Many thimbles of this kind have survived—so many that it might be thought it was the principal means of decoration—but presumably what happened is that this kind of thimble was cherished as a keepsake, whereas the more commonplace thimbles were simply worn and subsequently discarded.

The spirit of the eighteenth century promoted the thimble to the status of an object of *galanterie.* Small objects such as snuffboxes, cane handles, needlecases, etuis, and of course thimbles may appear trivial to the more serious-minded but they are inseparable from the rococo style. Porcelain was a most appropriate medium and it is in this context that Meissen thimbles need to be judged. Small, precious, and totally impracti-

178

English eighteenth-century enamel. A realistically decorated bird's egg inscribed "We live in hope," with token thimble to match. *Private collection*

cal, a Meissen thimble was an ideal present for a gentleman to give his *dame de coeur*. The inscriptions speak for themselves: "Je pense à vous" or "Mon feu durera toujours." Such inscriptions were usually in French, as befitted the requirements of fashion and elegance, but they might sometimes appear more prosaically in German: "Stich Dich nicht." Other manufacturers imitated Meissen, notably Chelsea, which made thimbles inscribed "Pour ma belle" or "Gage de mon amour."

It is in a kindred spirit that we must read a heroi-comical poem by Allan Ramsay (1686–1758) entitled "The Thimble." Allan Ramsay, who was the father of the well-known painter of the same name, published his poem anonymously in 1743.

A theme sublimer far demands my care,
I sing the Thimble armour of the fair.[2]

The poem is too long to reproduce here but it may be found in Gertrude Whiting's book *Tools and Toys of Stitchery* (see Bibliography). Allan Ramsay's poem created some controversy in the columns of *The Gentleman's Magazine* and led an anonymous contributor to write the following couplet:

Fair Lydia's Thimble, Ramsay, to thy name,
Shall be a passport thro' the gates of Fame.

In the same vein the following contribution

Wooden thimble case in the shape of an egg, inscribed "Love and Loyalty" on regency pink ground. Early nineteenth century. *Private collection*

179

also appeared anonymously in the May 1774 number of the same magazine:

On Stealing a Lady's Thimble

Of silver form'd by Pallas' care
And given to her fav'rite fair;
Inestimable present! true—
Yet with it what shall Cloe do?
Sure beauty ne'er was made to toil?
Alas! 'twou'd Cloe's finger spoil!
Then where's the fault, if Damon take
And keep the treasure—for her sake.
For her dear sake he grasps the prize,
And stands absolved by the skies.

Besides Meissen thimbles, there was a wide range of attractive gifts and toys made during the eighteenth century such as, for instance, combined thimble and needlecases, English enamel thimbles, and a variety of filigree thimbles of different kinds. Gold thimbles were also becoming more widely used and inevitably the status of a plain silver thimble was declining. Nevertheless the latter were still being offered as gifts, and James Woodforde records in his diary that as an undergraduate at Oxford in 1760 he became acquainted with two Oxford girls, Nancy Bignell and her sister Betsy and gave the girls a silver thimble each.[3] A year later he records giving his sister Jenny a present of three yards of ribbon and an ivory thimble; and two years afterward he gave her another present of four

hundred needles, four papers of pins, and two steel-top thimbles which he had bought in Oxford. It will be obvious, however, from the circumstances and nature of the gifts that by the eighteenth century the gift of a thimble was no longer of the same importance.

Improvements in manufacturing techiques at the end of the eighteenth century prepared the way for the mass production of silver and also of gold thimbles, which became more readily available. Until then gift and keepsake thimbles had been made to order to meet individual requirements, but with the introduction of mass production methods thimbles began to be made in standard designs, including designs specifically developed for gift thimbles. There followed a wide range of thimbles of varying patterns made in England during the nineteenth century which bear the words "Forget me not," "A keepsake," or some similar thought. These are usually in silver but sometimes in brass and other metals, including pinchbeck. This type of thimble was also made in countries such as France and Germany, notably the latter, where thimble manufacturers espoused keepsake thimbles as they did all other specialties of the kind. About the turn of the century Wilhelm Lotthammer of Pforzheim was offering for sale thimbles in the following standard inscriptions:

Andenken   Amistad

Nineteenth-century brass thimbles. *Left to right:* **Friendship; Live and let live; Blessings attend you; Love; Faith.** *Private collection*

180

Soldiers' keepsake silver thimbles. *Left*, **English, Boer War;** *center*, **Canadian, First World War;** *right*, **French, First World War.** *Private collection*

Gott schütze dich	Recuerdo
Vergiss mein nicht	Memoria
Gott mit dir	Dios te protege
Souvenir	No me olvidas
Dieu te garde	Con amor

Such thimbles might be made of .800 silver or more likely silver-plated nickel silver (alpacca) and, if necessary, other wording could be arranged. What is interesting is the omission of inscriptions in the English language, which serves to confirm that whereas German thimbles were exported to many countries, notably Spain and Spanish-speaking countries, they found little outlet in the English-speaking world.

With the growing use of the sewing machine, the thimble has lost much of its value as a gift and the practice of giving keepsake thimbles has fallen gradually into disuse. A few thimble manufacturers continued to make them, mostly at the cheap end of the trade, for example "The Cupid"—an English celluloid thimble with transfer decoration showing a cupid with garland—but this somewhat forlorn example was one of the last manifestations of an old tradition.

And lastly, to round off the subject of keepsake thimbles, some thimbles will be found inscribed with the Hebrew word *Mizpah*, which is first found in Genesis 31:49 and mentioned repeatedly in the Old Testament. A strict interpretation presents problems, but the word refers to the biblical story of the parting of Jacob and his father-in-law Laban and it recalls the ageless prayer that God may watch over the receiver and the giver while they are apart.

NOTES

1. Barnaby Rich, *My ladies looking glasse* (London, 1616).
2. "The Thimble—An heroi-comical poem" (published anonymously, February 1743, by Roberts).
3. *The Diary of a Country Parson, James Woodforde 1758–1781*, ed. John Beresford (London, 1924).

181

Souvenir Thimbles

THE TERM *SOUVENIR THIMBLE* MAY BE HELD TO include commemorative and keepsake thimbles, but these have already been described separately. Here the term is used to designate thimbles brought back from travels either as a reminder of a given locality or else as a present, to show that the traveler has not forgotten those at home. The typical souvenir is inscribed "A present from . . ." and it is in this sense that souvenir thimbles are described.

Souvenir thimbles were largely unknown during the eighteenth century and although the more wealthy were accustomed to visit fashionable watering places and there was a large trade in souvenirs, the latter seldom included thimbles. Exceptionally, at the end of the eighteenth century, the porcelain manufactory at Meissen made thimbles inscribed "Ich dachte am dich in Meissen" (I thought of you in Meissen) or "Andenken aus Meissen" (Souvenir from Meissen), which like all Meissen porcelain are beautifully finished, but this was unusual and presumably not many were made, because few have survived.

Similarly, during the first half of the nineteenth century, souvenir thimbles were still very uncommon. Although the Industrial Revolution was bringing together large numbers of people in surroundings from which they would have liked to escape from time to time, the only mode of transport was by coach or on horseback and the population therefore seldom strayed far from home. However, all this changed with the development of the railways, which revolutionized travel arrangements, and so fast did they expand that by 1840 there were already 1,500 miles of railway track covering the length and breadth of Britain. The effect cannot be underestimated. The spinning and weaving districts, for instance, soon established the custom of Wakes weeks, when a whole town at a time would set out on mass travel, and because photography was still in its infancy, there was an immediate and heavy demand for small and inexpensive objects as souvenirs of holidays and sightseeing trips. In an age when household sewing was an important activity, thimbles and thimble cases were an obvious choice, but the popularity of transferware cases came to limit the demand for souvenir thimbles: it will be obvious that a specially designed thimble case to hold a standard brass thimble, of a kind which was readily available in a choice of sizes, was in many ways preferable to a specially designed silver thimble which might or might not be available in the size required. Nevertheless some silver souvenir thimbles were made during the period 1840–60, notably plain silver thimbles in standard Victorian patterns with a plain turned-over rim and the name of some fashionable resort such as Bath or Cheltenham stamped round the border. There was also a range of plain white porcelain thimbles with gold lettering which are typical of the period. They are inscribed "A present from Towyn" (or Caernarvon, Llanfyllin, Dolwyddelan, etc.) and were presumably made

Russian niello inscribed "Caucasus" in cyrillic characters. Circa 1900. *Private collection*

in Stoke-on-Trent for sale in Welsh resorts, though examples ranging as far as Ramsgate have been noted. And from Ireland came bog oak thimbles inscribed Bray, Killarney, or more commonly Erin. Most of these have in common that they are souvenirs from the more select resorts, including the Welsh hills, which had such a great appeal for the Victorian middle classes. As yet they did not feature the English northern coastal resorts or the Isle of Man, which had a more popular appeal.

Another important type of souvenir thimble which was made about this time has a design die-stamped into a flat piece of silver, which was then rolled into a cylinder, seamed, and soldered to the top piece of a thimble made in the conventional way. The thimbles feature various historical buildings, houses and castles such as Dover Castle, Lichfield Cathedral, the Royal Pavilion at Brighton, Windsor Castle, and in good condition they are particularly elegant. Finger guards were also made in the same way. This series, which is

greatly sought after, should not be confused with another series which dates from the end of the nineteenth century and which features royal residences such as Balmoral, Osborne, and Windsor and such private residences as Abbotsford (Sir Walter Scott) and Newstead Abbey (Byron), as well as some of the Welsh beauty spots such as Tintern Abbey in Monmouthshire. The main difference between the two series lies in the construction. The latter is made by deep-drawing, the design is stamped around the border, and there may be some lettering round the rim. Thimbles of this kind are altogether less attractive but nevertheless they are both highly collected and in great demand.

There are many different occasions on which souvenir thimbles have been produced and none more interesting than one which was manufactured for the Ionian Islands on the occasion of the Great Exhibition of 1851. At that time the Ionian Islands, including the island of Corfu, were a British Dependency, and Lord Seaton, on

Silver, English nineteenth century. *Left to right:* **Osborne House, Brighton Chain Pier, unrecorded breakwater, Windsor Castle, Balmoral.** *Private collection*

Silver—shown at the Great Exhibition of 1851 on behalf of Ionian Islands. *Private collection*

Corcyra, the daughter of Asopus, who was carried off by Neptune to the island. She sits on a rock holding an olive branch in her right hand. On one side there is a cornucopia and on the other a galley, which symbolize prosperity and trade respectively. The letters Kερ stand for Kérkira.

b. Zante—a tripod. The letters Zακ stand for Zákinthos.

c. San Maura—A harp. Sappho died on the island. Another emblem is Bellerophon. The letters Λευ stand for Levkás.

d. Ithaca—The head of Ulysses. The letters Iθα stand for Itháki.

e. Cephalonia—Cephalus, son of Mercury, who killed his wife unwittingly, was condemned to dwell here. The letters Kεφ stand for Kefallinía.

f. Cerigo—The birthplace and domicile of Venus. The letters Kιθ stand for Kíthira.

g. Paxoi—the smallest of the islands and sacred to Neptune, hence the trident. The letters Πα stand for Páxoi.

It is hardly necessary to add that this is a rare item.

A somewhat different type of souvenir thimble arose following the invention of microphotography. René Dagron, a Parisian chemist and portrait photographer, played the leading role

behalf of the inhabitants, exhibited miscellaneous items including a silver thimble encircled with seven small medallions, showing the arms and initials of the seven islands comprising the Ionian group as follows:

a. Corfu—A female figure supposed to be

Silver—English circa 1900. *Left,* **Blackpool 1905;** *center,* **Jersey 1887;** *right,* **Isle of Man 1898.** *Private collection*

in the commercial exploitation of microphotography and specialized in the manufacture of peep-show rings and other peep-show novelties. He put his experience to more serious use during the Franco-Prussian War, when he was lifted out of Paris by balloon in order to organize a system of communications between the French Provinces and the beleaguered capital, using microphotography and pigeon post. Dagron's initiative was widely imitated, souvenirs of all kinds were made with peepshows and in 1880 W. Pursall took out a British patent (No. 118) for a novelty consisting of a thimble with a peep-show built into the cap. In England the small glass rod in peepshows is sometimes known as a Stanhope lens after the third Earl Stanhope (1753–1816), who is reputed to have invented it. Brass thimbles incorporating Pursall's patent were sold in various resorts, but few have survived and they are relatively scarce. This is not altogether surprising because Pursall patent thimbles were large and awkward owing to the need to house the lens and the plug of glass protecting the microphotograph and because the peepshow would necessarily get in the way of the needle. It follows that demand must have been

Nickel-plated brass with box. British Empire Exhibition, Wembley, 1924. *Private collection*

limited and the few that have survived are avidly sought after by collectors.

With the close of the Victorian era photography took over from transferware with the result that transferware cases became less popular and souvenir thimbles bearing the name of the locality gained at their expense: Jersey 1887, Llanrwst 1894, but above all the Isle of Man, which from 1890 to 1910 obviously provided a major outlet for resort thimbles, since at least six different designs have been recorded. Somewhat typical of the spirit of the time was the way James Usher, a Lincoln jeweler, promoted the Lincoln Imp. The Imp is a grotesque and legendary figure which features as a carving in Lincoln Cathedral, and in 1890 James Usher arranged to patent the design. He made spoons decorated with the Imp and many other articles including thimbles, an example of the latter being known in the original James Usher jeweler's box. In the United States likewise, there was a flush of resort thimbles: Brooklyn Bridge and Florida, both 1881 (KMD), Salem 1892 (Webster), Washington, D.C. 1893 (Simons) and others, but it was from Germany that the real impetus came. Travel was becoming more international and with the end of the Franco-Prussian War, the German thimble manufacturers dedicated themselves to the supply of resort thimbles on a massive scale. Generally speaking these were not specially designed thimbles but thimbles of standard patterns, with or without stone top, which were stamped with the name of the resort and gilded inside to make them more attractive. Besides being available at Continental spas such as Karlsbad, Wiesbaden, etcetera, they were available in many countries, notably in Spain and in Russia, for which latter country they were engraved in cyrillic characters. It may be added that souvenir thimbles were obviously popular in the Russian Caucasus, because besides German made thimbles, locally made niello thimbles were also available in considerable numbers.

In Britain, the outbreak of the First World War brought the trade in souvenir thimbles to a halt, and save for the one important exception of the Spa town thimbles which Henry Griffith and Sons developed from their Spa range, it was never resumed. Henry Griffith and Sons named the Spa range of thimbles after Leamington Spa where their factory was located, and by 1928 it

Silver with printed enamel decoration. *Left to right:* **Tallinn, Egypt, Naples, Jerusalem, Granada. German circa 1920.** *Private collection*

consisted of the Royal Spa, a heavyweight thimble wrought from thick gauge silver which retailed at two shillings, The Spa, a more popularly priced thimble retailing at one shilling, and the so-called 6d thimble about which there was so little to say that the Griffith advertisements were reduced to explaining that it served "not only as a comparison of values, but as an object of supreme value in itself." All three qualities were available in three different patterns, namely plain indentations, Louise style indentations and plain with a Louise style band. The Spa town thimbles were based on The Spa and were offered in the same three patterns with the names of the various towns or resorts in a milled band just above the rim. Sold at one shilling each, the same price as The Spa thimbles, the following place names have so far been noted:

Aberdovey
Aberystwith
Aylesbury
Babbacombe
Birmingham
Blackpool
Bournemouth
Bridlington
Brighton
Bristol
Bude
Chatham
Chester
Colchester
Colwyn Bay
Combe Martin
Croydon
Dewsbury
Eastbourne

Edinburgh
Felixstowe
Glastonbury
Gravesend
Great Yarmouth
Guernsey
Halifax
Inverness
Ipswich
Jersey
Killarney
Leamington Spa
Llandudno
London
Minehead
Newquay
Omagh
Oxford
Peebles
Penrith
Penzance
Portsmouth
Sandown
St. Leonards
Scarborough
Shrewsbury
Skegness
Southend-on-Sea
Southsea
Stratford-on-Avon
Teignmouth
Tenby
Wallesey
Westcliffe-on-Sea
Weston-super-Mare
Whitley Bay
York

There are undoubtedly other names to be added to this list. The most popular pattern was the one with part indentations and a Louise style floral band. The thimbles were hallmarked in Birmingham and bear the letters *E* (1929), *F* (1930), or *G* (1931) but by far the largest proportion, about 75 per cent or more, were hallmarked in 1930 indicating that the fashion for Spa town thimbles lasted only a short time. Spa town thimbles were also occasionally used for advertising by the addition of the name of a local firm, for example, Dickinson Newcastle. Sometimes Spa town thimbles have no hallmark and are merely marked "Sterling silver, made in England." At least one other thimble manufacturer sought to imitate the example of Henry Griffith but presumably with little success since specimens are rare. Henry Griffith also manufactured souvenir thimbles in the same style for sale on the P & O liners sailing between England and Australia. They included SS *Orion*, SS *Orontes*, SS *Oronsay* and SS *Orsona*. A ship's souvenir thimble was made which bears the name of RMS *Britannic*.

The German manufacturers, on the other hand, resumed where they had left off before the war and set about expanding and widening their range. Besides thimbles with an embossed border, they offered thimbles with enameled medallions and, more impressively, thimbles with the sides partly or wholly covered with multichrome enameled pictures of the locality. One series carries a transfer view of some well-known monuments with the name of the town concerned on the back, such as: Parthenon, Athens; Columbus Monument, Barcelona; The Pyramids, Cairo; The Dome of the Rock, Jerusalem; Duomo, Milan; and St. Peter's, Rome. Another series made of electroplated nickel silver carries an enameled shield displaying the arms of the locality or else a pictorial view of it. Almost every country is represented, including localities in Austria, Estonia, France, Italy, Spain, Switzerland and the Scandinavian countries, Brazil, Canada, New Zealand, and many others, but of course not Russia, which by then was cut off from the outside world. No one else could compete with them, and although the demand for souvenir thimbles has greatly diminished, they still hold a virtual monopoly.

Display of religious medallions of the type used to decorate thimbles. German circa 1920. *Private collection*

187

Silver with medallions. German circa 1920. *Private collection*

Ever since the Middle Ages it has been the custom for Christian pilgrims visiting shrines and holy places to purchase tokens or souvenirs of their pilgrimage or even holy relics. It is not surprising, therefore, that in more modern times there has been a flourishing trade in religious souvenirs or that during the latter part of the nineteenth century thimble manufacturers began to supply specially designed thimbles with a religious motif. These might take the form of an inscription stamped round the border or preferably some small shield or medallion attached to the side of the thimble of the kind that German manufacturers also provided for tourist purposes. Indeed the two kinds of thimbles have very much the same characteristics.

An advantage enjoyed by the German thimble manufacturers is that the heavy concentration of jewelers, manufacturing goldsmiths, and silversmiths in and around Pforzheim, encouraged the growth of ancillary suppliers. As a result, small specialized items or fittings which might otherwise have been difficult to find or to order at short notice were readily available. It was therefore a simple matter for the German thimble manufacturers at Pforzheim, and indeed for Gebrüder Gabler at Schorndorf not far away, to obtain a multiplicity of crested badges or emblems appropriate for each occasion. In particular, with the growth of transfer-type enamel decoration instead of hand painting, small medallions in varying sizes and shapes and with appropriate design provided a touch of originality and color which other manufacturers could not achieve. Thus the French manufacturers, who needed to rely on cast or engraved thimbles, found themselves at a disadvantage, if only because the Germans, using a standard thimble with the appropriate medallion soldered to it, could provide a competitive item quickly and at a fraction of the cost. Typical designs which are known to have existed include the following:

La Vírgen de Lujan (Argentina)
The Black Virgin of Montserrat (Spain)
La Vierge de Montaigu (France)
La Vírgen del Pilar, Zaragoza (Spain)
Notre Dame de Lourdes (France)
Our Lady of Fatima (Portugal)
The Black Madonna of Czestochowa (Poland)
Sainte Anne de Beaupré (Canada)

Other thimbles may carry emblems such as the cockleshell of St. James of Compostela or medallions relating to individual saints such as St. Joseph, St. Teresa, St. Anthony, or more generally medallions of the Blessed Heart of Jesus or the Virgin Mary.

Because the purpose was to provide a cheap souvenir of widespread appeal, the thimbles used were normally plain ones, sometimes of relatively poor quality silver but more usually silver-plated nickel silver (alpacca). Souvenir thimbles with a religious motif are seldom attractive enough to be worth collecting for their own sake but no collection can be considered as reasonably comprehensive without at least one representative of the genre.

Patent Thimbles

THE MODERN USAGE OF THE TERM PATENT IS NOR-mally confined to the grant of certain rights in inventions, but during the Middle Ages it had a much wider interpretation. "Patent" is derived from "letters patent," which once designated the document by which a sovereign conferred a privilege or right on one of his subjects. Letters patent were so called because being addressed to all the inhabitants of the realm rather than to an individual, the great seal was affixed in such a way that the text could be read without the seal needing to be broken. (From Latin through French, *patentem,* lying open). In this way the sovereign might confer a title, reward a service or help the establishment of a new industry, but during the reign of Queen Elizabeth I, letters patent became increasingly associated with the grant of monopolies for the purpose of raising revenue. Inevitably there were abuses and the resulting dissatisfaction led to the passing of the Statute of Monopolies (21 Jac.I c.3) in 1624. This act of Parliament declared the grant of a monopoly unlawful, but as an exception provided that exclusive rights could be assigned for "the sole working or making of any manner of new manufacture within this realm to the true and first inventor and inventors of such manufactures" and that such rights would be limited to a period of fourteen years. The act did not entirely solve the question of monopolies, which continued to be a matter of contention, but it did resolve that of invention patents, which thereafter were granted continuously in England under a system which developed more by custom than by statute.

An early beneficiary of English patent law was John Lofting (or Loftingh), a native of Holland who established himself in London about 1688 as a merchant and manufacturer of fire engines. He became naturalized and in 1693 was granted a patent for an engine (machine) to make men's, women's, and children's thimbles. The preamble to his patent (No. 319) reads as follows:

WILLIAM & MARY by the grace of God etc . . . to all whom these presents come, greeting.

WHEREAS John Lofting hath, by his humble peticōn represented vnto vs the great dutys charged vpon all thimbles imported from beyond the seas doth much discourage the merchants from bringing the same over, soe that the price of that cōmodity will come to be enhansed vpon our subjects, and that in Germany and other forreigne parts whence they have been heretofore imported into this kingdome, they are vsually made by a certaine engine or instruement hitherto vnknowne in our dominions, and hath humbly prayed vs to grant him our letters of Patents for the sole priviledge of makeing and selling the said engine or instruement,

KNOW YEE THEREFORE, that wee. . . .[1]

It will be seen from the above that John Lofting was not strictly an inventor. His machine was already known on the continent, but there was no provision during the seventeenth century for the protection of foreign inventions and trade rivals like the Dutch were considered fair game.

One of the first countries to introduce formal patent legislation was the United States, where the Constitution of 1787 gave Congress the power "to promote the progress of . . . the useful arts, by securing for limited times to . . . inventors, the exclusive rights to their discoveries." Following delay occasioned by the need for each individual state to confer authority to grant patents upon the central government, the necessary legislation was finally enacted in 1790.

In France the Revolution intervened to abolish the royal prerogative, and the French Constitution of 1791 was explicit in declaring the natural right of an inventor to the exclusive right to his invention. Most other countries also enacted laws on the subject of patents but it was not until 1852 that Britain, which in practice had led the way but which had never passed any formal legislation, finally followed suit.

As patent practice evolved so did the circumstances of the thimble-making industry. During the first half of the nineteenth century the industry's productive capacity increased enormously, supply was potentially greater than demand, markets became saturated, and partly because of the versatility of the age and partly because of the need to stimulate sales, inventors in Britain, the United States, and Germany, to name only

Gold by Charles Horner hallmarked Chester 1904. Inscribed "Patent applied for." Height 2.1 cm. *Private collection*

the three main thimble-producing countries, became increasingly active from 1850 onward seeking ways to improve thimbles and to devise gadgets to associate with them. Charles Iles in particular proved to be great innovators and as early as 1857 C. Isles, presumably a member of the Iles family despite the different spelling, took out a patent (No. 2111) for the manufacture of thimbles coated with a nonmetallic lining of suitable materials such as Keene's cement and gutta-percha. One of the problems associated with base metal thimbles is that they tend to harm the finger, and lining them with an appropriate coating offered a worthwhile improvement. Then in 1868 Charles Isles took out a patent (No. 1564) covering the method of manufacture and ornamentation of thimbles. In 1895 C. E. Iles took out a patent (No. 22397) for thimbles "ornamented by setting gems, artificial or stones, and the like on their ends or on their sides." This patent seems a little odd because the type of thimbles made by Charles Iles hardly called for such ornamentation. However, a nickel thimble is known with an imitation diamond set in the tip—a strange development which could only hinder sewing but might conceivably relate to the Iles patent. In 1898 C. E. Iles took out a patent (No. 4243) for a thimble with a lining, and the company evidently considered this development of some importance because at the same time they took the precaution of applying for a U.S. patent, which was granted in 1900 (No. 649310). Meanwhile, celluloid had come into use for thimble making and evidently Charles Iles foresaw its possibilities, because in 1899 they took out a further patent (No. 14818) covering machinery for the manufacture of celluloid thimbles. Then in 1908 they took out no less than three patents, the first (No. 1499) for the lining of thimbles with sheet celluloid or like flexible material, the second (No. 10821) for a ventilated thimble with one or more holes protected inside by steel wire gauze to prevent the entry of the point of the needle, and the last (No. 15826) concerning the fixing of a nonmetallic lining to a metal thimble. It will be noted that these three patents represented an attempt to adapt the advantages of celluloid to those of nickel silver. Efforts to improve the comfort of thimbles by providing ventilation were not new and as early as 1850 Charles Marsden, self-styled inventor and manufacturer, took

Cupronickel with flanges. The adjustable thimble. English patent No. 13605 dated 1892. *Private collection*

out a patent (No. 13341) for a ventilated thimble which he described as a thimble with an inner case between which and the outer case a space was provided for the escape of perspiration. Charles Marsden showed his thimble together with an elastic finger guard with a silver shield and sundry other items at the Great International Exhibition of 1851 and specimens still exist, but it failed to gain commercial acceptance. Charles Iles sought to achieve the same result with the help of celluloid. Both the Iles patent ventilated thimble and their nickel thimble with celluloid lining were produced in fair quantities, but they never went beyond the stage of being an interesting novelty. It is always easy to be wise after the event, but evidently customers who could afford it preferred a silver thimble, with or without an inner steel lining, and those who could not made do with plain celluloid.

The activities of Charles Iles as a leading manufacturer of base metal thimbles are obviously of interest but should not be allowed to obscure those of the many inventors who also developed ideas of their own. Besides John Lofting, the first person to make use of patent protection was John Piercey, a jeweler from Birmingham who as early as 1816 patented (No. 4077) a process for making thimbles from tortoise shell and who put his invention to use by

producing some attractive thimbles of this kind. Other inventors followed and by 1860 or thereabouts the initial trickle of patents became a flood. In 1861 B. Nicoll took out a patent (No. 416) for magnetizing various sewing tools including thimbles to prevent loss. In 1868 R. Charles patented (No. 3690) a glass-lined thimble. In 1878 A. M. Clark for Baillet patented (No. 2074) the first of the many inventions seeking to combine a thimble with a thread-cutting device. In 1884 Charles Horner patented (No. 8954) his famous thimble with an inner steel lining, and in 1892 Rosina M. Durham patented (No. 13605) an adjustable thimble-screw device with six flanges, which was also patented in the United States. Great hopes were placed in this latter invention and a company was registered specially to exploit it. According to the sponsors, it was well known that on a cold day the fingers are apt to contract, so that a thimble which might be of comfortable size in a normal temperature might become inconveniently loose. It was claimed that the adjustable thimble would last much longer than an ordinary thimble, being made of a special metal, heavily coated with pure silver or gold. The more interesting feature, however, was that when considering market prospects, the sponsors estimated that the annual production of thimbles for the supply of the world demand was approximately sixty million, from which of course it was only a short step to conclude that even a small share of the world market would result in a very profitable business. In the event, the adjustable thimble proved a failure, but the figure of sixty million is of considerable interest and well worth retaining.[2]

Then came an even greater surge of inventions, such as that of P. Gabler in 1899, who patented on behalf of Gebrüder Gabler (No. 2488) a method for attaching stone tops to thimbles, and such as Taylor's nonslip patent (No. 380) in 1904. The latter was a brass thimble with a ridge round the top to prevent the head of the needle slipping down the sides. Also Horace Bourne's patent (No. 19157) that same year. This was the Trueform thimble in the shape of a finger, which was designed to eliminate pressure on the fingernail and claimed to hold a certificate of merit from the Institute of Hygiene. There were numerous patents covering thimbles with needle-threading or thread-

THE

Trueform  Thimble.

(Bourne's Patent)

Something New and Interesting about Thimbles.

PROBABLY few people who use thimbles regard them of as much importance as they really are, or are aware of their great antiquity. We learn from the excavations that have been made from time to time, and also from writings, that both the Egyptians and Babylonians were magnificent embroiderers, and to enable them to produce such excellent results they must have used the thimble. Examples 2,000 years old have been found at Herculaneum of the same conical form as the thimbles of the present day.

Roman thimbles of the conical shape have also been found in England, and they are practically of the same design as those now in use.

Roman Thimbles from the Thames, now in the Cuming Museum at the Walworth Road Library, Southwark. Photographed by kind permission of the Southwark Public Libraries and Museum Committee.

One cannot but consider it remarkable that less inventive effort should have been spent over this most necessary and usual article, than over the other thousand-and-one things that are required in everyday life, and that it should have been left to the 20th century to make any real improvement in this line.

The ordinary thimble pinching up the nail. The dotted lines show natural shape of finger.

More especially is this so, when it is considered that medical testimony proves that the present conical form is most injurious to wear, as by reason of it pinching up the nail and pressing on the flesh unequally, it is a very frequent source of whitlows and other troubles such as cramp, chilblains, etc., due to the restriction of the free circulation of the blood.

The pressure also effects the nerves of the whole hand, causing a feeling of fatigue and lassitude.

Moreover, thimbles of the usual pattern in no way conform to the finger, and are most uncomfortable to wear, and also are very apt to come off, when the finger end has to be moistened so as to make them keep on for a time.

Another view showing the crude form of the present shape of thimble.

The Trueform Thimble,

A Comfortable Fit.

on the contrary, closely following, as it does, the shape of that part of the finger on which it is required to fit, is most comfortable and innocuous to wear, being *held on by surface contact* instead of pressure.

This Thimble is the only one which has obtained a certificate for **Hygienic Merit** from the Institute of Hygiene, 34, Devonshire Street, Harley Street, London, W.

Trueform thimbles in silver, brass, and cupronickel, circa 1905. *Private collection*

cutting attachments. In 1905 A. Nielson patented (No. 3826) a needle-threader consisting of a conical or funnel-shaped hole which was used to guide the thread through the eye of a needle inserted in another hole situated perpendicularly to it. In 1906 E. Dassler and A. Schneider patented (No. 14566) a thimble with an internal spring to grip the finger. In 1907 C. S. Bisson and H. W. Gallie patented (No. 6267) a thimble combined with a thread-cutter mounted in a slide recessed in the head of the thimble, and so on. The First World War failed to dampen the enthusiasm of inventors, who continued to patent improvements—mostly thread-cutting devices—and although the flow of inventions subsequently slowed down, it has continued to this day.

In the United States inventors were somewhat slower off the mark and the first thimble patent on record is dated 8 December 1857 (No. 18807). It was granted to John Devlin of Philadelphia and was described as an Improvement in Sewing Thimble. It provided for the application of a guard or fender to the outer side of a thimble, but the exact purpose remains unclear. Thereafter patents followed in quick succession and during the next hundred years some 150 patents of various kinds, including not fewer than 50 inventions designed to combine a thimble with a thread-cutting device. Many of these patents were the work of cranks but others, such as patent No. 247384 dated 13 June 1881 granted to Hugh McDougall, Brooklyn, N.Y., were evidently taken out for practical reasons. Hugh McDougall was a partner in the firm of Ketcham & McDougall, the well-known thimble-

makers, and he patented an improved method of manufacturing thimbles consisting in first so rolling a blank as to form a thick portion for the rim, or a thick portion and embossed ornamentation, next trimming the blank to the desired form, afterward bending the blank into tubular form and soldering its meeting edges together and finally closing the end of the tube. This patent was followed a year later by another one covering new and useful improvements in the art of making thimbles. Some of the finest thimbles made by Ketcham & McDougall have a raised and embossed design round the band and were presumably made by this process. Equally practical was patent No. 404910 granted to Charles Horner of Dorcas thimble fame, and patent No. 643310 granted to Charles E. Iles, both English thimble-makers seeking to protect the rights to their inventions in the United States. No purpose would be served by listing all the various patents available, but those interested may obtain such information from a privately published publication entitled *52 Thimble Patents*, by Bertha Betensley,[3] or else from the files of the Commissioner of Patents, Department of Commerce, Washington, D.C. Unlike English thimbles, which are normally marked with their patent number, American thimbles carry the date on which the patent was granted.

Similarly in Germany the files of the Patents Office (class 52A, 58—09) are replete with inventions relating to thimbles, many of which duplicate those to be found elsewhere. Possibly the most innocuous is the thimble provided with a rubber lining on the grounds of hygiene. Then there is the thimble which provides greater pro-

Silver nonslip thimble. Provisional patent, hallmarked Chester 1906. Height 2.1 cm. *Private collection*

tection for the finger by means of a helical blade which prevents the needle from slipping. There is also a thimble with adjustable fitting. Another guarantees the sewing of a straight seam by means of a stud and a needle-guiding groove. There is the thimble which is held securely on the finger by means of a clamping device and another whose interior shape adapts itself to the finger. There is a thimble with a device to help pull the needle through stiff fabric and another with a contrivance to make button holes. Lastly there is the Magneto thimble, which has a small magnet alongside to help pick up pins which was also patented in Austria, France, Britain, and North America.

German thimbles do not always carry a patent or registered design number, though they may be inscribed DBP which stands for Deutsches Bundesland Patent (DRP or DRGM prewar) and indicates that the design was registered with the German Patent Office. In France, the letters *Bté* or *Breveté* indicate that the thimble is patented and the letters *SGDB* standing for "Sans garantie du gouvernement" are a warning that the authorities take no responsibility for the merits or otherwise of a patented article.

While the patent system protected the rights of inventors, it did nothing to protect designers with new and original ideas for designs, so that during the nineteenth century several countries felt it desirable to enact legislation for the purpose. In England from 1842 to 1883 a diamond-shaped mark was introduced and may be found on specially designed articles to indicate that the design was registered at the London Patent Office and to prevent piracy. Some thimbles manufactured on the occasion of the Great Exhibition of 1851 bear the mark, but it is otherwise seldom seen on thimbles. With the introduction of the Patents Designs and Trade Marks Act of 1883, the diamond-shaped mark was replaced by registered numbers and the date of registration may be estimated from the fact that the numbers are consecutive, starting in 1884 and reaching 600000 by about 1910.

Registered numbers are not infrequently found on English thimbles and are useful first in helping to date them in a negative sort of way—a thimble cannot be older than the date on which the design was registered—and secondly by enabling the researcher to trace the maker by reference to the Patent Office's records. Thus, for instance, it can be shown that a steel-lined Pat thimble marked Rd 73626 was necessarily made by Charles Horner and that it was made in or after 1887. In fact, of course, this is Charles Horner's famous Dorcas "Diamond" pattern. For a more difficult example, there was long some doubt regarding the ownership of a trademark featuring three thimbles in a shield, which is often found on English nickel thimbles. The finding of this trademark on a thimble stamped Rd 108544 soon revealed that the design had been registered on 20 September 1888 by Charles E. Iles, who were therefore obviously the owners of the trademark as well. There are many interesting English thimbles with registered design numbers, e.g., Rd No. 202312, a thimble decorated with stones inset round the rim; Rd No. 212144, decorated with green holly leaves and red berries in enamel; and Rd No. 222445, a well-known and rare silver thimble in the shape of a Scottish thistle.

The situation in the United States is somewhat less straightforward. Faced with the same problem of differentiating between invention and design, the U.S. Patent Office came to register designs much in the same way as normal patents,

194

Silver-plated thimble with box. The Threader. Height 2.3 cm. *Private collection*

but calling them design patents and allocating them a separately numbered series. Like normal patents, design patents are numbered consecutively but with a *D* prefix and they had reached D230000 in 1974. As with normal patents, it is the date which appears on the thimble. There is therefore room for confusion and all the more because certain features which would have rated full patent status during the nineteenth century,

e.g., a thimble with a needle pulling device, ranked as a design patent thereafter. Some care is therefore indicated.

From perusal of the U.S. Patent Office records it is interesting to note that from 1889 onward Simons Bros. made extensive use of the design patents to protect new and original designs, among which may be mentioned the following:

Patent No.	Date	Design
19121	28 May 1889	Vertical ribbed base
19470	3 December 1889	Enriched border
19750	1 April 1890	Design of lower rim
21742	2 August 1892	Chicago World's Fair
21746	2 August 1892	Ornamental scroll pattern
28721	31 May 1898	Egg and dart rim
32540	31 August 1898	Mark "Priscilla"
37680	31 November 1905	Cherubs with garland

Cupronickel—German collapsible thimble circa 1920. *Private collection*

Other manufacturers granted design patents include Stern Bros. & Co. (No. 21408) dated 5 July 1892, for the Chicago World's Fair design, and Ketcham & McDougall (Nos. 42978/79/80), all dated 3 September 1912 and all relating to the design of a thimble with an asymmetrical projection forming an overlay round the edge of the thimble.

Needless to say that to take out a patent for the purpose of protecting the rights to some extraordinary idea does little to further its practical application. Not all inventions which were patented reached the commercial stage, though judging from those that did, there are obviously many customers who are ready to buy gadgets which an experienced needlewoman would reject out of hand. When turning over the pages of patent office records, it is astonishing to find what fancies have been woven round such a simple and straightforward article. In practice these so-called improvements have seldom met with success.

NOTES

1. Patent of John Lofting—Engine for making thimbles. No. 319 dated 4 April 1693.
2. *The Spinning Wheel* (London), 4 March 1893.
3. *52 Thimble Patents*, written and published by Bertha Betensley, 3444 S. Rd. 1050 West, Westville, Indiana 46391.

Advertising Thimbles

THIMBLES BEARING THE NAME OR DESIGNATION OF the donor or of products made by him have been used extensively for advertising goods or services, particularly in the United States. Such thimbles are normally made of some cheap material like aluminum or plastic, though advertising thimbles of brass, nickel, and also silver are not uncommon.

The available evidence suggests that the use of thimbles as a means of advertising started at the turn of the century, and one of the first enterprises to use thimbles for advertising was the Prudential Insurance Company in the United States. The latter commissioned one million brass thimbles in 1904 and another million in 1908, which it distributed through its agents. The Prudential thimbles were inscribed "The Prudential Insurance Company of America" or "The Prudential Insurance Company of America. Made in U.S.A." Many of these thimbles have survived in excellent condition.

In Europe the use of brass thimbles for advertising dates from about the same time and served to advertise a variety of products, notably sewing requisites—for example, Anker Naihmachienen (German sewing machines), Barbour's Linen Thread (British), Cablé Louis d'Or (French thread), Güterman's Naihseide (German silk thread), J. P. Coates (British), etcetera. In similar vein a French needle manufacturer sponsored a brass thimble inscribed "Cousez avec l'aiguille scientifique." Other products such as "Lutona Cocoa," "Chaussures Bailly," "C.W.S. Tea,"

"Javel," "Mazawattee Tea," "Cointreau Liqueur," and "Ceylindo Tea" were also advertised and so were a number of individual firms. The thimbles might be plain or sometimes with a painted band round the rim after the manner of aluminum advertising thimbles (see below). The manufacturers of Hudson's Soap were more ambitious. Besides bringing out several varieties of thimbles, some of which are rarer than others, they also brought out a combined needle, spool, and thimble case with their name on it and capped by a thimble inscribed with the words "Hudson's Soap" round the rim.

Nickel is sometimes used for advertising thimbles, but more rarely. Abel Morrall, which themselves made base metal thimbles, produced a nickel advertising thimble with "Use Morrall's needles" round the rim.

Silver thimbles, being more expensive, were not give-away items but were normally produced for the purpose of a sales campaign, such as for instance that of Lipton Tea, which offered a Lipton Tea silver thimble in exchange for a number of Lipton Tea packet labels. Other well-known products sold in Britain which have silver thimbles bearing their name include Andrews Liver Salt, Hovis Bread, Lifebuoy Soap, Quaker Oats, and Heinz 57 Varieties. In a like spirit the American *Needlecraft Magazine* for April 1923 offered a heavy-duty sterling silver thimble with border decoration to any reader bringing in four subscriptions. In September 1924 the same magazine was offering a somewhat lighter thim-

Silver advertising. *Left,* Hovis 1910; *center,* **James Walker, the London jeweler, 1925;** *right,* **Andrews Liver Salt, 1926.** *Private collection*

ble for two subscriptions. A thimble inscribed "Story Journal" may have a similar background.

Another series of silver advertising thimbles arose in Britain during the 1920s when jewelers sought to promote sales by presenting a silver thimble to customers purchasing jewelry. James Walker, for instance, offered a silver thimble bearing the company name to any purchaser spending more than five shillings—a comparatively small amount when set against the value of the thimble, which was then about four pence. Jewelers in other countries did the same, notably in the United States where, however, some jewelers were apparently content to supply brass thimbles, for example, Lippman's Jewelers, Harrisburg, PA.; Rudolph's and Walter J. Shopnitz, Waterloo, Iowa. The grip which German thimble-makers exercised on the Spanish market is well illustrated by the fact that at least one Madrid jeweler commissioned his silver thimbles from Germany.

Aluminum, being a soft metal, is not really suitable for thimble making because it does not stand up to wear and tear, but the very softness of aluminum means that it can be used to stamp out thimbles in quantity at very low cost. During the interwar years aluminum thimbles became very popular with advertisers of branded products, who would encourage shopkeepers stocking their goods to give them out to their custom-

ers. The advertisement usually appeared in raised letters round the side and there would be a colored band—red, green, blue, and black being the favorite colors—which served to offset the lettering. Sometimes there is no colored background, or else the lettering is printed direct on the metal. Aluminum thimbles may have a simulated stone or glass top, the more common colors being blue, red, green, and amber. They may also have a needle-threading attachment of the wire loop variety. They were used extensively in Britain and a complete list of all British firms and/or products advertised by means of aluminum thimbles would include over a hundred names. Many were made by C. E. Iles in the 1930s, which was the heyday for advertising thimbles in Britain. Others were imported from Germany. Aluminum advertising thimbles were also used extensively in other countries, notably the United States. Lists of known varieties of American aluminum advertising thimbles have been compiled by American collectors and circulated privately.

In the United States plastic advertising thimbles have also proved very popular and to a large extent have displaced the aluminum kind. They are made in a wide variety of colors and used to advertise many different products and services. The use of plastic thimbles for advertising is largely confined to North America.

198

Brass advertising thimbles circa 1910. *Private collection*

A peculiarly American custom associated with advertising is the use of thimbles urging voters to vote for a political candidate, or the so-called campaign thimbles. Sewing requisites have long served to give expression to political feelings: for instance, some womenfolk of the Jacobite party in England sported pin cushions or lace bobbins inscribed "God Bless Prince Charlie" and other mottoes of the kind. But the novelty aspect of the campaign thimble is that it is intended to further the election of the person named. The introduction of campaign thimbles is reputed to have followed on the repeal of the nineteenth Amendment of the United States Constitution. This amendment, which was ratified in 1920, was designed to extend suffrage to men and women alike and those candidates wishing to attract women's votes are said to have hit on the idea of using thimbles—each stitch hopefully helping to impress their name on the mind of the voter. In a similar vein the thimble whistle is an aluminum campaign thimble with a built-in whistle and was patented in 1935. Political trivia of this kind, including buttons, badges, and other give-away items, are widely collected in the United States. The leading publication is the *Illustrated Political Button Book* by Dick Bristow, and it includes the illustration of several political thimbles. It is not possible to list here all the campaign thimbles which have appeared both in aluminum and in plastic, but American collectors have compiled lists for private circulation.

Nobody can pretend that advertising thimbles show any great degree of workmanship or beauty. Nevertheless, they are an interesting manifestation of the twentieth century and provided they are in good condition deserve a place in any representative collection.

Finger Guards

THIMBLE COLLECTORS WILL OCCASIONALLY FIND A small silver appliance resembling a ring, one side being perhaps an inch wide and curled at the tip and the other not much wider than an ordinary finger ring. This is a finger guard (also known as a finger shield or finger protector) and it was worn in the days before sewing machines, when much plain sewing and hemming had to be done by hand. It fitted on the first finger of the left hand, that is, the hand not wielding the needle. The material would be held between the thumb and the tip of the finger in such a way that the part of the material to be sewn rested on the metal and the finger was thus protected from the needle point. Finger guards are no longer used and there are not many people today who would even recognize one, but in Victorian times they were in everyday use. Any well-fitted needle-work box included both a thimble to protect the middle finger on the right hand from the blunt end of the needle and a finger guard to protect the first finger of the left hand from its point. They were usually made of silver but sometimes of silver gilt, gold, bone, or ivory. They are also known in brass, though these are rare and were never popular since they tended to dirty the material. An odd specimen is known made of mother-of-pearl, but this was presumably designed to match other mother-of-pearl fittings in a workbox and would have been impractical.

English silver finger guards seldom carry a hallmark, though they sometimes carry a maker's mark, notably that of Joseph Taylor of Birmingham (IT) who was active in the early part of the nineteenth century. The mark (IT) in a rectangle dates from about 1790 and the same mark (IT) in an oval from about 1810. Other marks noted include that of Taylor & Perry also of Bir-

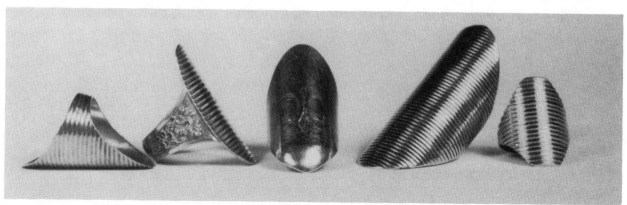

Silver ring-type finger guards. *Left to right:* **Simons Bros.; Continental; eighteenth century with fleur-de-lys; Dutch by van Zeuten en van Leuve 1820–30; unknown origin.** *Private collection*

Silver finger guards. *Left to right:* **Bright cut, early nineteenth century; Joseph Taylor circa 1810; unusual model circa 1810; Brighton Pavilion; Charles May 1868.** *Private collection*

mingham (T&P), who also worked during the early part of the nineteenth century and, more interesting, the mark (ML) which is usually Mathew Linwood but on this occasion the letter *L* has an unusually large serif and the mark stands for the Nathaniel Mills/Langston partnership. Experts in early nineteenth-century English silver have long wondered what type of articles were made by the partnership. It was thought that they specialized mostly in small objects, and this now seems to be confirmed by the discovery of their mark on a finger guard which is thus dated about 1803. Other English manufacturers of finger guards include George Unite (GU) and James Fenton (JF).

Continental finger guards are somewhat different in design and appear to have developed separately. In France, where a finger guard is known as a *Doigtier*, Savary des Bruslons, writing about 1700, describes this as a piece or small cylinder of brass, open at both ends and highly polished, which dressmakers, seamstresses, upholsterers, tailors, and other needleworkers both male and female use to protect the second (*sic*) finger of their left hand for fear of its being caught by the point of the needle.[1] Ladies, he adds, normally have finger guards made of gold or silver. It would seem therefore that the finger guard was known on the Continent throughout the eighteenth century. Unlike English finger guards, Continental guards consist essentially of a ring to slip over the first finger of the left hand with a broad oval on which the material was made to rest. A good example made by van Zente en van Leuve of Amsterdam (1820–30) is illustrated. This type of finger guard was also used in the United States, where it was made by Ketcham & McDougall, Simons Bros., and others.

Bone ring-type finger guard with design of an anchor and two stars. Probably prisoner-of-war work, circa 1810. *Private collection*

English finger guards were made throughout the greater part of the nineteenth century and there is some variety of design. Some finger guards covered the finger more extensively than others and in extreme cases the finger might be almost completely enclosed. Finger guards were not as ornate as thimbles, probably because ornamentation was likely to catch the point of the needle, but all finger guards are not necessarily plain and some finely engraved specimens may occasionally be found. The more ornate finger guards tend to be somewhat later, and as a general guide, the plainer the finger guard, the earlier it is likely to be. In the same way as some mid-nineteenth-century thimbles may be decorated with representations of royal palaces and the like, so more rarely finger guards may also be decorated in this way. A good example, depicting the Brighton Pavilion, is among those illustrated.

Exceptionally and very rare, late eighteenth century thimbles were sometimes supplied with two matching finger guards together in a presentation case. These were of course gift items, and usually of gold decorated with multicolored enamel. There is a Swedish gold thimble (steel top) with two finger guards of this kind dated 1798 in the Kunstindustriemuseet in Copenhagen and several others in private collections.

An amusing novelty dating from about 1800 consists of an emery cushion mounted on a silver base on which screws first a finger guard and then a thimble. The underside served as a letter seal, after the fashion of the time.

More recently the finger guard has given way to the imitation tortoise-shell or celluloid finger protector, but these are also becoming obsolete in an age when plain sewing is normally done by machine.

NOTE

1. Jacques Savary des Bruslons, *Dictionnaire universel du commerce* (Paris, 1723–30).

Just a Thimbleful

SMALL CUPS AND MEASURES HAVE LONG BEEN MADE in the form of a thimble, and one of the best examples is the cup illustrated on page 164 which was commissioned on behalf of the Tailors' Guild of Nuremberg in 1586. The original is in the possession of the Germanisches National Museum at Nuremberg, and there is also a brass gilt copy made in 1876, which belongs to the Gewerbe Museum of that same town. The cup is about five inches high and is obviously a close replica of the thimbles which were made in Germany during the sixteenth century. There is also another cup of this kind in the Berlin Kunstgewerbemuseum which is of gold plated copper; it is inscribed "Vivat Die Ehrsame Schneiderzunft," or "Long live the worshipful guild of tailors," and dated 1601.

It is likely that some early pewter measures were made in the form of a thimble. Certainly the thimble was accepted as an indication of measure—witness the directions in a military manual dated 1617: "Take half a thimbleful of Gunpowder" (Markham, *Cavalry II*) and Dryden's somewhat less prosaic "Yes, and measure for measure, too, Sosia; that is a thimbleful of gold, a thimbleful of love" (*Amphitryon*). Small glass tumblers used to serve strong liquor were known as thimbles during the reign of the Stuarts, and a century later Jonathan Swift wrote of Gulliver drinking from the thimble of Glumdalclitch at the Green Eagle Inn. Clearly the association of thimbles and drinking measures is one of long standing.

Silver-plated spirit measure in the form of a Regency style bright cut thimble. Height 7.1 cm. *Private collection*

During Victorian times cups and measures in the form of a thimble and made of pewter or slag glass were popular novelties and often bore the inscription "Just a Thimbleful," meaning a very little drop—usually of spirits. "Only a thimble" was sometimes used in common parlance in place of a thimbleful. Thomas Hood (1799–1845) wrote in "A Tale of a Trumpet":

Tis true to her cottage still they came . . .
And never swallow'd a thimble the less
Of something the Reader is left to guess.

203

The pewter measures appear in various forms, the most striking being elegant reproductions of Regency bright cut silver thimbles complete with monogram, but with the monogram inverted since the measure might be expected to stand on its base. There is also a measure in the shape of a Scottish thistle thimble and inscribed "A wee drappie." Others are plain, with little decoration other than the indentations.

Slag glass measures are associated with Sowerby & Co. of Gateshead, which used the mark of a peacock's head in relief to denote their products. Between 1860 and 1880 Sowerby's made pressed glass articles in vitro-porcelain, which was a form of glass incorporating steel slag, that is, waste from iron furnaces, to give an opaque striated purple effect. More rarely Sowerby measures may be found in opaque blue or yellow glass or in transparent white or yellow tinted glass. Some glass measures of this kind are unmarked and it is an open question whether they were also made by Sowerby's or by some other firms such as Greener & Co. or George Davidson & Co. which also made slag glass.

More commonplace are the Goss and crested china thimble shapes. Goss is a term used rather loosely to denote any form of miniature white porcelain bearing an armorial crest. Strictly speaking, it should only be applied to those items made at the Goss works in Stoke-on-Trent. In 1887 Adolphus Goss secured permission from boroughs and cities of Britain to reproduce their coats of arms on small items of porcelain and these souvenirs became immensely popular with the public. Their success led a host of imitators to follow suit. Possibly because thimble shapes are not strictly miniatures, being larger than life, Goss did not make them, but thimbles were al-ready popular as souvenirs and several types of heraldic porcelain thimble shapes were soon available. The largest, which stand about 5 cm high, are somewhat heavily potted and usually inscribed "Just a thimble-full" on the inside. They have no makers' mark but were made by Willow Art China and they are perhaps the least interesting. The next, which stand about 4 cm high, are mostly inscribed "Arcadian China." They were made by Arkinstall & Sons between 1904 and 1924. The mark is a terrestrial globe inscribed "A&S Stoke-on-Trent" and surmounted by a crown, or later a rose instead of a globe. Arkinstall made a thimble shape on the occasion of the British Empire Exhibition in 1924 which is marked with a rose. Other brands include Porcelle, Sussex China, and Swan China, the last-named made by Charles Ford, Stoke-on-Trent (1900–1904), with a mark in the shape of a swan and the initials CF. The smallest, which is also the most attractive, is only slightly shorter but narrower in shape. Most of these were made by Wiltshaw & Robinson, whose mark was a swallow in a circle inscribed "W&R Stoke-on-Trent" and surmounted by a crown. This mark was in use from about 1890 to 1910. Similar thimble shapes were also made by Willow (1903–5) and by Locke & Co., using a mark corresponding to 1900–1904.

The mention of Locke & Co. serves to recall that they were manufacturers of porcelain from about 1895 to 1904. The firm was founded by Edward Locke at the Shrub Hill Works, Worcester, and instead of developing his own production, Locke sought to copy the style of the Royal Worcester Company. Quite typically, Locke imitated the Royal Worcester blush ivory and since Worcester had a long tradition of thimble mak-

Porcelain thimble shapes by Arkinstall & Sons 1904–24. *Private collection*

Porcelain thimble shapes by Wiltshaw & Robinson 1890–1910. *Private collection*

Porcelain thimbles and thimble shapes by Locke & Co., Worcester, 1900–1904. *Private collection*

ing, it is not surprising to find that he made thimbles and also thimble shapes in this manner. Eventually Locke's activities in pirating Royal Worcester designs and production became so troublesome that the Royal Worcester Company took them to court and Locke was obliged to close down.

More recently spirit measures in the form of thimbles have become a popular novelty. Such measures are made in many different materials from electroplate to silver. In the United States, where a spirit measure is known as a jigger, Simons Bros. have made spirit measures in sterling silver and even in 14 carat gold. Collectors may sometimes be puzzled by large silver thimbles, too large to wear on the thumb, let alone the finger, but nevertheless too small to be used as a measure. These are specially designed for sufferers from gout or arthritis and are intended to fit comfortably over a bandaged finger.

Spirit measures have also been used as tourist items and for advertising. A brass measure inscribed "Just a thimble-full from the Isle of Man," Rd. No. 707065, dates from shortly before the First World War, and a measure decorated with a large lion was sold to commemorate the British Empire Exhibition at Wembley in 1924. In Germany a spirit measure inscribed "Alter Weinbrand XX" and made by Gebrüder Gabler was evidently used for advertising.

In the United States the Westmoreland Glass Co. made thimble shapes of opaque glass in a variety of colors with hand-painted flowers on the band. These were first made in 1920 following the "Prohibition" Amendment and continued in production until Prohibition was ended in 1933. They were known as "Just a Thimblefull." In 1973 the molds were brought out again and a new supply was made, but production has since been discontinued.

No doubt it was the tradition of "Just a Thimbleful" which induced the inhabitants of Walthamstow to engage in a somewhat specialized contest. According to the *Guinness Book of World Records,* the record amount of water emptied from a "village pond" with a No. 1 size sewing thimble (3.5 cc) is 424 gallons 7 pints by a team of twelve from the Town Hall Fountain in Walthamstow in twelve hours flat on 26 November 1977. No doubt this is a praiseworthy achievement, but should the good folk of Walthamstow believe that a No. 1 size thimble is the biggest available, they would be well advised not to pit their efforts against Chester, which possesses what must surely be one of the largest thimbles on record. This thimble is made of silver and stands six inches high. It is inscribed "The Thimble, Chester 1916" and it served as an emblem on an ambulance which the women of Chester sponsored and sent to France during the First World War. After the war, the emblem was returned and it now forms part of the Chester municipal silver collection.

The tradition whereby a tailors' guild will often have drinking vessels or a cup in the shape of a thimble is well established in Germany and so is that of the tailor drinking a thimbleful. There is a well known German song about a nine times nine tailor who drank yet another thimbleful and thereafter danced on the point of a needle. The tradition extends to other German-speaking countries: for instance, the Zurich tailors' guild have a cup in the shape of a thimble which no doubt means to them as much as the regimental silver means to a British army officers' mess. It is appropriate to recall that in the town of Pforzheim in Baden Württemberg, which was almost totally destroyed during the Second World War, one of the first cares of the local tailors' guild as soon as reconstruction started was to commission a cup in the shape of a thimble. No doubt other tailors' guilds in Germany did the same; given the circumstances this was an expression of hope and confidence in the future which did them credit and which their forebears in the sixteenth century would certainly have understood and approved.

Thimble Cases

IT IS BY NO MEANS CERTAIN WHEN SPECIAL CASES were first made to hold thimbles. There are references to caskets of wood, leather, and crystal containing thimbles in the inventories of the fifteenth and sixteenth centuries, but such caskets were not necessarily thimble cases in the sense employed here, namely, that of a small decorated container which is designed especially to hold a thimble and nothing more. It is reasonable to believe, however, that the goldsmiths and jewelers who lavished their art on decorating and embellishing thimbles must have designed suitable cases to hold them. There is some confirmation for this belief in a fifteenth-century inventory from Catalonia which mentions "una capseta petita ab un didal per a cusir."[1] The juxtaposition of a small box with a sewing thimble suggests that they were made for each other.

By the eighteenth century the more expensive thimbles were normally presented in a thimble case. Some beautiful specimens are occasionally glimpsed passing through the salesroom, such as "a rare Meissen gold-ground gold mounted thimble case reserved with pairs of lovers in landscapes on the gold ground, the interior with lovers playing cards, the gold mount with bright cut decoration." Or again, "a fine Meissen gold-mounted thimble case painted in sepia and flesh tint with figures in landscapes with moulded scroll cartouches, the mount with bracket thumb-piece." Thimble cases of this kind, however, are exceptional and offend against the precept that a thimble case should be less valuable than the thimble it is designed to hold. Where a thimble is meant for practical use this is an obvious constraint and it will explain why a gold (or silver) thimble case will seldom be found to house a gold (or silver) thimble. The preferred material for all kinds of cases and etuis during the eighteenth century was shagreen (*galuchat*) a material tanned from fishskin and usually dyed green. Shagreen thimble cases were widely used to house gold thimbles (also porcelain) and were shaped like an etui in which the thimble could stand upright; they usually have a pink velvet lining and one of their more pleasant characteristics is that inherent feel of quality which is so often the mark of the eighteenth century.

Besides shagreen, ivory was popular and also leather, but it was wood which was to supply the basis for a wide range of thimble cases. This was a time when a number of small towns in England and on the Continent had acquired a reputation for the remedial properties of some local springs and had developed into fashionable holiday resorts and as places of escape from unsanitary conditions prevailing in the larger cities. A few of these, such as Tunbridge Wells, being situated in wooded areas already had a woodworking industry and the one stimulating the other, they developed a substantial trade in souvenirs. In his *History of Tunbridge Wells,* dated 1766, Benge Burr wrote:

> The trade of Tunbridge Wells is similar to that of the Spa in Germany and chiefly consists in a variety of toys in wood such as tea chests, dressing boxes, snuff boxes, punch ladles, and numerous other articles of the same

207

kind. Of these great quantities are sold to the company in the summer and especially at their leaving the place, when it is customary for them to take Tunbridge fairings to their friends at home.

Needless to say that these fairings included a wide range of sewing tools and numbered thimble cases of different kinds. It is of course very difficult to distinguish the date and provenance of small woodware, but certain types of Tunbridge ware are sufficiently distinctive that they offer little problem. Deserving of special notice is the less expensive, paint-decorated woodware of the type sold at Tunbridge between 1790 and 1820 or 1830 made of natural wood, clear polished and decorated with oil paint, red, yellow, green, and black usually being the preponderant colors. Thimble cases in this style are known in the shape of an egg, of an acorn, of a barrel, and there are also wooden thimbles of about the same period and manufacture. The thimble cases are sometimes inscribed "A Present from Brighton" or "A present from the Roman Pavement," in Regency style lettering on a pink background. Also deserving notice is the type known as stickware. The process was developed in about 1830 and is related to a type of Tunbridge work known as end-grain mosaic. In this process sticks of varying natural woods but contrasting

colors, such as rosewood, beech, and mahogany, were glued together in a block and turned on a lathe, the pattern depending on the arrangement of the wood and the depth of cutting. Thimble cases in this style are known in the shape of an egg or a barrel, or they may be acorn-shaped with the screwtop made of stickware and the body otherwise plain. Stickware continued to be made throughout the nineteenth century.

Following on the development of Tunbridge ware but separate from it came the development of Scottish woodware, which is also known as Mauchline ware because for a long time production was concentrated on Mauchline, a small town in Ayrshire. There are two kinds: the older is clan tartanware which was first produced in the 1820s and consists of paper decorated with clan tartans and glued to wood, usually sycamore. So perfectly was the gluing done that it is almost impossible to tell the joins. Thimble cases were produced in a variety of designs and like most tartanware were sold primarily in Scotland. They were made chiefly from 1840 to 1880, though in all probability clan tartanware continued to be produced until the end of the nineteenth century. The other is transferware, which is again usually sycamore and is decorated with transferred pictures. It was first introduced

Woodware thimble cases. *Left,* **tartan;** *center,* **transfer;** *right,* **fern decorations.** *Private collection*

Bone thimble case decorated with polychrome foliage and flowers with a bird perched on a branch. The case is in two parts, the top screwing over a base which bears similar decoration underneath. Possibly English about 1800. Height 4.2 cm. *Bethnal Green Museum*

in the 1830s and remained popular until toward the turn of the century, though one factory remained in production as late as 1933. Transferware was basically intended to simulate pen and ink drawings to meet the demand for cheap souvenirs of all kinds. Thimble cases were produced in a variety of designs and date mostly from 1850 to 1900. It is likely that the first engravings had local Scottish associations, for example, thimble cases inscribed "Burns Cottage—bought at the cottage," or "Made of Wood grown on the banks of the Doon," but they rapidly embraced most places of historical interest, as well as holiday resorts throughout Britain. The range is too vast to quote and suffice it that there are literally hundreds of designs to be found applied to thimble cases. Moreover, not content with saturating the British market, transferware ranged abroad. Transferware thimble cases were sold for export to France, to the United States (The Washington Monument—Washington, D.C.; The Common, Greenfield, Mass; Old Tip Top House, Mt. Washington,

N.H.; The Flume, Franconia Notch, N.H.; Summit of Mt. Washington, etc.), and to Australia. Although the yellow finish of varnished sycamore is not necessarily to everybody's taste, the transfer applied pictures are of the highest quality and faithfully record the scenery and fashions of the time.

While transferware set out to simulate pen and ink drawings, it was itself imitated by means of photographic reproductions, both black and sepia, which were glued to the wood and varnished over. There was also a development known as fernware whereby fern leaves were used as decoration instead of transfer prints. Both kinds of decorations were used on thimble cases, but they did not prove successful and are relatively scarce. For those wishing to delve further *Tunbridge and Scottish Woodware* by Edward and Eva Pinto (London, 1970) is the best book of reference.

Besides the Scottish woodware which depends entirely on decoration for its effect, other types of thimble cases were produced from better quality wood such as mulberry, for which the nature of the wood itself and the quality of the workmanship are the main points of attraction. Such thimble cases are normally in the shape of an egg, an acorn, or a barrel, and may have matching thimbles turned from the same wood. Alternatively there may be room inside for spool and needlecase. Collectors should beware of modern thimble cases made of wood which are sometimes passed off as early or mid-nineteenth century; suffice it to say that the wood is poor, the finish is rough, and such cost-cutting devices as push-on caps instead of screw threads help to reveal the deception.

Reverting to the early nineteenth century, tortoise shell and mother-of-pearl were fashionable materials and not surprisingly were used to decorate thimble cases. These are mainly of two kinds. One consists of a small rectangular casket 4 cm long by 2.5 cm wide which is made of wood with a hinged lid. The casket is overlaid with mother-of-pearl or abalone in varying patterns and the inside is trimmed with velvet, with the edgings finished in bone. The other kind consists of a small octagonal box about 2.5 cm across, of similar construction and overlaid with mother-of-pearl or abalone. Later in the nineteenth century this kind of casket was made of tortoise shell, a material which was also used to make small upright boxes, resembling a miniature knife box, to hold needles and a thimble. Tortoise shell and mother-of-pearl caskets are attractive, but as for all delicate objects of this nature condition is important and really fine specimens are rare.

Thimble cases made of multicolored beadwork were also popular during the nineteenth century and can be very attractive. These were made principally in France, although beadwork is also known from England and possibly also from Russia. They consist of two halves made of bone, which screw together in the shape of an egg and each half is covered in beadwork. The beads themselves are threaded on fine wire wound round the bone core, each row attached to the next with silk stitching. Occasionally the case is fitted with a small cylindrical container which projects at one end to hold needles and which is also covered in beadwork. There are two main pitfalls for which to watch. One is that beaded cases were not all necessarily made for

thimbles (for example, some were made to contain miniature rosaries) and are not shaped inside to hold a thimble. The other is that a beaded case with a bare half is merely a case which has lost its beads and is worthless. Unfortunately beadwork is easily damaged and here again specimens in really fine condition are rare.

Bone was an early substitute for ivory and was used to make thimble cases from the end of the eighteenth century and possibly earlier. Bone thimble cases are normally in the shape of barrels, acorns, or eggs and it is believed that some were carved by French prisoners during the Napoleonic Wars. In one type of bone thimble

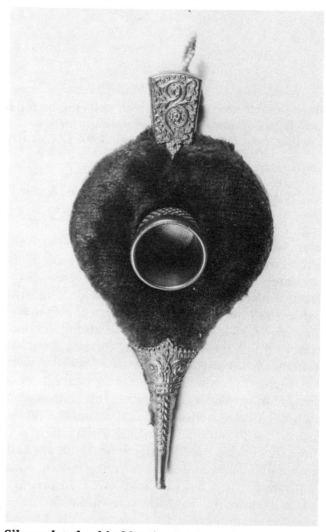

Silver-plated thimble in presentation thimble-holder. "Le Soufflet." Registered design No. 138883. Charles Iles circa 1920. *Private collection*

Elaborately carved vegetable ivory thimble cases with thimble to match and one coquilla thimble case with peep-show fitting. Mid-nineteenth century. *Private collection*

used chiefly during the Victorian era and a thimble case inscribed "A present from the Thames Tunnel" dates from 1843 or thereabouts, which was the date when Brunel's tunnel under the Thames was finally opened. Some vegetable ivory thimble cases are fitted at the top with a peephole (Stanhope) showing a view of a fashionable holiday or tourist resort of the period. Vegetable ivory cases may also be found in the shape of an egg, but these are merely polished without any carving and so tend to be somewhat plain and unattractive. Attempts were made to use color on vegetable ivory cases but this was not successful, and more often than not all that is left is the vestige of a design.

Silver thimble cases do not appear to have been much in demand during the early part of the nineteenth century, but possibly following the discovery of the Comstock Lode in 1859, which led to a fall in the price of silver, silver thimble cases became more popular. Typical of the late Victorian era is the silver thimble case in various designs but more commonly cylindrical and about one inch high when closed. Inside the ornately decorated container there may be a raised support on which the thimble rests when not in use. These containers were particularly popular in the United States where they were produced in large quantities during the late

case, the bone was dyed red on the outside and the design carved after dyeing so that it appears white against a red background, but otherwise attempts to use color on bone were largely unsuccessful. Such thimble cases may be inscribed "A trifle from a friend" and be decorated in Regency style.

Another substitute for ivory besides bone was the so-called vegetable ivory (or corozo nut) and a large number of thimble cases were made of this substance. Because the corozo nut is relatively small, thimble cases made from it are normally constructed in two halves which screw together and the thimble rests inside. Also possibly for this reason vegetable ivory thimble cases are often made in the shape of an acorn, the plainer cases having a simple design worked on the cup part of the acorn, leaving the body itself perfectly smooth. Others are more elaborately worked and carved all over. Vegetable ivory was

Vegetable ivory thimble and thimble case, the latter in the shape of a beehive with bone fittings. *Private collection*

nineteenth and early twentieth century. In 1921–23 the Webster Co. of North Attleboro, Massachusetts, were selling them wholesale at $2.25 each.

For those who found the cost of a silver thimble case beyond their means, base metal was an alternative. Also typical of the late Victorian period is a range of small thimble cases made of metal sheeting in the shape of an egg or a rectangular box fitted with a small metal chain. The sheeting, which was impressed with a light design, was molded to shape and held within a brass framework. The inside fittings designed to hold the thimble were made of cardboard and other similar materials in bright colors. These cases, which were available as cheap souvenirs, were made to hold a brass thimble and were sold, it is believed, from 1890 to 1910. A specimen to commemorate the Diamond Jubilee (1897) bears a small picture of Queen Victoria inset at the top and another has a small medal commemorating the Franco-British Exhibition held in London in 1908 attached to a chain. Cases which have lost their inside fittings or their chains are best avoided. Somewhat similar cases with the same framework and the same internal fittings but with the yellow metal sheeting replaced by a shell of mother-of-pearl may also be found and date from approximately the same period. The mother-of-pearl cases are cleaner and more attractive than the metal cases, which get dirty, but they suffer from the disadvantage that the mother-of-pearl is readily cracked or broken. They may sometimes be found with blue mussel shell instead of mother-of-pearl. Both types were made on the Continent but it is not clear whether they originated from France of from Germany.

Coming closer to Edwardian times, a favorite fabric was plush, which is a variety of cloth woven like velvet but differing from it in having a longer and more open pile. Not surprisingly,

Thimble case made of mussel shells in brass mountings with brass thimble. Probably French circa 1900.
Private collection

therefore, a range of thimble cases were made in plush or plushlike materials, usually in rich golds or purples, and souvenir plush cases were sold on the occasion of Edward VII's coronation with a medallion photographic reproduction on the outside. Plush thimble cases might be plain rectangular gift boxes to hold the thimble or else they were specialty boxes—for example, in the shape of a book and clasp with a thimble resting inside. Subsequently thimble cases were made in somewhat less opulent velvet-type fabrics, and during the 1930s Iles offered a range of thimbles in presentation cases of this kind. One of the more popular was the Threader thimble, a thimble with a hook-type threader attachment described as a "nickel plated, nickel silver, silver chased thimble" which was offered in a shell-shaped velvet-covered thimble case complete with instructions. Unfortunately plush and velvet thimble cases tend to become threadbare and dirty, but anyone fortunate enough to own one in mint condition will know that new they could look very attractive.

Lastly, this account of thimble cases would not be complete without mention of those small rectangular thimble cases with metal frames and with a brown leather, or sometimes a velvet (purple or red), covering. They may be inscribed "Souvenir" or else have a small nameplate. More elaborately, the case may be bound with miniature straps and a small carrying handle at the top. They date from about the turn of the century.

So far this account has been mostly concerned with thimble cases as such, and it is now necessary to turn to thimble stands. The thimble stand is not really a thimble case but rather a special type of thimble holder with the thimble resting as if on a pedestal ready for use. It has been said that the thimble stand is a relic of the days when the thimble was still a domestic treasure and a household necessity rather than a personal possession, but this is obviously overstating the position. No doubt during the nineteenth century there may have been the odd thimble stand with a thimble ready for use on it. It is after all conceivable that there were the odd needlewomen who preferred to keep their thimble at hand rather than keep it in their work basket. But for every such there must have been hundreds for whom a thimble stand was an amusing trifle, a

Wooden thimble stand. *Private collection*

gift or souvenir to keep on a mantelpiece but surely of no practical application. That this must be correct is confirmed in the design of thimble stands themselves. There are some wooden pedestals and covers which are reasonably functional but the large majority are totally impractical. The little brass donkey plodding patiently along with a thimble secured on each side may have been a happy memory for the owner, but it is futile to suggest that it fulfilled any practical role in the household.

213

It would be interesting to know, for instance, why so many thimble stands were made in the shape of an egg cup with an egg resting inside. These might be made of wood, possibly lignum vitae, turned in the shape of an egg cup with a polished vegetable ivory egg fitted on top. The egg part unscrews and the thimble is found on a velvet-covered mount inside the cup itself. Or they might be made of ivory, like a pedestal egg cup holder which is engraved with an elegant design of stars and United States shield, dated 1883. Some lesser thimble stands of this kind merely have the egg of white painted wood. But egg cups are only one of the many manifestations of thimble stands.

Thimble stands in the form of a sailing ship with mother-of-pearl sails and a seashell for the ship itself were a German contribution in late Victorian times. The thimble fits into a wire holder and there is usually some metal rigging and a small metal anchor. There are models with one, two, or three sails, the mainsail carrying some inscription, e.g., "Kaiser Wilhelm Kanal" (The Kiel Canal, also called the Kaiser Wilhelm Canal, was opened in 1895); World's Columbian Exposition (held at Chicago in 1893), or simply "A gift from Eastbourne." They were made in Germany.

From thimble stand to thimble holder is only a short step. Besides the thimble stands as such there is a wide range of thimble holders and a popular subject around the turn of the century

was the slipper or shoe. The more common model was in the shape of modern "mules" and made of pressed glass about 5.8 cm long and usually in white, green, blue, or dark amber glass. It is believed they were made in Britain but must have been exported widely, as some were made for the Pan-American Exposition at Buffalo, N.Y., in 1901,[2] and another is known inscribed "Marienbad," a fashionable spa in what is now Czechoslovakia. The pressing was in two halves which were brought together, and when cooled the sole and heel were ground lightly so that the shoe could stand steady. The glass was then hand-painted or otherwise decorated and the thimble fitted into a special cavity approximately where the foot would slip into the shoe. Another model, somewhat similar in both shape and size but more elaborate, was made with a base of pewter or similar metal, covered with leather or fabric, the latter decorated with hand embroidery and fitted with a small leather sole. Still more elaborate were small-scale but otherwise accurate models of shoes and slippers made up in a variety of fashions and fabrics. These might include an inner sole made of flannelette which served as a needle holder. Glass thimble holders in the shape of a shoe recall the Cinderella story, but unfortunately the glass slipper springs from a misunderstanding. When Charles Perrault wrote his *Contes de ma Mère l'Oye* (1697), which popularized some traditional fairy tales, he wrote of a "pantoufle en vair" (a fur or

Pressed glass thimble-holders in the shape of shoes. *Private collection*

214

Thimble-holder made of satin with beads. English nineteenth century. *Private collection*

subject with a local association. A tourist item recalling Hitler's Germany was a miniature walking boot and in it a silver thimble worked with swastikas. The latter may well have come from the Austrian side of the frontier, because the German National Socialist party did not allow the swastika to be used for commercial purposes in this way. Dutch wooden clogs are also carved as thimble holders.

A more sophisticated type of thimble holder emerged toward the end of the nineteenth century and was mass-produced in a variety of designs. There was, for instance, the thimble holder in the shape of a horseshoe for luck, a pair of bellows (Le Soufflet, Rd 138883), a heart shape (The Cupid Heart Case, Rd 210332), a slipper (The Fairy Slipper, Rd 128010), all designed to hold a "silver cased thimble." These were cheap souvenirs (the mention of silver cased thimble, i.e., a base metal thimble with a silver coating, is evidence of that), and they usually show much wear and tear. The few specimens that have survived in mint condition are well worth collecting.

But besides the above there was also a wide range of thimble cases and thimble holders of miscellaneous shapes such as baskets, bottles, railway rolling stock, electric bulbs, buckets, hats and hatboxes, mandolins, leather balls, beer mugs, muffs, sedan chairs, lanterns, acetylene lamps, and miniature hampers. The list is seemingly inexhaustible, and one can only wonder at the scope of Victorian versatility and imagination.

A somewhat different form of thimble holder arose as a fitment for the chatelaine (also known as an *équipage* or *ménagère*) which a lady might carry hooked to her waist. In earlier times pockets were nonexistent and it was customary for the lady of the manor to carry various items, notably her keys, hanging by a cord attached to the waistband. She might also carry a needle in a needlecase:

Lors trais une aiguille d'argent
D'un aiguiler mignot et gent,
Si pris l'aiguille è enfiler.[3]

Good needles were rare and valuable, and if a lady carried a needlecase, then why not scissors as well, and a thimble in a thimble case? One thing led to another and eventually the

sable slipper), not "en verre." Sable was worn by kings and princes, so that the good fairy gave royal fur and not glass slippers to her favorite.

Thimble holders were also made of wood, chiefly in Switzerland, southern Germany, and the Tyrol, where woodcarving has always been an important cottage industry, practiced during the winter months when outdoor occupations are at a standstill. Some are more properly thimble cases, being carved in the shape of an acorn, walnut, pine cone, or mushroom, but for the most part the thimble is open to view resting in the carving of an edelweiss, eagle, bear, or other

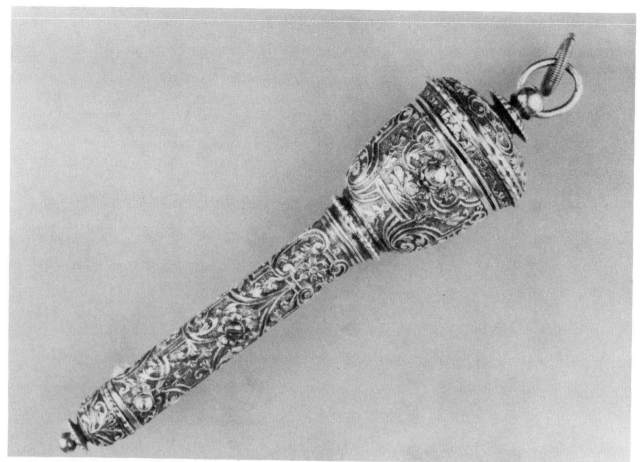

Combined thimble and needlecase from a chatelaine. Silver gilt with enamel. Eighteenth century. *Private collection*

chatelaine developed into an article of fashion, sometimes to carry a watch, watch key, and seal and sometimes to carry sewing implements, including a thimble in a separate thimble holder. From 1700 to 1750 the chatelaine grew more elaborate. In 1712 George Willdey, at the Great Toy Shop next ye Dogg Tavern in Ludgate Street was selling scissors and thimbles in decorated cases with chains and clasp to swing at the waist, and in 1715 Lady Mary Wortley Montagu described a chatelaine which was obviously the height of extravagance:

Behold this Equipage by Mathers wrought,
With fifty Guineas (a great pen'worth)
  bought.
See, on the Toothpick Mars and Cupid strive,
And both the struggling Figures seem alive.
Upon the bottom, see the Queen's bright
  Face,
A Myrtle Foliage round the Thimble Case,
Jove, Jove himselfe does on the Scissors
  shine;

The Metal and the Workmanship Divine![4]

These lines serve to confirm that the design of chatelaines tended to rococo scrolls and flourishes, executed sometimes in gold but more commonly in pinchbeck or gilded brass (ormolu). Some magnificent eighteenth-century chatelaines will be found in many museums, including the Louvre in Paris, but mention should be made of the chatelaines in the Special Collection (Osobaya Kladovaya) of the State Hermitage Museum in Leningrad. These are quite exceptional, and there is also an outstanding gold-mounted porcelain chatelaine in the porcelain collection at the Hermitage which features a porcelain thimble, both attributed to the Vienna factory. Inevitably the fashion for chatelaines attracted the attention of the English enamelists, who produced some colourful chatelaines with matching etuis and thimble eggs in painted enamels (Bilston) with flowers or miniature pas-

216

Thimble-holder from a chatelaine. Gilded metal with mother-of-pearl. Late eighteenth century. *Colonial Williamsburg Foundation*

toral scenes in gilded rococo scrolls set against pink or turquoise background. Subsequently, changes in the style of clothing led to the wearing of chatelaines being abandoned and by 1810 they were out of fashion. They remained out of fashion until late Victorian times, when there was a brief revival. From about 1895 to 1905 it became fashionable for women to wear a somewhat elaborate chatelaine holding sewing instruments and writing material. Thimble holders from this period, mostly silver, cut steel, or gilt metal are not uncommon. There are even thimble holders decorated with leather. In their simplest form they consist of a small metal bucket with a fabric lining, usually dark blue or purple, which served to hold the thimble. Others have a lid fitted with a hinge. They were mostly attached to the chatelaine by a small chain. Silver thimble holders of this period were chiefly made in and around Birmingham, and among the

maker's marks that of George Unite is the most frequent.

Finally, this account would not be complete without some reference to the type of box which a jeweler would normally provide, assuming that his customers were not looking for anything fancy in which to present a thimble. Whereas previously thimbles had stood upright, from the first half of the nineteenth century onward jewelers began to provide a plain shagreen or leather-covered case in which the thimbles lay on their side. The name of the jeweler normally appeared printed on a silk facing inside the lid. Slightly larger and more rudimentary cases were made to house porcelain thimbles. Leather cases of this kind remained in use throughout the second half of the nineteenth century. About 1900 celluloid boxes came to be used in plain cream or colored celluloid, and they might also bear a short inscription. One box of this type used for

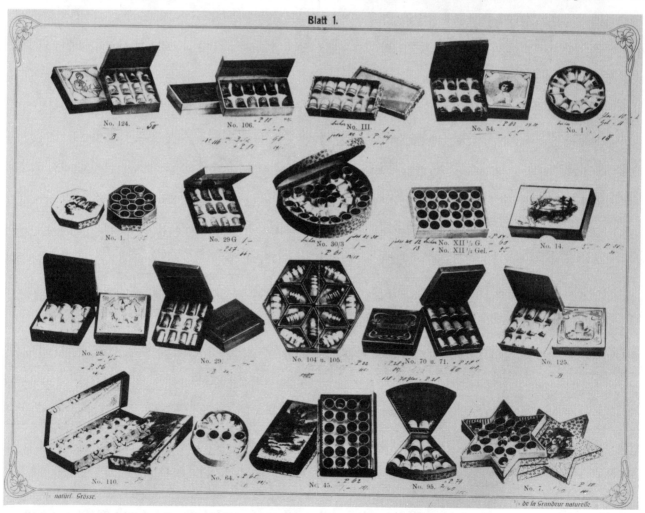

Page from a cardboard-box manufacturer's catalog. *Private collection*

218

Thimble case and tape measure combined. Brass in the shape of a beer tankard (stein). Made in Austria circa 1930. *Private collection*

brass hinge is lightly engraved. However, celluloid cases were not really suitable for the better-class thimbles and leather covered cases remained in use with some modification of style, fashionable jewelers providing cases of varying shapes and in more modern designs. Meanwhile Charles Horner had introduced small individual cardboard boxes for his branded steel-lined thimbles. By the time of the First World War other thimble manufacturers had adopted the same practice. At first some of the boxes bore the name of the jeweler, but by the 1930s most thimbles were sold in boxes supplied by the manufacturers under a brand name. These in turn have disappeared and the few which have survived are eagerly sought by collectors.

Although thimbles are often written about in collectors' magazines and journals, thimble cases are seldom mentioned, with the result that they are not so heavily collected. This makes it possible for the collector to enter a field which is perhaps less crowded and where there may be better opportunities.

souvenir purposes is inscribed "A present from the Crystal Palace," and it is a measure of the care with which they were made that the small

NOTES

1. Archives of the Cúria Fumada de Vic. 1491.
2. Ruth Webb Lee, *Victorian Glass* (Northborough, Mass., 1944).
3. *Roman de la Rose*, Edit. Méon, verse 90 (c. 1260).
4. Lady Mary Wortley Montagu, "Thursday, The Bassette Table," *Town Eclogues* (1715).

Thimble-Rigging

THE THIMBLE BEING ASSOCIATED WITH THE VIR-tues of good housekeeping, it is perhaps unfortunate that among the more seamy activities found on race courses was the sharper's game of thimbling. This sleight-of-hand trick was played with three small thimble-shaped cups and a tiny ball or pea. The ball was placed on a table and covered with one of the cups. The trickster then started moving the ball from one cup to another and challenged bystanders to guess which cup covered the ball and to bet on their choice. Needless to say, the person who bet was seldom allowed to win. The game was known in England at the time of Queen Anne, when it was called thimbles and buttons, and it may conceivably have been imported by Continental gypsies during the reign of Queen Elizabeth I. Gay mentions it in his *Trivia* (1716), and Dickens, writing of Hampton racecourse, refers to "a little knot [of bystanders] gathered round a pea and thimble table to watch the plucking of some unhappy green horn."[1] It was also practiced in the United States toward the end of the nineteenth century: "It's the rabble that follow the circus that gives me trouble. The cheats, the three-card monte experts and that damned thimble game."[2] More recently the game of thimbling has fallen into disuse and been replaced by the equally unsavory card game known as hunt-the-lady. But the name has stuck, and over the years the term *thimble-rigging* has come to be used allusively about any kind of mean cheating or jiggery-pokery. It is not inappropriate therefore to note that the vogue for thimble collecting and the relatively high prices which unusual thimbles will fetch have attracted the attention of the unscrupulous, nor is it inappropriate to warn against the activities of individuals and firms who have set out to cash in on the demand for thimbles and to prey on the unwary.

It would be hard to include under the heading of thimble-rigging those thimbles which are manufactured for the tourist trade. To give an example, most American collectors know the ornate silver thimbles sold to tourists in Mexico, and even if Mexican needlewomen may prefer plainer and more utilitarian thimbles, it is difficult to object to what has become almost a type of souvenir. Other countries which go in for tourist thimbles include Greece, Holland, Portugal, and Spain. There are presumably enough thimble collectors traveling around the world to make it worthwhile for duty-free gift shops at international airports such as Amsterdam, Athens, Lisbon, and Madrid to stock them. The Greek tourist thimbles are distinctive and colorful, the Dutch are pleasantly reminiscent of Delft (although made in Germany), and as regards Spain, the yellow metal "Toledo" thimbles will be equally well known. Provided that they are sold only for what they are, namely, inexpensive souvenirs, they are harmless and acceptable. It might also be hard to include under the heading of thimble-rigging the commemorative thimbles which are offered for sale, though there is something unpleasantly bogus about the many so-

***Derby Day* (detail) by William Powell Frith (1819–1909).** *The Tate Gallery, London*

called commemorative thimbles which are produced in increasing quantities and on every conceivable occasion. The commemorative thimble has a respectable history and genuine commemoratives are to be welcomed, but far too often the one and only purpose of these so-called commemoratives is to exploit thimble collectors. In a sense they are reminiscent of the special stamp issues which plague stamp collectors, but whereas commemorative stamps can be used to mail a letter, most commemorative thimbles are totally useless. Moreover, the advertisements offering them for sale are often equally objectionable. This applies particularly to porcelain thimbles when every possible means of suggesting that the thimble is made individually by hand may be used to obscure the only point that really matters, namely, that it is not a hand-painted design but a worthless print. However, even here there is still a limit, and in 1980 Messrs. Peter Jones China (Mail Order) of West Parade, Wakefield, which admitted supplying a thimble with a false description "hand-painted" were fined by Birmingham magistrates. Quite different is the position of the collector who is seeking to buy older thimbles and who may be offered thimbles faked or improved to be passed off as rare or exotic items for sale at correspondingly high prices. Unfortunately, by its very nature the antiques trade attracts more than its fair share of sharks and tricksters, and the budding collector needs to keep the doctrine of *caveat emptor* well before him. The traditional advice of dealing only with experienced and reputable firms is of course perfectly sound, but it hardly meets the

circumstances of the thimble collector who as a specialist may need to cast his net wider, even if it means exercising more caution. Some advice may therefore be helpful.

In the first place it is important to recognize that a thimble in mint condition is worth considerably more than a worn or damaged thimble. This is the same as for coin-collecting, where a worn coin, unless it is particularly rare, is almost worthless. Beware, therefore, of the silver or gold thimble with signs of wear or with holes in it. It is always good practice to hold a thimble to the light to see if it is holed and avoid the so-called sanctimonious (holy) thimbles. Disregard suggestions that holes may be there for a purpose. The holes of a patent ventilated thimble are unmistakable and a thimble with regular holes was either faulty in the making or else the design has encouraged wear at the weakest points. Beware also of thimbles which have been repaired. It is almost impossible to repair a silver or gold thimble without leaving some trace. Always look carefully, preferably with a glass, for the telltale solder marks on the inside. A worn or repaired thimble may still be collectable but its value will be correspondingly reduced, and a dealer—unless he knows you—will not necessarily draw your attention to its condition.

Beware also of modern items being passed off as antiques. Fake antiques have always been a problem, and never more so than in times of scarcity. Genuine wooden thimbles are relatively rare, yet wooden thimbles abound, they are difficult to date, and it is obvious that many of the wooden thimbles on offer are worthless rub-

Contemporary thimbles as sold to tourists. *Left to right:* **Spanish brass, Chinese cloisonné, English Worcester porcelain, Mexican silver, Greek wirework and enamel.** *Private collection*

222

bish. Equally pernicious are new mintings of old thimbles. Great care should be exercised in buying French thimbles, because a whole series of French silver thimbles, notably the "Fables de la Fontaine" and associated designs, have been cast from molds prepared from the original dies. Reproductions of this kind are like the reprints of old engravings; at best they are superficially attractive, but they are of little value and of no interest to the serious collectors.

Even more care should be exercised when buying enamel or porcelain thimbles. Such thimbles are expensive and nowhere is the art of the restorer more in evidence. Repairing chipped, cracked, broken, or otherwise damaged porcelain is almost an industry on its own account and a good restorer is capable of repairing a piece of porcelain and glazing over the cracks so that the repair is virtually indistinguishable except under an ultraviolet lamp. Restorers will also repair chipped or damaged enamel. In any event it is the buyer's responsibility to satisfy himself regarding the quality and condition of what he is buying. Bear in mind that while dealers may not choose to draw your attention to a flaw, a reputable dealer will never tell you a deliberate untruth. If in doubt, ask whether a thimble has been repaired and listen carefully to the reply. Look at a porcelain thimble against a strong light when a hidden crack may become apparent as a shadow within the body of the porcelain. Study the surface carefully for any disturbance in the design and check the gilding. It is not easy for a restorer to match the color and texture of the gilding exactly, and this will often give the game away. Above all take your time. It is only after the most careful examination that you can decide whether the porcelain thimble you are offered is cheap at $250 or expensive at $50. With experience the pitfalls will become obvious, but even the expert can be taken in occasionally.

The art of the restorer is not necessarily put to dishonest uses and is therefore in a different category to outright fakes and forgeries. A plain silver thimble may be worth twenty dollars but a silver thimble set with turquoise is worth a hundred dollars or more. All that are required therefore are some old beads, together with an appropriate adhesive, to transform an ordinary thimble into something which is seemingly more valuable. Such fakes are crude and can usually

Coquilla with gold shield, French early nineteenth century. Note that original shield was evidently lost and replaced by a new ill-fitting shield. *Private collection*

be distinguished under a magnifying glass, because the adhesive will show around the stones. They are also often given away by the pattern of the silver thimble, which does not fit. But if the pattern is right and the thimble is presented sufficiently cleverly, for instance in a thimble case, it may be dangerous, and dealers themselves are sometimes misled.

Another source of deception is the apocryphal stories which may be woven around an ordinary thimble in order to make it seemingly more interesting. A typical example is the bronze colored thimbles decorated with an iron cross design and inscribed "Gott mit uns" which come from Germany. These are straightforward base metal thimbles (not necessarily iron) and quite collectable in their own right, but the story which sometimes goes with them that they were given to German housewives in exchange for gold thimbles to finance the cost of the First World War is an invention. Stories of this kind go back at least as far as the War of Independence against Napoleon in 1813, when gold wedding rings were exchanged for similar rings of iron. The familiar quotation "Gold gab ich für Eisen"

(I gave gold for iron) may have originated at this time and was engraved on the new rings. It is possible that wedding rings were again requisitioned in 1914–18, but this would not have applied to thimbles, if only because Continental Europe was relatively poor and thimbles made of precious metal were comparatively rare. At most, when a girl left school she might be given a silver thimble by her relations, which was greatly treasured and which was not used for sewing because it was regarded as too precious. Gold thimbles were virtually unknown and it would never have been worthwhile to collect them in this way.

Another story much in the same vein concerns wedding ring thimbles. Silver thimbles in the United States are sometimes decorated with a thin band of gold applied round the base as a means of ornamentation. This is a peculiarly American practice which is seldom found elsewhere and which has led to some curious misrepresentations, as witness the following paragraph from an antiques magazine:

Another traditional thimble was the silver and gold 'Wedding band' thimble. The rather tall thimble has a silver top ending in a gold band round the base. It was given to a young woman on the occasion of the betrothal by her fiancé. At the time of the marriage the gold band was cut off to serve as a wedding ring. These are occasionally found making one speculate as to why they are still intact.[3]

The above is obvious nonsense, but its sentimental appeal has led unscrupulous dealers to solder a gold wedding ring round a plain silver thimble and to offer the result to those gullible enough to swallow their story. The fact is that the association of silver thimbles and wedding rings is a mere figment of imagination and there is no such thing as a wedding ring thimble.

But probably the biggest source of cheating arises from plain outright misdescription. Thimbles are not normally valuable enough to warrant a receipt giving a full description, so that dealers are free to embroider at will. Countless celluloid or bone thimbles, for instance, have passed as ivory, which would not have happened if the dealer felt accountable. Often enough the error is deliberate, but it would be wrong to exclude genuine confusion. Telling one material from another is not always easy, particularly with

Early-nineteenth-century English porcelain. Damaged and repaired. Note the disturbance to the gilding. *Private collection*

regard to metals, where even the legitimate descriptions are often misleading. Terms such as gold filled, gold cased, and rolled gold, for instance, have become accepted over the years but they are traps for the unwary. The only certainty about terms of this kind is that they refer largely to base metal. Similarly with German silver, nickel silver, electroplated nickel silver (EPNS) and others which serve to describe base metal with or without a thin layer of silver. Other terms such as gold-plated silver, silver-plated nickel, and nickel-plated brass are perhaps less confusing, but the situation is not helped by the fact that thimble-makers themselves were never loath, particularly in Germany, to adorn and improve the appearance of their silver thimbles by treating them with a light coating of gold, either on the inside or the outside or both. This treatment could hardly be called gilding, because it was extremely light, and more often than not in the nature of a wash, but the difference between that and silver gilt is essentially a matter of degree. A famous deception concerning coated thimbles was perpetrated when the impresario P. T. Barnum presented the midget Tom

Thumb and his wife Lavinia Warren in Paris. Little brass thimbles, lightly washed with silver and sold as copies of Lavinia's silver thimble, soon showed the base metal underneath and the unsuspecting buyers realized that they had been deceived. Nowadays silver is hardly expensive enough to be worth faking, but gold or genuine silver gilt items are sufficiently valuable that great caution is necessary.

Misdescription need not be confined to the nature of the material, and of course age and provenance are also a fertile source of prevarica-

Damaged silver (cable) thimble with stone fitted at top to conceal holes. Note solder mark half way down the front. *Private collection*

tion. There is undoubtedly a tendency among dealers (as also among many collectors) to ante-date their thimbles, and far too many so-called eighteenth-century thimbles are in fact nineteenth-century. Bearing in mind the difficulties associated with dating thimbles, this is perhaps excusable: who can blame a dealer when some leading museums and even some popular reference books on thimbles do not necessarily know the difference? As in all forms of collecting, the only real safeguard is knowledge and experience. The strange thing is that after a time the expert develops an instinct for what is genuine, and it is possible to know that a thimble is "wrong" before being able to rationalize the precise reasons for rejecting it. This happens more often than one might think, but again the key is knowledge and experience.

It would be ungracious to end this chapter without paying due acknowledgment to the many dealers who are just as anxious as the collector to see fair play and who themselves are often the prey of the unscrupulous. Fortunately, careless or dishonest dealers are in the minority, but it would be foolish to pretend that they do not exist, and if this chapter can help to curtail their activities it will have served a useful purpose.

NOTES

1. Charles Dickens, *Nicholas Nickleby* (London, 1838), chap. 50.
2. James A. Michener, *Centennial* (London: 1974), Secker & Warburg.
3. "Sewing Antiques," in *Spinning Wheel Complete Book of Antiques,* ed. Marilyn Estes Smith, 548.

Thimbles in Museums

HOWEVER WELL THIMBLES MAY BE DESCRIBED OR however good the photographs and illustrations which may accompany such description, there is nothing to compare with actually seeing thimbles and if possible handling them.

Unfortunately, to see thimbles is easier said than done. Few museums have them, and when they do, the thimbles are usually relegated to the so-called reserve collection, which in effect means that they are stored away and can only be seen by appointment. Moreover, if thimbles are on show they may not necessarily be grouped together but scattered around the museum with other unrelated objects. The difficulty is that thimbles being needlework tools, they should normally come under textiles, but some specialized museums which do not have a textiles department own thimbles in the context of their specialty, and others such as the Victoria and Albert Museum, which does have a textiles department, nevertheless keep their thimbles dispersed among several departments. The ideal solution is to be found at the Swiss National Museum in Zurich, where the textiles department administers a small collection of thimbles together with other needlework tools—the best are on display and the remainder are in store. At the other extreme, the Archaeological Museum in Madrid have a noteworthy collection of early Moorish thimbles, which was known and commented upon at the end of the nineteenth century but which the Museum authorities subsequently forgot about until they were rediscovered a few years ago. Others, such as the Archaeological Museum in Florence, have lost all trace of thimbles which were known to be in their possession. Thimble collectors should perhaps be forgiven if they sometimes feel that archaeologists would do better by excavating the cellars of their museums.

Not surprisingly perhaps, the three most important collections of thimbles in the hands of museums are all located in the United States. They are the following:

a. *The collection belonging to the Textiles Department of the Colonial Williamsburg Foundation in Virginia*

The thimbles in the safekeeping of the Textiles Department of the Colonial Williamsburg Foundation were received by them as part of an important collection of sewing tools given by Mrs. R. E. Tomlinson. An account by the assistant curator of textiles of the sewing tools subject of the gift was published in the magazine *Antiques*.[1] Mrs. Tomlinson's collection included several former collections, notably that of Mrs. DeWitt Clinton Cohen, and since Mrs. DeWitt Clinton Cohen was a friend of Gertrude Whiting, the latter used some of the Cohen thimbles to illustrate her writings on the subject. It follows that many of the thimbles illustrated in *Tools and Stitchery* may now be found at Colonial Williamsburg. The thimbles in the collection have been carefully written up, but unfortunately many of

Thimbles from the British Museum. *Top row (left to right):* brass, spiral of large hand-punched indentations, claimed to be seventeenth century, height 1.7 cm; silver, indentations in the form of small circles, a cartouche flanked by two birds, maker's mark, English seventeenth century, height 1.6 cm; silver, indentations in the form of small circles, floral design round the base, height 2.0 cm. *Middle row (left to right):* brass chevron, design, rim inscribed "Be not idell," height 3.1 cm; brass sewing ring, decorated with an eagle with wings displayed, rim inscribed "Dio supra el Tuto," Italian, height 1.6 cm; bronze, spiral of small indentations, height 2.1 cm. *Bottom row (left to right):* bronze from Herpes, Charente (S.W. France), beehive-shaped thimble with smooth top, hand-punched indentations and punched wavy line round the rim, height 2.3 cm; silver, linked squares design over small waffle-shaped indentations, English seventeenth century, height 2.9 cm; silver, raised collar round base, hand-punched indentations round sides, molding at top, height 2.2 cm. *British Museum*

the descriptions follow those of Gertrude Whiting. All praise is due to Gertrude Whiting for being the first person in the English-speaking world to write about sewing tools, but much of what she wrote on the subject of thimbles was either naïve or plain mistaken. Many of her errors have been reproduced in the Colonial Williamsburg records, and the Williamsburg descriptions should therefore be taken with a pinch of salt.

There are only sixteen porcelain thimbles in the Colonial Williamsburg collection, but these include two eighteenth-century Meissen, a unique late-eighteenth-century thimble from the Royal Porcelain Factory at Naples which is decorated with a view of the Bay of Sorrento, and six Sampson Hancock Derby which, although not particularly outstanding in themselves, nevertheless constitute what is probably the finest and most representative group of these thimbles available anywhere. Among the enamels there are four Bilston and another eighteenth-century thimble of unknown origin. The gold thimbles feature several outstanding items, including a copy of the thimble presented by Paul Kruger to Queen Wilhelmina and also a number of highly interesting thimbles from Latin America. The collection includes fourteen thimbles in ivory, bone, and vegetable ivory, two tortoise-shells, a Piercy's patent, two mother-of-pearl with pansy decoration, a cut-glass and a vegetable ivory with polychrome decoration. It includes many silver thimbles, notably a seventeenth-century item decorated with a tulip, a seventeenth-century German decorated with putti, two nineteenth-century English, one depicting Lichfield Cathedral and the other unidentified, sundry Russian niellos, a nineteenth-century Chinese with wirework enamel, and some American scenic thimbles. There are also eight filigree thimble toys including one filigree thimble and scent bottle combined bearing the date 1811. Finally there are sundry items such as Korean tea cozies, a finely decorated Italian iron thimble, a Byzantine dome thimble, some interesting sewing rings, a brass filigree thimble with unusual design, and last but not least, sundry brass thimbles, possibly seventeenth-century Italian or Spanish, which are certainly worthy of further research. It is unfortunate that it has not always proved easy for visitors to inspect this lovely collection.

b. *The Alden Collection of Porcelain Thimbles at the Boston Museum of Fine Arts*

The thimbles belonging to the Museum of Fine Arts, Boston, came to them as the bequest of Louise D. Alden in 1962 and are known as the Alden Collection. The collection consists entirely of porcelain thimbles except for three late eighteenth-century English enamel (Bilston) thimbles. Its importance may be judged from the fact that it includes no less than twenty-three eighteenth-century Meissen, most of which are of the highest quality. The remainder are mostly good English nineteenth-century thimbles, but the collection does include about a dozen very ordinary twentieth-century Worcester and some damaged items, which can only be regarded as an eyesore in a collection of this quality. It is estimated that the world over there are probably only two hundred and fifty Meissen thimbles in being, so that the Alden Collection is obviously exceptional, and seeing that porcelain thimbles are so easy to display, it is a matter of regret that the Alden Collection remains out of sight in the Museum's basement.

c. *The Mary Gallatin Hoppin Collection of Thimbles at the Smithsonian Institution, Washington, D.C.*

The thimbles in the safekeeping of the Smithsonian Institution came to them as the bequest of Mrs. Mary Gallatin Hoppin and are known as the Mary Gallatin Hoppin Collection of Thimbles. The collection consists of some 420 items, a few of which are of the highest quality, but the bulk so trifling that it is beneath notice and can only be regarded as an embarrassment. Furthermore, although the donor kept meticulous records of where the thimbles came from and on what occasion, her ideas about the thimbles themselves were wildly incorrect. In other words, the collection badly needs the services of a strong-minded curator to put some order into it. To give an example, there are about a hundred porcelain thimbles in the collection—rather more than in the Alden Collection—and it includes eleven eighteenth-century Meissen, but at the other extreme there are forty twentieth-century Worcester, mostly contemporary and totally devoid of interest. It also includes a couple of dozen plastic thimbles besides countless contemporary tourist items of no conceivable value. Nevertheless, there are some interesting thimbles to be found here and there. In addition to the eleven Meissen already mentioned, there is a Mennecy and at least one other eighteenth-century French porcelain, four English eighteenth-century enamels (Bilston), two early Hispano-Moresque, two Byzantine domes, several nineteenth-century silver from Asia Minor, and a few interesting English nineteenth-century porcelain, as well as some early nineteenth-century English silver thimbles. The collection is on display at the National Museum of American History.

In addition to these three collections there are also some smaller collections in the United States, notably at the Slater Museum, Norwich, Connecticut, where there is a small collection on permanent display; the Washington Historical Society, Washington, Connecticut (The Hunt Collection); the Munson-Williams-Proctor Institute, Utica, New York (The Proctor Collection); the Hyde Collection, Glens Falls, New York; and the Cummer Gallery of Art, Jacksonville, Florida, which latter somewhat improbably owns eight porcelain thimbles, all eighteenth-century, and six of them Meissen of the highest quality. Other American museums also own thimbles of

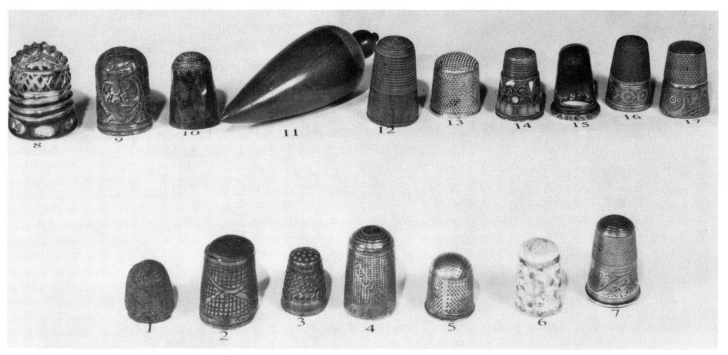

Thimbles from the Greg collection of Handicrafts, Manchester Museum:

1. **Medieval brass thimble**
2. **Seventeenth century brass**
3. **Unknown origin**
4. **Silver inscribed "The gift be small goodwill to all," seventeenth century**
5. **Silver, English seventeenth century**
6. **English nineteenth-century porcelain**
7. **English silver thimble and vinaigrette—early nineteenth century**
8. **Glass, probably English nineteenth century**
9. **Unknown origin**
10. **Cut steel thimble, probably French nineteenth century (There is a similar thimble in the collection of the Bethnal Green Museum.)**
11. **Thimble and thimble case, mulberry wood, nineteenth century (See *Treen and other Wooden Bygones* by Edward H. Pinto, London 1969, plate 339.)**
12. **As above.**
13. **Eighteenth-century gold**
14. **Russian silver with enamel, nineteenth century**
15. **Silver finger guard, probably English nineteenth century**
16. **Said to be Spanish but more likely German decorated in Spain**
17. **As above. *Manchester Museum***

interest but these are often individual items, not collections, and as such are hardly worth the trouble and expense of a special visit.

Besides the United States, England is one of the few countries where there are museums possessing a collection of thimbles. The collections in England are smaller and comprise mostly English thimbles, but the individual items are older and often of great rarity. The Victoria and Albert Museum possesses some fine thimbles, but unfortunately they are widely dispersed among several different departments, including ceramics, textiles, and the museum's offshoot in Bethnal Green. The British Museum has a collection which comes under the Department of Medieval and Later Antiquities and so has the Museum of London and also the Cuming Museum in South London. Outside London the two best collections will be found in the Manchester Gallery of English Costume and in the Strangers' Hall of the City of Norwich Museum. These are small but good quality collections of interest to those wishing to see some older English thimbles.

Elsewhere in Europe there is not a great deal to be seen. Most archaeological museums possess a few thimbles, beginning with the prestigious Musée des Antiquités Nationales at St. Germain-en-Laye, which is the leading Gallo-Roman museum in France, the Heerlen Museum in Holland, and the Rheinisches Landesmuseum at Trier in Germany. Unfortunately most (if not all) of these so-called Roman thimbles are medieval or later, but they are no less interesting for all that. The Museo Arqueológico in Madrid has, as earlier mentioned, a fine collection of eighteen Hispano-Moresque thimbles which date from the tenth to twelfth centuries. The Musée Le Secq des Tournelles at Rouen, which specializes in iron and steel, has a unique collection of twenty-eight decorated steel thimbles, mostly Italian eighteenth century. The Swiss National Museum at Zurich is also noteworthy, not perhaps for the quality of its collection of thimbles but because of the care and enthusiasm with which the Costume and Textiles Department has developed its collection of sewing tools, including thimbles. The State Hermitage Museum at Leningrad also has a few thimbles, including at least one Meissen. It would be quite impractical to list all the museums which own thimbles, nor would there be much purpose, but the above will serve to give some indication of what is available.

As explained above, the main problem about thimbles in museums is that they do not fit under any convenient description. Perhaps for this reason the thimble has received little attention as an

Silver-gilt thimbles designed to commemorate the Pforzheim Schmuckmuseum thimble exhibition in 1979 and the tour that followed. *Left to right:* **Pforzheim, Schwäbish-Gmünd, Hanau.** *Private collection*

230

object of historical and cultural significance, which will explain the importance of an exhibition held under the name of Fingerhüte und Historisches Nähzeug and staged by the Schmuckmuseum Pforzheim in November 1978. Pforzheim, which is situated on the edge of the Black Forest, is the principal center of the goldsmith and jewelry trade in Germany. It possesses what is probably the only specialized jewelry museum to be found anywhere in the world, and the museum serves both as a showcase for its own valuable collection of jewels and also to display the work of local craftsmen. From time to time the museum authorities hold a more specialized exhibition, and because thimbles have long been made in Pforzheim, they readily agreed to the suggestion of a former master goldsmith and thimble-maker that the museum should hold an exhibition of thimbles. In order that the thimbles should be presented to the best advantage and for purposes of decoration, the scope of the exhibition was enlarged to include a few sewing tools and embroidery, but it was essentially an exhibition of thimbles which were loaned by German museums, notably some late sixteenth-century thimbles from the Kunstgewerbemuseum, Berlin, by some local German thimble-makers past and present, and by private collectors. The exhibition, which was undoubtedly the first professionally organized thimble exhibition ever held, was subsequently transferred to the Deutsches Goldschmiedehaus, Hanau, near Frankfurt, and then to the Städtischsmuseum at Schwäbish-Gmünd. It aroused remarkable interest and received extensive coverage in the German national press, wireless, and television. It was also noticed most favorably in several neighboring countries, and it is to be hoped that the success of the Pforzheim exhibition may persuade museums fortunate enough to possess a collection of thimbles to accord them more recognition.

NOTE

1. Sandra C. Shaffer, "Sewing Tools in the Collection of Colonial Williamsburg," *Antiques,* August 1973.

Thimbles for Other Uses

THERE ARE A NUMBER OF APPLIANCES WHICH FIT on the finger and look very much like thimbles but which are not necessarily designed to protect the finger from the point of a needle. Among these may be mentioned the following:

—The wig-maker's thimble has a pointed end in order to lift the underlying canvas and facilitate the insertion of the needle.

—The plate photographer's thimble has an attachment designed to lift the plates without touching them. It was used in earlier times when photographers worked with wet glass plates. Once in the developing tray they were difficult to lift away from the smooth bottom of the tray until a thimble with a pointed claw was invented to help the photographer reach under the sticky wet glass by first raising the edge with the claw.

—The ophthalmologist's (eye surgeon's) thimble has a curved T-shaped attachment about 2.0 cm long to enable the eyelid to be held back during examination or surgery.

—The tobacco stemming thimble is an open top thimble made of thin metal sheeting. It was worn on the thumb and forefinger by workers in tobacco plants when stripping the heavy veins from the leaves before the tobacco is processed.

—The tambour thimble is designed for tambour work or crochet embroidery. In her *Encyclopédie des ouvrages de dames* Thérèse de Dillmont de-

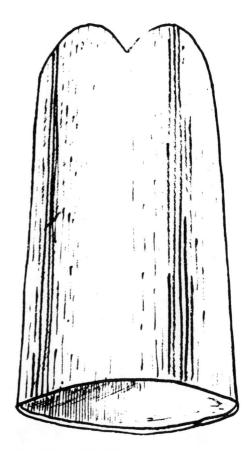

Sketch of tambour thimble. *Private collection*

232

scribes a special type of thimble, worn on the forefinger of the right hand, made of a piece of coiled metal which was not joined and could therefore be expanded as required. It was open at the top like a tailor's thimble and had a notch cut at the highest part of the sloping top, which was worn above the fingernail. This notch was used to guide the movements of the tambour needle and press down the fabric as each loop was worked. See also *Les broderies et les dentelles (cours en quarante leçons)* by Mlle Marguerite Charles et M. Laurent Pagés, Paris, 1905, which illustrates a tambour thimble.

—The thimble for handling paper was patented in 1895 (No. 8486, by J. Garton) and similar types of thimbles made of rubber with small asperities are widely used for leafing over sheets of paper, counting notes, or other similar applications. They are made in a range of sizes and are sometimes known as finger cones or fingerettes.

—The pipe-smoker's thimble is one of the many forms of tampers for a pipe.

—The thatcher's thimble is made of tin, and four worn on fingers of the left hand were used by thatchers in Norfolk until well into this century. The thimbles were used chiefly by the thatcher's assistant to protect his fingertips from thistles when handling the straw or rushes. A leather glove would have worn out too quickly. A set of thatcher's thimbles may be seen in the Bridewell Museum at Norwich.

—A thimble valvulotome similar to a tailor's thimble is used as a surgeon's instrument in a heart operation known as mitral valvulotomy. See *Mitral Valvulotomy—The Technic with Particular Reference to the use of a Thimble Valvulotome* by William W. L. Glenn, *Annals of Surgery* 145, no. 4 (April 1957).

—The ticker-tape thimble was devised by the American cable company Western Union to cut the ticker tape for their telegrams. There was a razor attached and the staff used it to slice the tape. The thimbles were marked "Western Union."

—A husking thimble was patented by J. H. Gould of Deerfield, Ohio, in the mid-nineteenth century. In the operation of husking corn it was the practice to hold the ear of corn in one hand and to slit the husk lengthwise with a fingernail of the other hand. This method damaged the end of the finger and wore out the nail, causing

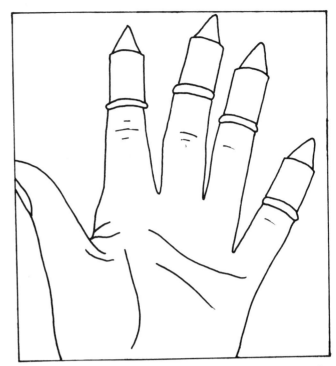

Sketch of Norfolk thatcher's tin thimbles. *Private collection*

Thimble used in a heart operation. *Private collection*

the operator pain and injury. The husking thimble consists of a thimble which fits over the finger, and the small cutter at the end is used in place of the nail, resulting in a quicker, easier job.

—The harvester's thimble, somewhat similar to the thatcher's thimble, which was sufficiently widely used in Spain that it gave rise to a proverb: *Cuando segares, no vayas sin dedales*. For a detailed account of the use of the harvester's

Indian woman's dress made of buckskin and decorated with thimbles. Klamath reservation, nineteenth century. *Field Museum of Natural History, Chicago*

thimble, see *Revista de Filológica Española* (Madrid) 15:271.

This account of thimbles serving for other purposes than needlework would not be complete without some reference to thimble bells.

Thimbles have been used for many strange purposes, but none stranger than the practice which grew among American Indians at the end of the eighteenth century to use thimbles to adorn clothing. Small holes were pierced through the top of plain commercial thimbles so that they could be hung on thongs over a bead in the manner of a bell. These thimble bells were attached to various items such as the edge of a bodice or the hem of a dress, skirt, bag, or beaded ceremonial stole. A complete dress so ornamented may be seen at the Field Museum of Natural History in Chicago. The dress, which originates from the Klamath Reservation, is said to date back to 1850, and it has some forty thimbles hanging from it as pendants, all unused, of different sizes and not identical. Similarly, the Denver Art Museum has an Indian medicine man's pouch made of otter skin, decorated with thimbles. These are brass and punched through the top with beaded thongs. It appears that from an early date itinerant peddlers were visiting Indian territory and the thimbles were traded and adapted for a purpose for which they were not intended. The use of thimble bells to adorn clothing is well attested. Cushman refers to "the monotonous tinkling and rattling of the thimble bells and terrapin shells" in Indian dancing. In Choctaw there was a special word to denote thimbles worn for decoration, and they were so called because of the tinkling sound.[1]

Even more curious, the practice of adapting thimbles into thimble bells was also followed in parts of Russia. Garments have been found from Russia's northern areas with thimble bells attached and during the nineteenth century travelers reported seeing women from villages on the banks of the Volga wearing dresses decorated with thimbles. The simultaneous and independent development of such an odd practice would be totally puzzling if it were not for underlying similarities between the two areas. Not only does association of bells with ritual activities lie deeply buried in mankind (e.g., Morris dancing), but it occurs frequently in Shamanism, a religious phenomenon which found its chief expression among the Siberian and Ural-Altaic people. The shaman's or spiritual leader's costume would be decorated with sundry metallic objects, notably bells, which were reputed to repel evil spirits. Shamanism also held sway among North American aboriginal tribes, and it becomes less surprising therefore to find primitive people in both areas reacting in the same way.

NOTE

1. H. B. Cushman, *History of Indians* (1899), 501.

Collecting Thimbles

A WISE COLLECTOR DOES NOT SEEK TO rationalize his motives and should be content that his collection brings him pleasure and satisfaction. Nevertheless, it is permissible to ask why thimble collecting has become so popular, and the reasons are not far to find. Apart from the general attraction of smallness and quality in an age that revels in largeness and mass production, a special and added fascination of thimbles is that they are one of the earliest domestic tools of mankind. There is an underlying sense of purpose and industry about thimbles which distinguishes them from mere trifles, and up to a point the fact that the thimble is becoming obsolescent also adds to its significance in the eyes of collectors. Because the thimble is universal and because it was used by rich and poor alike throughout the centuries, it has become an integral part of our civilization. Generations of craftsmen have devoted their skill to producing better and more attractive thimbles, ranging from plain utilitarian objects to the height of the goldsmith's and jeweler's art. Beautiful, precious objects have always been collected, but thimbles have the added attraction that they have always held an honored place in the household.

Another factor which undoubtedly adds to the popularity of thimble collecting is the excitement of the chase. This applies to some extent to all forms of collecting, but the thimble being so small, distinctive, and universal, it is ideal for the purpose—the same qualities which established hunt-the-thimble as a favourite game in the nursery. Today hunt-the-thimble is an adult pursuit engaging the attention of many collectors throughout the world. The United States is undoubtedly the most thimble-conscious country. Certainly it is the only one with both national and regional thimble collectors' clubs, and it even has mail-order businesses directed specially at thimble collectors. However, collectors will also be found in many other countries, and the truth is that thimble hunting has become so popular that good thimbles are increasingly scarce. It is tempting to think of old ladies treasuring the silver thimble which belonged to their great-grandmothers—"un dée en argent tch' apparténait à ma grand'grand'méthe," as an old saying from the Channel Islands goes. No doubt there are more thimbles coming forward all the time, but in practice much of the better and older material has long been in the hands of collectors. The trade in thimbles is well organized and any newcomer to thimble collecting should bear this in mind.

It is not the purpose here to discuss how to set about collecting thimbles or to suggest the different types of thimbles in which a collector might specialize. The enormous variety makes it difficult at first to know which thimbles to collect and where and how to start. A good beginning is to look at thimbles in museums and private collections and to become aware of thimbles. The first criterion must be to collect what you like. Neither is it intended to consider the question of price, because prices can vary enormously.

The Mecca for small antiques collectors: Portobello Road Market, London, at eight o'clock on Saturday morning. *Private collection*

There is, however, one rule about buying thimbles which is worth remembering: keep to thimbles in good condition and concentrate on beauty and quality. Examine a thimble both inside and outside, remembering that the inside is often the more revealing of its state of preservation. Silver thimbles with holes in them, for instance, should be avoided, and so should thimbles which have been repaired. Look for thimbles with aesthetic appeal, thimbles which also have an appearance of richness and solidity. Then after buying a thimble bring it home, clean it carefully both inside and out, study it and gloat over it to your heart's content; if it continues to give you pleasure and if you can regard the price you paid for it with equanimity, you can be sure that it was a good buy. If, on the other hand, you find your pleasure diminishes, if you start thinking that the price you paid may have been excessive, it was probably a bad buy. There is no market price for thimbles. It is easy to get carried away in the excitement of the chase and each collector must set his own limits. Above all, disregard talk about thimbles being a good investment. This is the sort of nonsense which is put

Convention badge. *Private collection*

about by journalists who are short of copy or by dealers who are trying to persuade you to pay more than you can afford. The wise collector should forget about market trends and concentrate on buying carefully and sensibly within his means.

237

A wealth of thimbles. *Private collection*

should be carefully examined and cleaned when necessary. Cleaning an old brass thimble will merely destroy the patina—but most silver thimbles need to be polished if they are to look their best. Cleaning silver thimbles can be tiresome because of the difficulty of reaching tarnished areas within the indentations, but once it is clean the thimble will remain in good condition and can be polished again easily.

Some collectors find that systematic record keeping increases the enjoyment they get from their collections and they catalog each new acquisition as it arrives. There is no set form for cataloging thimbles, but the following is a checklist of the points to be covered:

Having started a thimble collection, the collector will be faced with the choice of where to house it. Some collectors keep their thimbles in specially designed display cabinets, others in boxes, drawers, or cases, and yet others find it preferable to keep their thimbles in a safe deposit. This is really a matter for the individual, but velvet-lined boxes divided into small compartments—say fifty to a box—are very convenient. Furthermore, thimbles are easy to look after and require little attention. New additions

—Name of collection and/or reference number
—Composition of thimble (gold, silver, brass, etc.)
—Origin (if known)
—Condition (state if damaged)
—Brief description of thimble
—Inscriptions and/or hallmarks (if any)
—Country of manufacture (if known)
—Name of manufacturer (if known)
—Size number (if any)
—Date when it was made
—Height (in centimeters) and/or weight (in grams)
—Cross references (if any)

Putti with thimbles. *Private collection*

To the above it may be desirable to add the following:

—Brief commentary on thimble and its attribution
—Details of any photographs available
—How, when, and where acquired
—Value for insurance purposes.

The following are two examples of catalog references taken from international museums:

British Museum, Department of Medieval and Later Antiquities,

81, 11-4, 4 Silver. Two ovals containing a head: one obliterated other crowned and inscribed C.R.2. English, 17th century. Height 1.8 cms.

Kunstgewerbe Museum Berlin, Inv. No. F2321:

Silver-gilt thimble with detachable cap and inside under a transparent cover a shield with flowers and near it the date 1606 and the letter VGMN. The sides surrounded by ornamentation and at the rim the inscription "IVNKFRAU (Miss) IVSTINA VON HERTEN." Height 2.0 cms.

Thimbles can be examined satisfactorily with the naked eye, but a glass of the type used by watch repairers with a magnification of ×5 or ×10 will be found useful when looking at hallmarks. A simple millimeter gauge is also useful when measuring the height for cataloging purposes. Otherwise there is no special equipment required for thimble collecting unless it is desired to keep a photographic record.

A detailed account of how to photograph thimbles is beyond the scope of this book. But a few hints may nevertheless be found helpful. The first consideration, as in all kinds of photography, is of course that of equipment, but for amateur purposes a normal 35-mm single lens reflex camera (SLR) with a built-in exposure meter, preferably of the type that measures the brightness on the focusing screen or at the film plane, and with a set of extension tubes for close-up focusing, will serve admirably. With such equipment it is possible for the image size recorded on the film to be approximately the same size as a thimble and to work in either black and white or in color.

Thimble photography can be carried out either outdoors, preferably on a bright day, or else indoors under artificial lighting conditions. The main advantage of outdoor photography is that lighting presents fewer problems. Rather than set up the camera in an open position, it is best to work in a shady spot because shade gives more even lighting and will serve to bring out the details of the thimble. The disadvantage is that the intensity of the light may vary according to the time of day or the weather and that working outdoors there are too many extraneous factors to disturb the photographer and take away from his concentration. Close-up photography requires the utmost precision and control of a kind more suited to a laboratory, so that where possible working indoors is preferable.

The biggest problem with indoor photography is undoubtedly the question of lighting and, if working in color, that property known as the color temperature. Flash lighting is not usually satisfactory because for close-up work the amount of light is too large to handle conveniently and its effect too uncertain. It is therefore necessary to fall back on a light source of the photoflood variety. Photoflood bulbs have a high intensity with a short life. Their color temperature is 3,400 Kelvin units and they are intended for use with Tungsten type color film. Normal outdoor or flash color film is not usually suitable. However, since Tungsten type color film is usually balanced at 3,200 Kelvin, it may be necessary to use a No. 81A filter or its equivalent, and this in turn requires correcting the film speed or exposure in order to achieve accurate color reproduction. Professionals often use what is known as a light tent to obtain completely uniform diffuse lighting, but if this is not available two reflectors, each fitted with a 275 watt No. 1 photoflood bulb and positioned above and behind on each side of the camera at a distance of twelve inches from the subject, will yield good results. Achieving a high intensity of light in this way creates considerable heat, so that good ventilation is needed to keep both the photographer and his equipment reasonably cool. This, however, is the lesser of two evils because if light intensity is low, exposure times may have to be increased to the point where reciprocity failure may enter the exposure equation. In this event an additional exposure time must be added (tables are available to compute this additional

Thimble boxes and records. *Private collection*

time) for accurate color or black and white reproduction, but it is an unnecessary and added complication.

Another problem associated with close-up photography is sensitivity to vibration. The magnification produced using close-up equipment also magnifies any disturbance, so that the least vibration results in a blurred image. For good results, therefore, the camera should be mounted on a tripod—a small table-top tripod is often the most convenient—and a cable release must be used to trip the shutter. Similarly the thimble should rest in a stable position on a small sturdy stage which will need to be placed at a convenient height. A piece of paper is fastened to the front of the stage and curled upward and backward to form a background. The subject being so small, there is no need for a large piece of paper. Standard A4 is more than sufficient and any good quality mat surfaced paper without watermark in white, or possibly some neutral color, is suitable.

When positioning the camera it should be aimed very slightly down on the thimble. This will allow part of the crown to be seen and will also have the advantage that a thimble having slanted sides, the side will be more closely parallel to the plane of the camera and allow more accurate focusing. As the camera is brought closer to the subject the depth of the field narrows, and though this can be compensated for by stopping down the lens, nevertheless at very close distances an extremely narrow depth of field is inevitable. The lens should therefore be stopped down to the smallest aperture and care taken that the greater part of the thimble lies in the zone of sharpness. In practice it is best to set the focusing ring at whatever setting gives the desired reproduction ratio and to bring the image into focus by drawing the thimble and the stage on which it rests forward or backward as necessary.

As in all photography, accurate exposure measurement is essential. This is often a problem in

240

close-up photography, because the lighting of the background may influence the setting, but it is less so with thimbles, which because of their shape can readily be made to fill much of the frame. It follows that for best results thimbles should be photographed individually and a one-to-one reproduction ratio is indicated, both for being more convenient and to give maximum detail. Particularly with color film, exposure is critical and the less background there is, the less likely it is to affect the meter. Incidentally, in using an automatic exposure camera, care should be taken to cover the eyepiece, as light straying inside can affect the meter and lead to underexposure. In general, mat surfaces are easier to photograph and for this reason silver thimbles are best left unpolished. To dull bright metallic thimbles a special "dulling spray" may be obtained from most photographic suppliers, which can be washed off after use. Alternatively where dulling spray is not available, highlights can be toned down by dabbing an unduly bright silver thimble with plasticine or builders' putty, which will achieve the same effect.

The pleasure of collecting can be enhanced considerably by photography. For one thing, it is a curious fact that a photograph will often reveal details which are by no means so obvious without it. Quite literally, the collector is made to view the thimble in a different light. But equally important, because of the difficulties of time and distance, it is not always possible for collectors to meet each other, and the exchange of photographs is one of the best ways to keep in touch. A keen collector will necessarily wish to correspond with others, and no amount of description can ever take the place of a photograph.

Finally, if a collector is really interested in

Designs for thimbles. After an engraving by Joh. Theo. de Bry (1528–98).

thimbles he will study the pieces in his collection, exchange views with other collectors, and seek out information in archives, libraries, and museums. As will be obvious from reading this book, much remains to be discovered, and it is to be hoped that many more collectors will feel inspired to probe the records and help recall the importance and exclusiveness that has attached to the thimble throughout its history.

Appendix 1
Thimble Dictionary

TRANSLATION OF THE WORD FOR A THIMBLE IN ALL main spoken languages, together with notes on derivation and on the native languages of Africa and America.

Afrikaans	**vingerhoed**
Albanian	**gishtëz**
Anglo-Saxon	**(th) ŷmel**
Arabic	**kustuban** (see note d)
Armenian	**madnotz**
Basque	**atz-andel**
Bengali	**angushtáná**
Bohemian (Czech)	**náprstek**
Bulgarian	**naprustnik**
Calabrese	**iritale**
Catalan	**didal**
Chinese	**su chi ing, jumting** (Canton), **tzeng koo** (Shanghai)
Cornish	**bysgon**
Creole	**dé**
Croatian	**napršnjak**
Danish	**fingerbol**
Dutch	**vingerhoed**
English	**thimble, tailor's thimble** (t), **sewing ring** (t) (see note a)
Eskimo	**tîkerk, pudjortok** (t)
Esperanto	**fringringo**
Esthonian	**sôrmkübar**
Finnish	**sormustin, syyrinki** (t)
Flemish	**vingerhoot**
French	**dé, dé fermé, dé ouvert** (t)
Gaelic	**meuran**
German	**fingerhut, nähring** (t)
Greek (Classical)	**See note b**
Greek (modern)	**daktilithra**
Gujarati	**angoothiyum**
Hawaiian	**komo, komo humuhumu, komo lima**
Hebrew	**etzbaon**
Hindi	**angulitran, angusthana**
Hungarian	**gyüszü**
Icelandic	**fingurbjörg**
Indonesian	**tudung, sarung djari, bidal**
Irish	**méaracán**
Italian	**ditale, anello (da cucire)** (Tuscany) (t)
Japanese	**yubi wa, yubi sashi, yubinuki**
Javanese	**bidal**
Korean	**kolmi**
Latin (Classical)	**See note b**
Latvian	**uzpirkstenis, fingerröd**
Lebanese	**omeh**
Limousinian	**dedau, da**
Lithuanian	**pirštukas**
Malay	**bidal, lidal** (Selangor), **sarong jari** (Kedah)
Maltese	**holga talhjata**
Manx	**farvair, mairane** (t)
Mongolian	**huruuvch**
Nepalese	**anwaltunhu**

243

Norwegian	**fingerbøl**
Persian	**angushtana, angushtdān**
Polish	**naparstek**
Portuguese	**dedal**
Rumanian	**degetar**
Russian	**naperstok**
Samoan	**atigi lima**
Sanskrit	**See note c**
Serbian	**naprstak**
Siamese	**plok suam niew**
Slovak	**náprsok**
Slovenian	**naprstnik**
Spanish	**dedal, dedal abierto** (t)
Swahili	**kastabani, subana, tondoo** (see note e)
Swedish	**fingerborg, syring** (t)
Tahitian	**ponao**
Tamil	**virarchimizhi, virar-munaippun**
Thai	**polk suam niew**
Tibetan	**lćuṅ-mo, mdzub-rtén**
Tongan	**nge'esi-nima**
Turkish	**yüksük**
Ukrainian	**hanépcmok, nanepcmin**
Vietnamese	**cái dê**
Welsh	**gwniadur, bysleder**
Yiddish	**fingerhut**
Zulu	**isigaka so munwe** (see note e)

NOTES

a. A small letter (t) after a word denotes that the word refers to a tailor's thimble.

b. Classical antiquity—Although the names of various sewing requisites figure in Classical Greek and Latin and although there is even a hieroglyphic depicting a needle (**mehtep**), nowhere is the written word for a thimble to be found. The words **digitale** and **digitabulum** may be found among others in Low Latin.

c. Sanskrit—It is not known whether the word for thimble existed but the following are of interest:

anguli	finger
anguli-tra	woman's finger guard
angulitrâna	"
angulî	finger
angulîya	finger-ring
angúshtha	thumb

d. Arabic—Dozy, *Supplément aux dictionnaires arabes*, gives **kustuban** (Persian **alkushtbaneh**, later **ankushtuwaneh**), also **kushtuban** and **kustuwan** (plural **-āt**) A Thimble. The word **kustuban** does not appear in Lane's *Arabic-English Lexicon* and presumably therefore it does not feature in Lisan al Arab, which indicates that it is a postclassical word, i.e., that it dates from after about A.D. 850.

e. African Languages—The thimble does not appear to have been known in Africa until it was introduced under the influence of the Mediterranean civilizations. Some African languages have therefore adopted the foreign word, e.g., Kikongo, Lingala, Lontomba, which employ the French word **dé,** and Sotho, which employs the word **fimpele,** derived from the English **thimble.** Others have transposed the foreign word into the local idiom, e.g., Zulu which employs the name **isigawa so munwe,** that is to say "a hat of the finger," after the Afrikaans **vingerhoed.** In Swahili the word **kastabani** (also **kustabini**) is used, obviously derived from the Arabic. Or else **subana** (also **subano**), also possibly from the Arabic, for a trifle of no importance. The word **tondoo** may be found. In Kikuyu the word is **thubana** (also **thubano**) after the same root as **subana.**

f. Native American Languages—Similarly, the thimble does not appear to have been known in either North or South America until the arrival of the Europeans. Some native American languages have therefore adopted the foreign word, e.g., Guarani, which employs the Spanish word **dedal,** or else, as in the case of most North American Indian languages, the word was transposed into the local idiom as in the following examples:

Atakapa	**ka-u wōc** To cover, put into, finger
Choctaw	**ibbak ushi foka** Finger, about
Hopi	**malatchi toque pai** Finger, sack
Osage	**shá-ge u-gtho** Finger, in which, to put

In Choctaw the word **tạli kạssa** was used to denote thimbles worn as ornaments and are so called for the tinkling sound of thimble bells. (See H. B. Cushman, *History of Indians* [1899], 501.) Other North American derivations are reported as follows:

Alaska—Eskimo	**oknikmiladon**
—Tlinqit	**kik shanok audee**
Apache	**deh'dah'l** (Sp. Dedal)
Cherokee	**ah-li-ye-su-sto-wo**
Chickasaw	**ilbuk achoshowa**
Coushatta	**illbesteelka**
Cree	**kaskik wa suna bisk**
Creek	**estenk-svhepak'kv**
Dakota	**napostay** (Sl. Naperstok)
Micmac	**bookasooties**
Mohawk	**ion-nes-snon-so-roks-ta**
Navajo	**hala-basa-ana**
Onondaga	**nonnio'sta**
Ojibwa	**gandaig wa ssowin** (Eng. Sewing)
Ottawa	**gon-de-ne-oun**
Seminole	**estenk-sv-hepak'kn**
Sioux	**nah-pa-sh'don**
Winnebago	**nap ho-wa-ghook**

Appendix 2
Manufacture of Sewing Thimbles
By F. H.

THE DIES AND DEVICES DESCRIBED IN THIS ARTI-
cle are employed in the production of thimbles
used in sewing. The shape of the work after each
consecutive operation up to the seventh may be
seen in Fig. 2. Other operations, as shown in
Figs. 8 and 9, are required to knurl the thimble
and stamp little depressions into the end, as
shown in the enlarged half-section view, Fig. 1.

The diameter of the blank A, Fig. 2, is 1½
inches, and the area 1.767 square inches including the part trimmed from the end in the fifth
operation. The material from which the thimbles are drawn is sheet copper, 0.0140-inch
thick. A limited number of thimbles are made
from silver of the same thickness, in the same
dies. The presses used are of the inclinable type.

The die used for the first operation is shown
in Fig. 4. The material is fed to this die in strip
form, the blanks being cut out and drawn to the
shape shown at B, Fig. 2. The piece is removed
from the punch by the blank-holder B, Fig. 4,
and from the die, by the knock-out pin C. The
diameter of the die equals the outside diameter
of the drawn cup.

The die shown in Fig. 5 reduces the diameter
approximately 20 percent. The work is placed
on the blank-holder E by the operator. The
press slide descends far enough to permit the
cup to be stripped from the punch by the spring-

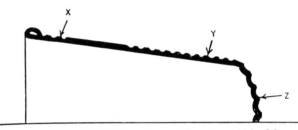

Fig. 1. Enlarged Half-section of Sewing Thimble.

actuated strippers F. The cup remains in the
hole G of the die until the next piece of work
passes out through the die and slides through a
large hole in the back of the press. Thus the
operator is not required to remove the work.
The blank-holder is operated by a spring pressure attachment. The diameter of the die in this
case also equals the outside diameter of the cup,
and the diameter of the punch is the same as the
inside diameter of the cup which is shown at C,
Fig. 2.

The die used for the third operation, shown in
Fig. 3, resembles the one used for the second
operation. It consists primarily of the parts I and
K. The small strippers are so arranged that the
work is removed at once after each down stroke.
The diameters of the punch and the die are
equal to the inside and outside diameters of the
cup, respectively. These dimensions make no allowance for clearance. The dimensions given at

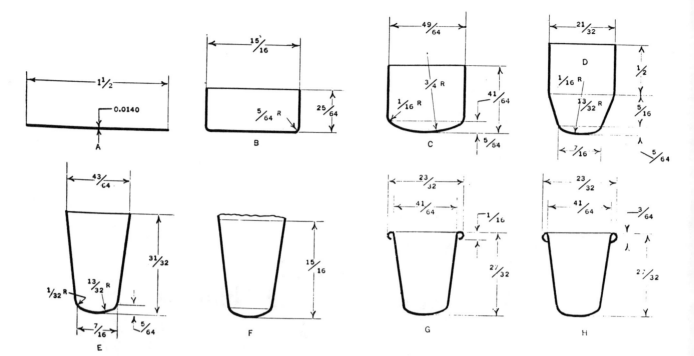

Fig. 2. Shape of Work after each Consecutive Forming Operation.

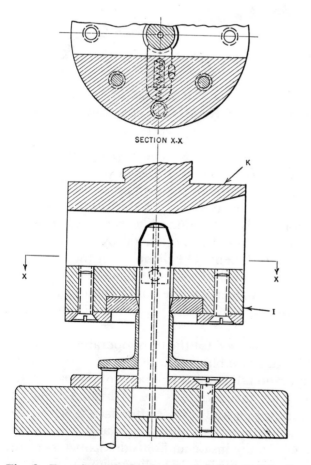

Fig. 3. Forming Die for Producing Cup D, Fig. 2.

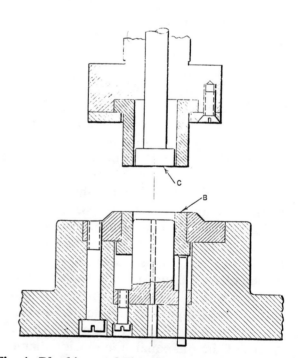

Fig. 4. Blanking and First Forming Operation Die.

246

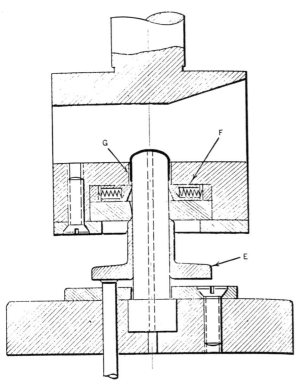

Fig. 5. Die for Drawing Work to Shape C, Fig. 2.

D, Fig. 2, apply to the inside diameters.

In Fig. 6 is shown the forming die used in the fourth operation. This gives the lower part of the thimble its final shape. When the operation is completed, the stripper M lifts the cup so that it may easily be removed by the operator. The knock-out pin N is provided to eject the work from the die.

As a preparation for the following operation, the cup F, Fig. 2, must be trimmed. It is, therefore, placed on the arbor P, Fig. 8, which is held in the chuck of a trimming machine and revolved at high speed. The stop Q holds the work in place while it is being trimmed to length by the tool R. The inward movement of the circular cutter R is effected by means of a foot-treadle. The work is held in a similar manner for the rolling and curling operations.

From the trimming machine the cup goes back to the press, where the trimmed edge is curled in the die shown in Fig. 7 to the shape shown at G, Fig. 2. The work is placed on the holder T, Fig. 7, and the curling operation is performed by the die U when the press slide descends. The work is removed from the die by the pin V. The

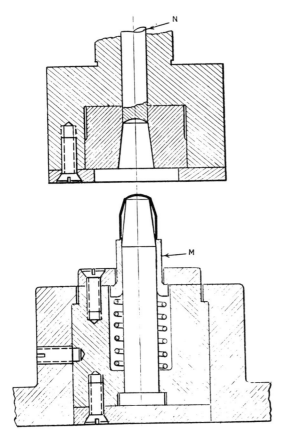

Fig. 6. Die for Producing Shape shown at E, Fig. 2.

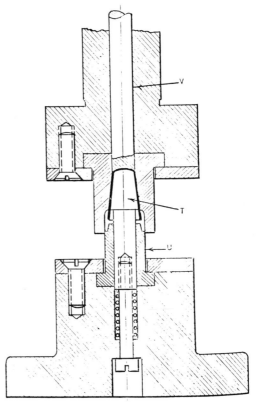

Fig. 7. Die for Curling Edge as shown at G, Fig. 2.

247

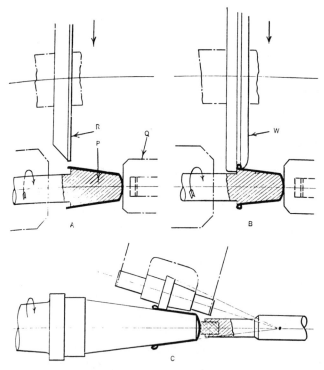

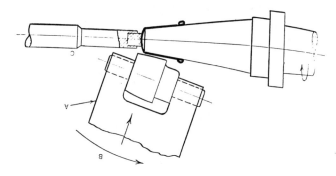

Fig. 8. Trimming, Finish-curling, and Knurling Tools.

Fig. 9. Knurling indentations in Thimble.

finish-curling operation is performed as shown in view B, Fig. 8. The roller W used for this purpose has a groove that produces the required roll or curl, as shown at H, Fig. 2.

A screw press is employed for stamping the depressions on the bottom of the thimble at Z, Fig. 1. These depressions show up somewhat, on the inside of the thimble, while those at Y, which are obtained by knurling, do not change the appearance of the inside of the thimble. Generally, an artistic design is knurled on the thimble at X close to the curled edge. A cylindrical roller (which is not shown) is employed for this purpose if the design is narrow as compared to the length of the thimble. If the design is comparatively wide, a roller of conical shape must be employed, as shown in Fig. 8. The taper and the circumference of the roller are the same as for the thimble, so that the peripheral speed of both is the same at all points.

The last operation consists of knurling the thimble at Y, Fig. 1, on a special machine. The engraved roller for this operation is shown in Fig. 9. It will be noted that this roller has a slightly curved surface. The roller-holder A is forced against the work by a toggle link, and is backed up by a strong spring. This arrangement makes it possible to adjust the pressure and allow the necessary play for the roller. In addition, the holder is given a circular movement, as indicated by the arrow B. The different points on the roller are thus brought into proper contact with the work by the circular movement.

The work is held in place by a stop C having a point made of leather. The machine spindle revolves at high speed, and an automatic feeding device is employed which gives an output of 2,000 pieces per hour. Previous attempts to produce the required knurling with a straight roller pressed against the work failed to give satisfactory results. The thimbles made from copper are given a thin coating of silver after they have been completely formed.

Reproduced from 19 January 1928 issue of *Machinery*.

Bibliography

D'Allemagne, H. R. *Les Accessoires du Costume et du Mobilier.* Paris, 1928.

Andere, M. *Old Needlework Boxes and Tools.* Newton Abbot, 1971.

Bond, S. *History of Sewing Tools.* London: Embroiderers' Guild, 1967.

Cocheris, P. W. *Histoires Sérieuses sur une Pointe d'Aiguille.* Paris, 1886.

Groves, S. *The History of Needlework Tools and Accessories.* London, 1969.

Holmes, E. F. *Thimbles.* Dublin, 1976.

Hughes, G. B. *More about Collecting Antiques.* London, 1952.

Johnson, E. *Thimbles.* Princes Risborough, 1982.

Lundquist, M. *The Book of a Thousand Thimbles.* Des Moines, Iowa, 1970. *Thimble Treasury.* Des Moines, Iowa, 1975.

Rath, J. A. *Antique and Unusual Thimbles.* Cranbury, N.J., 1979.

Syer Cuming, H. "On Thimbles," *Journal of the British Archaeological Association,* 35 (March 1879): 238–42.

Whiting, G. *Tools and Toys of Stitchery.* New York, 1928.

Index

Page numbers in italics refer to illustrations.

Abalone, 93, 210
Adjustable thimble, 191, *191,* 194
Advertising, 51, 62, 153, 155, 161, 197–99
Agate, 120, 122
Allemagne, H. R. d', 86, 249
Alpacca. *See* Nickel
Aluminum, 31, 51, 62, 144, 154–55, 161, 197, 198
Amber, 130, *158*
Ammam, Jost, 26, *27,* 133
Archery, 16, 20
Ashmolean Museum (Oxford), 17, 18
Australia, 50, *50*
Austria, 102, 123, 129, 132, *219*

Bakelite, 128, 157, 158
Bateman, Hester, 40, *41*
Battersea enamel. *See* Bilston enamel
Becke, Bernhard von der, 140, 141, 146, 165
Belleek porcelain, 80
Benschoten, Nicholas van, 9, 108
Bethnal Green Museum (London), *165, 209*
Bilston enamel, 82, *83, 179,* 216, 228, 229
Bodkin, 15, 38, 58
Bog oak, 128, 158
Bolsover, Thomas, 52
Bone, 9, 18, 66, 115–16, 129, 148, 160, 162, 200, 209, 210, 211, 224, 228
Boulton, Matthew, 40, 147
Bourne, Horace, 153, 191, *192*
Boxwood, 128, 129
Brand names, 36, 50, 106–13, 152, 153, 155, 159, 160, *192, 195*
Brass, 15–23 passim, 24–27 passim, *28,* 30, 37, 38, 39, 51, 54, 56, 57, 65–67 passim, 69, *71,* 84, 87, 99, 133–44, 146, 163–66 passim, *169,* 175, *180,* 185, 191, *192,* 197, 198, *199,* 200, *212, 227*
Brazil, 130
Britain, 37–53, 56, 57, 76–80 passim, *83, 89,* 91, *96, 97, 100, 101,* 102, *104,* 106–14 passim, *118, 129, 130,* 139, 143, *153, 155,* 173, 174, 176, *179,* 180, 182–84 passim, 191, *192,* 204, 205, *227, 229*

Britannia Metal, 52
British Archaeological Association, 52, 126, 137
British Museum, 23, 118, 173, *227,* 230, 239
Bronze, 15–23 passim, 66, 93, 133, 145, 164
Bry, Jos. Theo. de, 28, *29, 99, 241*
Byzantium, 19, 20, 21, 139, 163, 228, 229

Cable thimbles, 42, *42, 43*
Calamine. *See* Zinc
Casein, 114, 158, 160
Casting, 21, 25, 26, 133, 134, 135, *135, 137,* 138, 139
Castle thimbles, 41, 183, 201
Celluloid, 95, 129, *153,* 156, 157, *158,* 160, 161, 181, 190, 191, 202, 218, 219, 224
Cellulose acetate, 51, 159
Chatelaine, 215, 216, *216, 217,* 218
Chelsea porcelain, *74,* 76, 179
Children's thimbles, *169, 170*
China, 16, 84, 115, 165, *165, 222,* 228
Chrome, 51, 148
Clan tartanware. *See* Scottish woodware
Cloisonné, 84, *222*
Coalport porcelain, 80
Collecting, 9, 53, 64, 80, 81, 85, 104, 177, 219, 222, 237–42
Colonial Williamsburg Foundation, *31,* 41, *55,* 76, 78, 82, 84, *88, 91,* 94, 118, 127, *141, 145, 217,* 226, 228
Commemorative, 43, 60, 64, 92, 173–77, 182, 212, 213, 222
Coney, John, 56
Copenhagen porcelain, 75, *75*
Copper, 24, 65, 66, 99, 133, 136, 137, 150
Coquilla nut, 129, 130, *211, 223*
Coral, 88, 158
Corinth, 19, *19,* 20, 163
Cornelian, 84, 93, *121,* 122
Corning Glass Works, 118
Corozo nut. *See* Vegetable ivory
Crêpy-en-Valois porcelain, *68,* 75
Cuming Museum (London), 52, 126, 230
Cupronickel. *See* Nickel

Dame's thimmel, 170

Deep drawing, 21, 40, 100, 120, 139, 142, *142*, 143, 147–48, *151*, 245–48
Delaporte Frères, 69, 147
Denmark, 25, 75, 80, *99*
Derby porcelain, 76, 77, *77*, 78, 80, *80*, 228
Design patent, *43*, 106–14 passim, *123*, 152, *153*, 162, 194–96, 205, 210, 215
Dillmont, Thérèse de, 115, 148, 232
Dolls' thimbles, 172
Dorcas, 49, 106–14, 120, 148
Dreema, 112, *113*
Dura, 112
Durham, Rosina M., 191

Earthenware, 81
Eber, Friedrich, 32, *34, 35*, 36
Ebony, 128, *158*
Ecuador, 129
Egyptian Museum (Cairo), 15, 16, *16*, 20
Electro-plating, 51, 150–53 passim, 155, 187, 195, 205, 224, 248
Enamel, 36, 43, 51, *63*, 68, 82–85, 87, *90*, 169, 180, 194, 223. *See also* Bilston enamel
England. *See* Britain
Eskimos, *115*, 116, *126*, 127, *127, 148*

Fabergé, Peter Carl, 82
Fabric, 131, *131*, 132, 165
Féau, A., 69, 70, *70*, 71
Fenton, James, 46, *47*, 48, 49, *49*, 88, 114, *123, 170*, 201
Filigree, 28, 40, *40*, 41, 84, *141*, 169, 228
Finger guards, *89*, 96, 200–202
Finger shield/protector. *See* Finger guard
Finger stall, 17, 125, 126
Flinders Petrie, Sir William M., 15, 16, 20
Fontaine, J. de La, *71*, 222
Foskett, Henry. *See* Foskett, Samuel
Foskett, Samuel, 46, 49, 88, *101*, 114
France, 65–72, 75, *87*, 91, *93, 94*, 102, 103, *128*, 147, 148, 190
Fürstenberg porcelain, 74

Gabler, Gebruder, GmbH, 31, 32, 33, 36, 149, *149*, 153, 159, 167, *168, 169, 171*, 188, 191, 205
Gallo-Roman thimbles, 9, 18
Galuchat. *See* Shagreen
Garnet, 123, 124
Germanisches Landesmuseum (Nuremberg), *164*, 203
German silver. *See* Nickel
Germany, *22*, 24–36, 73, 74, *85*, 91, *99*, 103, *121, 123*, 129, *135*, 140, 141, 146, 147, *149, 152, 164, 169*, 179, 185, 186, 187, 188, 194, 203, *230*
Gilded brass, 68, 87, 90, 216, *217*, 218
Glass, 118–19, 120, 228
Gold, 31, 38, 46, 49, 57–62 passim, 67, 68, 69–72 passim, *83*, 86–92, *93*, 96, 98, 103, 112, *121*, 147, 148, 149, 175, 176, 177, 180, *190*, 200, 207, 216
Goldsmith Stern. *See* Stern Brothers & Co.
Great Exhibition (1851), 41, *43*, 51, 174, 175, 183, *184*, 191, 194
Greece, 101, 220, *222*
Greif, Helmut, 32, 36, 176
Griffith, Henry and Sons, 46, 49, *49*, 88, 112, *113*, 185, 186, 187
Guillart le Deillier, 66, 69
Gutta percha, 156, 157, 190

Hallmarks, 40, 46, 49, 50, 62, *90*, 91, 92, *100, 101*, 102–4, 108, 152, 175, 187, 200
Halstead, Benjamin, 58, *58*, 59, 90
Hammering. *See* Stamping
Holland, 30, 37, 38, 54, 55, *55*, 103, 135, 136, *137*, 138, 139, *170*, 176, *200*, 201, 222
Horn, 117, *117*, 129
Horner, Charles, *44, 45*, 49, 106–13 passim, 151, *190*, 191, 193, 194, 219
Houghton John, F. R. S., 38, 53
Hungary, *21*, 80, 102
Hurd, Jacob, 56, 57

Iceland, 25
Iles, Charles, 51, 52, 144, 148, 151, 152, 153, *153*, 154, 155, 157, *158*, 159, 160, 190, 191, 193, 194, 198, 213
Indentations, 21, 22, 25, 26, 27, 33, 40, 42, 54, 67, 70, 71, 94, 100, 117, 141, 143, *143*, 159, *160*, 161, 165, 248, *248*
India, 20, 101, 110, 115, 117
Inscriptions. *See* Mottoes
International trade, 21, 25, 36, 37, 38, 39, 55, 56, 57, 58, 110, 136, 137, 138, 146, 147
Inventories, 37, 55, 56, 57, 76, 86, 99
Iran. *See* Persia
Iraq, 102, *104*
Ireland, 126, 128, 158, 183
Iron, 16, 17, 30, 37, 54, 56, 99, 133, 145–49, 164, 228
Italy, 75, 76, 80, 118, *119*, 120, *121, 145*, 146, 228
Ivory, 9, 18, 57, 66, 94, 95, *95*, 115, 117, 129, 156, *157*, 160, 162, 200, 207, 228

Japan, 127, 131, 132, *143, 155*, 161, 165
Jiggers. *See* Spirit measures

Kam Museum (Nijmegen), 18, *24*, 24
Keepsake, 36, 53, 73, 93, 155, 160, 178–81, 182, 213
Kestner Museum (Hanover), *28*
Ketcham and McDougall, 59, *60*, 61, 64, *64*, 89, 154, 176, 185, 193, 196, 201
Korea, 127, 132, 228
Kunstgewerbe Museum (West Berlin), *28, 29, 66*, 90, 231, 239

Latten, 65, 66, 134
Leather, 16, 17, 20, 21, 37, 125–27, 131, 161, 165, 207, 218, 219
Letter seals, 41, *87, 99*, 202
Linwood, Matthew, 40, 201
Locke & Co., 204, *205*
Lofting, John, 38, *39*, 56, 137, 138, *138*, 164, 189, 191
Lotthammer, Wilhelm, 32, *32*, 180, 181
Low Countries. *See* Holland
Lowe, Edwin, Ltd., 50, 51
Ludwigsburg porcelain, 74

Magnet, 153, *155*, 191, 194
Maker's marks, 21, 31, 32, 33, 36, 39, 40, 41, *41*, 46, 57, 59, 61, 62, 74, 77, 78, 80, 102, 103, 104, 106–13, 151, 152, 153, 200, 201
Manchester Museum, 178, *229*, 230
Mauchline ware. *See* Scottish woodware
May, Charles, 46, 49, 88, *89, 101, 201*
Meissen porcelain, 53, 73, *73*, 74, 77, 81, 178, 179, 182, 207, 228, 229
Mennecy porcelain, 74, *75*, 229
Mercers, 25, 39, 66, 146
Metropolitan Museum of Art (New York), 15

251

Mexico, 102, 220, *222*
Mills, Nathaniel, 42, 201
Mongolia, 125, *125*
Moors, 17, 19, *20,* 21, 54, *134,* 226, 229, 230
Morrall, Abel, 148, 152, 153, 160, 197
Mother-of-pearl, 68, 71, 93, *93,* 122, 147, 200, 210, 212, 217, 228
Mottoes, 28, 38, 39, 54, 76, *83, 99, 136,* 160, 178–81, *227, 229*
Mulberry wood, 128
Musée d'Art et d'Histoire (Geneva), *21*
Musée des Antiquités Nationales (St. Germain-en-Laye), 18, *18,* 230
Musée Le Secq des Tournelles (Rouen), 146, 230
Museo Arqueologico (Madrid), 21, *134,* 226, 230
Museum of Fine Arts (Boston), 57, 87, 228
Museum of London, 173, 178

Naples porcelain, 75, 76, 228
National Museum (Copenhagen), *115,* 116, *126, 127, 148*
National Museum (Tokyo), 131, *131,* 132
Needle, 15, 16, 17, 19, 20, 21, 23, 55, 56, 57, 65, 66, 69, 86, 99, 121, 126, 146, 152, 163, 165, 180, 201, 215
Needlecase, 17, 30, 41, 84, 86, *129,* 178, 210, 214, 215, *216*
Needle pusher, 15
Needle threader, 153, 155, 191, 193, 198
Needlework boxes, 94, 115, 128
Nickel, 31, 33, 46, 51, 71, 148, 150–53 passim, 175, 185, 188, 191–96 passim, 197, 205, 213, 224
Niello, *101,* 102, *104,* 183, 228
North American Indians, 234, *234,* 235, 244
Norway, 25, 83, *84,* 103, 121
Novelties, 26, 27, 30, 39, 40, 41, 84, *87,* 138, 180, 202, 228
Nuns' Thimbles, 128
Nuremberg, 17, 24–29 passim, 54, 134, 135, *135,* 139, 163, *164,* 203
Nymphenburg porcelain, 74

Olney, Amsden & Son, *49,* 148, 152
Ormolu. *See* Gilded brass

Palais Royal, 93
Palm protector, 166
Papier-mâché, 129
Patents, 51, 61, 62, 96, *97,* 106–14, 137, 138, 139, 153, *153, 157, 158,* 159, 162, 175, 185, 189–96
Payne, Graham, 81
Pearl, 88
Pebble thimble, 121
Peepshow thimble. *See* Pursall, William
Pemberton, Samuel, 40
Persia (Iran), 20, 83, *83,* 101
Personal thimble, 64, 161
Petersdochter, Marichger, 136
Petit point, 132
Pewter, 52, *52,* 176, 203, 204
Photography, 239–41
Piercy, John, 96, *97,* 191, 228
Pinchbeck, 57, 58, 90, *97,* 180
Plastics, 31, 51, 62, 114, 129, 131, 144, 155, 156–62, 165, 190, 197, 198, 202, 228
Platinum, 69, 92
Polystyrene, 155, 159, 160, 161
Porcelain, 53, *53,* 73–81, 85, 178, 182, 204, 218, 222, 223, *224*
Portugal, 54, 102, 103, 220
Powell, William, 78, 79

Prince's metal, 52, 137
Princeton University, 19, *19*
Prix du Dé d'or, 72
Pudding charms, 172
Pursall, William, 95, 185

Regemorter, Babtista van, 135, 136
Registered design. *See* Design patent
Religious thimbles, 36, 155, *187,* 188, *188*
Revere, Paul, 87
Rheinisches Landesmuseum (Trier), 18, 230
Rhode Island Historical Society, 55, *55*
Richardson, Joseph, 40, 56, 57, 87
Ring and chain attachment, 101, *101*
Ring-type thimbles. *See* Tailors' thimbles
Roman thimbles, 9, 10, 17, 18, 19, 20, 230
Rouy et Berthier, 68, 147
Rumpe, Johann Caspar, 140, 141, 144, 165
Russia, 82, *84, 90,* 92, 101, *101,* 102, 103, 148, *170, 183,* 185, 228, 234

Saglio, Edm., 9, 10, 18
Sampson Hancock, 77, *77,* 78, *80,* 228
Sandalwood, 128
Savary des Bruslons, Jacques, 66, 163, 201
Scent bottle, 41, *87,* 228
Schmuckmuseum, Pforzheim, *230*
Schot, Jan Claess, 136
Science Museum (London), 42, *42*
Scottish thimbles, 121, 194, 204
Scottish woodware, 208, *208,* 209
Scovill Manufacturing, 144
Scrimshaw, 116
Seals. *See* Letter seals
Sears Roebuck, 90, 154
Sèvres porcelain, 75, *75*
Sewing boxes. *See* Needlework boxes
Sewing kits, 30, *35,* 41, *95, 128,* 149
Shagreen, *67,* 68, 207, 218
Sheffield plate, 52
Silver, 26–36 passim, 38–50, 54–64 passim, 67–71 passim, *84, 85,* 87, 88, *121,* 122, *123,* 148, 151, *164, 165,* 168, *169,* 172, 173–77 passim, 180, *181,* 182–87 passim, 193, *194,* 197, *198,* 200–202 passim, 203, 205, 206, 207, *227, 229, 230*
Silver gilt, 29, 33, *35,* 43, 46, 69, 70, 72, *72,* 86, 90, 91, 96, 164, 200, 224, *230*
"Silver Thimble, The," 168
Simons Brothers Co., 59, *60,* 63, 89, 90, 91, 153, 171, 175, *175,* 176, 185, 195, *200,* 201, 205
Simulated stone tops, 122, 154, 198
Size numbers, 39, 51, 69, 70, 76, 108, 151, 152
Slater Museum (Norwich), 229
Smithsonian Institution, 228
Soergel and Stollmeyer, 32, 33, *152, 171*
South America, 80, 102, *103,* 228
Souvenir, 36, *43,* 92, *101,* 102, 153, 155, 182–88, 219, 220
Sowerby and Company, 204
Spain, 19, 20, 21, 54, 65, 94, 99, 102, 133, *134, 149,* 177, 181, 198, 220, 222, *222,* 228, 229, 230
Spindles, 15, 17, 126
Spirit measures, 203–6
Stamping, 21, 26, *27, 30,* 56, 133, *135*
State Hermitage Museum (Leningrad), 74, 216, 230
Steel, 16, 17, 20, 51, 68, 69, 145–49, 218
Steel tops, 33, 40, *41,* 42, 56, 57, 58, 70, 90, 94, 106, 120, 147, 148, 152

Stern Brothers & Co., *60*, 61, *62, 63*, 196
Stickware. *See* Tunbridge ware
Stone, 15, 43, 68, 71, 86, 88, 120–24, 194
Stone tops, 33, 42, 70, 84, 93, 120–22, 129, 148
Swann, James, 49, 88
Swansea porcelain, 77
Sweden, 25, 91, 92, 103, *121*, 202
Swiss National Museum (Zurich), 74, 226, 230
Switzerland, 74

Tagua. *See* Vegetable ivory
Tailors' thimbles, 16, 17, 19, 20, 30, 54, 55, 57, 69, *115, 117*, *125, 125, 126*, 127, 131, *131*, 132, *132*, 146, 148, *148*, *155, 155*, 161, 163–67, *227*, 228, *233*
Tambour thimble, 232, *232*
Tape measure, 41, 219
Taylor, Joseph, 41, 200, *201*
Taylor and Perry, 87, 200
Taylor's nonslip, 191
Thailand, 102, 122
Thatchers' thimbles, 233, *233*
Thimble bells, 234, 235, 244
Thimble case, 64, *67*, 68, *116*, 130, *179*, 182, 207–18 passim
Thimble holder, *210*, 214–17, 218
Thimble-rigging, 90, 91, 151, 210, 220–25
Thimble shapes, 81, 203–6
Thimble stamps, 56
Thimble stand, 213, *213*, 214
Thread cutter, 191, 193
"Threader Thimble," 51, 153, *195*, 213
Thumb thimbles, 10, 20, 125, 126, 205
Tin, 133
Tortoise-shell, 96, *96*, 97, 156, *158*, 191, 210, 228

Toys. *See* Novelties
Transferware, 182, 208, *208*, 209
Tunbridge ware, 128, *129*, 208, 209
Turquoise, 88, *89*
Turtle-shell. *See* Tortoise-shell
Tutania, 52

Unite, George, *101*, 201, 219
United States, 54–64, 89, 91, 103, *109*, 154, 156, 157, 158, 159, 175, 190, 193, 194, 195, 196, 198, 199, 226, 228, 229, 233, 234

Vegetable ivory, 94, 95, 129, 211, *211*, 228
Ventilated thimbles, *153*, 190, 191
Victoria and Albert Museum, *20*, 76, 82, 226, 230
Vincennes porcelain, 75, *75*
Vulcanite, 157

Waite Thresher and Co., *60*, 61
Walker and Hall, 112
Webster Company, *60*, 61, 185, 212
Wedgwood, Josiah, 81
Weigel, Christoph, 26, 28, 29, 30, *30*, 36, 133
Whistle thimble, 199
Whiting, G., *179*, 226, 249
Willmore, Joseph, 88
Wood, 66, 128–30, 147, 207, 222
Worcester porcelain, 53, 76, 77, 78, *78*, 79, 80, 204, 205, *222*, 228

Zinc, 24, 133, 139, 150
Zurich porcelain, 74